HIT
FACTORIES

HIT
FACTORIES

A JOURNEY THROUGH
THE INDUSTRIAL
CITIES OF BRITISH POP

KARL WHITNEY

WEIDENFELD & NICOLSON

First published in Great Britain in 2019 by Weidenfeld & Nicolson
an imprint of The Orion Publishing Group Ltd
Carmelite House, 50 Victoria Embankment
London EC4Y 0DZ

An Hachette UK Company

10 9 8 7 6 5 4 3 2 1

A CIP catalogue record for this book is
available from the British Library.

ISBN HB 978 1 4746 0740 7
ISBN eBook 978 1474 607421

Typeset by Input Data Services Ltd, Somerset

Printed and bound by Clays Ltd, Elcograf S.p.A

MIX
Paper from
responsible sources
FSC® C104740

www.weidenfeldandnicolson.co.uk

For my parents,
May and Tom

Contents

Prologue
THE RECORD PLANT

When I first heard that there had once been a record pressing plant not far from where I lived, I wondered exactly where it had stood. I soon found out a little bit more about it, just enough to start piecing together its story. Built by the RCA company to manufacture vinyl records, the plant had been closed down when the demand for them declined. I found a former employee who was able to describe where the building had been. It was possible that its ruins lay overgrown in an industrial estate somewhere near the A1 motorway. But if I was to find out what remained, I first needed to pinpoint it precisely. Then I had to go to the site, to see it with my own eyes. After searching for a while, I found an old map on which a rectangular building was marked as 'Record Factory'. I compared that map with recent satellite photos of the area. An expanse of waste ground on the satellite photo fitted perfectly over the record factory on the old map.

One weekday morning I took a bus from central Sunderland, the largely working-class city in north-east England in which I live, then changed to a local bus that dropped me at a stop not far from my destination in a corner of Washington, a new town built between Sunderland and Gateshead in the sixties and seventies. I passed through the grounds of a disused office block whose windows had been smashed so that the wind whipped through the open apertures. Some teenagers standing in the office block's rear car park broke glass bottles and shouted at one another. I reached a road, and crossed, passing between clusters of overgrown bushes and came to the site of the building.

Whatever had been there was cleared – the walls, the roof – except for a wide expanse of tiled flooring that led from where I was standing to a hill of rubble and muck above which was a B&Q car park. Trees and weeds sprouted through cracks in the tiles. A shopping trolley sat stranded on one corner of what had been the factory floor. Long abandoned, the site wasn't fenced in and thus was freely accessible to the public. Although I hadn't anticipated encountering anyone, I immediately saw a man walking his dogs across the tiled surface. At one end of the expanse some skateboarders had built a series of ramps and rails, a secluded skatepark in which they could do tricks. Although not marked on the map as a public amenity, a post-industrial public park had taken root on the ruins of the music industry.

Some fragments of the factory's floor tiles lay scattered around at my feet, and I picked four of them up and stuffed them in the pockets of my jacket. When I returned to my office I piled them up one on top of the other, and they sat on a book shelf for a few months as I got on with other things. But my mind kept returning to the record plant.

After a while I began to wonder if, starting from this derelict site on the edge of an industrial estate, I could begin to trace the life and death of the British music industry through its physical locations, and through that come to understand Britain. I would travel around visiting the venues, the studios, the terraced houses and the students' unions: the landscape of pop. I would travel to regional cities, avoiding London, to see what I could find out about the importance of local scenes to the development of musical acts.

The terrain of pop that I was in the process of sketching closely mirrored the map of cities that were central to British industry: the coalfields of the North East, the shipyards of Glasgow and Belfast, the steel factories of Sheffield, the foundries of Birmingham, the car plants of Coventry, the ports of Hull, Bristol and Liverpool, the mills of Manchester and Leeds. Not coincidentally, many of the musicians drawn from these places came from working-class backgrounds. Music provided a cultural activity that could be systematised into a product; their talent was a raw material to be refined. For the most commercially successful artists, this often involved relocating to London, a trajectory that paralleled the brain-drain of higher-skilled and better-educated workers from the regions to the capital.

But before I could get started, events – two celebrity deaths and a referendum – conspired to focus my mind on the journey that I would soon take.

A few months after my visit to the site, David Bowie died. Audrey Young, the former employee of RCA who had told me where the plant had been, had also informed me that Bowie had visited the Washington factory when he first signed to the label. Employees were shepherded into the workers' canteen, where they watched Bowie cut a cake. Celebration over, employees returned to their jobs. His first record for RCA, the joyous *Hunky Dory*, was the beginning of a run of truly great records for Bowie, whose career had previously suffered a number of false starts.

Young also told me about how the RCA plant had been reprieved from closure in August 1977, when the company's best-known artist Elvis Presley died. On holiday at the time,

Young learned of the star's death when she passed the factory and saw that the flags were at half-mast. The plant took on extra staff to meet demand and hung on for a couple of years more. I thought of this series of events when I heard Bowie's death announced in early January 2016. Radio stations suddenly changed their programming: DJs made heartfelt tributes to the singer, favourite records were played, interviews were dug out from the archive. Retailers began to sell out of copies of *Blackstar*, an album that had been released by Bowie two days before his death. The demand for his back catalogue increased in the same way – seven of his albums reached the Top 40 in the week after his death, a record that equalled Elvis. Perhaps this is what it was like when Elvis died, I thought.

But the experience of Bowie's death was different. It felt like the death of a certain kind of artist, one whose career had been enabled and sustained by a record industry that simply didn't exist in the same way any more. The demand for Bowie's records meant that some stores quickly ran out of physical product, but it wasn't as if you couldn't hear his work on the radio or online. A few months later a friend messaged me as I sat at my desk to tell me that Prince had died, and I spent the next few hours streaming his albums. This was a very contemporary form of mourning.

Digital had changed things: made music more instantly accessible, but taken the money out of the business. In 2002 I paid €22 for a new CD that had just been released. Ten years later the price for a new release was half that, and anyway you could listen to it online for free. For artists whose fame predated digital music, this was a problem, but less of a problem than for those who were just getting started. The older artists had benefited from an industry in which money oiled the wheels of publicity. As a result their presence was still vivid for generations of people

– glowing afterimages burnt into our minds by a much larger and more powerful industry. Those beginning their careers were entering a business in which audiences were fragmented and in which radio play no longer guaranteed sales. You didn't need sales for a hit, but the returns were so much lower from online streaming. Although digital sales – the single mp3 download through platforms like Amazon and iTunes – provided a decent royalty rate to artists on a per-song basis, they allowed listeners to cherry-pick favourite tracks to download from an album without having to pay for the whole thing. And, anyway, with the increasing portability and convenience of streaming apps enabled by greater mobile data allowances, why would you buy an mp3 at all? Instead, the money in music lay in live performances, but again this privileged the legacy artists who people already knew and put new acts on their first or second albums at a disadvantage. Nostalgia for old acts pervades the digital world, the ghosts of old records emerging remastered from the machine.

The lesson I was beginning to draw from my visit to the ruins of the record plant was that it was a valuable glimpse of a stage in the development of an industry whose relationship to its physical product was now much changed. It was like a fossil. Bowie's death had brought home to me that what I was looking at was the history of a certain idea of the music industry – one that was in the process of passing away, if it had not already gone.

The more I considered it, the more the RCA factory embodied this transition, and the challenge of what would come next. The manufacturing of records was the very kind of light industry that it was hoped would take root, hastening the transition to new industries. The physical manufacture of the vinyl record took place in factories where conditions didn't quite resemble those of other industries. To a large degree the pressing of vinyl was automated, observed by workers who kept the machines running as smoothly as possible. The finished discs were then listened to on headphones connected to high-fidelity record players to ensure the sound quality was good enough, that there were no glitches.

But there was another level to be considered when looking at the manufacture of records, and that was the music itself. Pop music was a light industry whose products projected a dream life, a cultural vision of the consumer and their relationship with the world. These visions were concocted by groups of people not unlike the listener, often from a similar socio-economic background, in studios and venues and rehearsal rooms – the factory floors of a nascent creative industry. In pursuing a musical career they had chosen to participate in an industry that was still in its infancy, and this audacious gamble had paid off in a few notable cases.

Not far from the RCA factory in Washington is the semi-detached house in which Bryan Ferry of Roxy Music grew up. His father was from a family of farm labourers who had worked in the surrounding countryside, but who took a job taking care of the horses at a local mine. In his teens Ferry began playing gigs with local bands, eventually joining well-known local rhythm and blues combos that had a substantial following in Newcastle. The close attention he paid to pop-art style and vintage fashion was sharpened by his degree in Fine Art at Newcastle University and part-time jobs working at tailors' shops in Newcastle city centre. His trajectory from post-war industrial life to pop star glamour is one that many wanted to emulate, and some did. Ferry's trajectory wasn't just that of an exceptional person, but an example of the dizzying possibilities of post-war social mobility. In the current moment, such a trajectory had come to seem unthinkable.

I wanted to retrace the social history of the places I visited: did others experience the journey from an industrial working-class background to fame in a similar way to Ferry? Why did different sounds emerge from different places? Why did blues take hold in Newcastle in the sixties, or heavy metal and reggae in Birmingham in the seventies, Marxist punk in late-seventies Leeds, or synth-pop in Sheffield in the early eighties? What could looking at those scenes tell you about the cities themselves? And what had changed since their musical heyday? I soon realised that if I was going to travel through these musical cities, I needed to take a parallel journey through the records that came from those places, some of which had been familiar to me for many years. What could be learned from listening to them? What would they tell me about the places they emerged from? Were they an effort to reflect those places or an escape from them?

I was by now certain that discovering the record plant had only been the beginning of my journey through British pop's industrial past. It provided a window into a world, a brief glimpse of a deeper history that I had become determined to explore. I needed to plot in as much detail as I could my journey across the country, so I printed out a map of the UK and Ireland and pinned it to my wall, marking on it the cities I wanted to visit. Over time I began to retrieve the sheet of paper from the wall and trace a trajectory between the cities, filling in where I'd go and what I'd do when I was there. I sat at my desk imagining my journey.

First I would take the bus to Manchester, the birthplace of the industrial revolution, along whose streets I would follow the story of the legendary Factory Records and its mercurial spokesman Tony Wilson. Returning to the North East, home territory for me since my move to England, I wanted to walk through the Georgian sandstone streets of Newcastle on the trail of journalist Nik Cohn, who had been a student in the city, then investigate the blues clubs that gave the world The Animals and Bryan Ferry, before catching up with Tom Caulker, a local music promoter and DJ whose career has spanned three decades. After that I would make a trip to the nineteenth-century industrial powerhouse of Leeds, visiting its arcades and universities to explore the history of the city's Marxist punk of the late seventies, followed by a short hop to the steel city of Sheffield, where I would retrace the Yorkshire city's electronic music heritage, from Cabaret Voltaire to Warp Records, including the stories of two of the city's greatest pop bands, The Human League and Pulp.

I took out a ruler and drew a line from Sheffield towards the North Sea. Taking the train from Sheffield to the east coast I would arrive in Hull, 2017's UK City of Culture, and the port city from which hailed three-quarters of Ziggy Stardust and the Spiders from Mars, The Housemartins and Everything But The Girl. Then I would journey north of the border, to Glasgow, the former shipbuilding city that became an EU Capital of Culture and which was home to a distinctive brand of bright and melodic guitar pop that stretched from Orange Juice to BMX Bandits, Teenage Fanclub and beyond. I planned to talk to members of the latter two bands and meet the former manager of Belle and Sebastian to discuss the challenges of band management, the importance of small venues to the Glasgow scene, and the drastic changes in the music industry wrought by digital.

Crossing the Irish Sea to Belfast in Northern Ireland – part of the United Kingdom rather than Great Britain, and as much an Irish city as a British one – I would look back to the Belfast blues scene of which Van Morrison was a central part. I'd travel to his home neighbourhood to retrace his steps around the east of the city, in the shadow of the shipyards in which his father once worked. Then I'd make my way to the west of the city to see how the Troubles had divided Belfast and split up its music scene, and find out how punk had bridged the divide.

After the Second World War, immigrants from Commonwealth countries travelled to Britain in search of work. In Birmingham newly arrived Jamaicans, Indians and Pakistanis found jobs in the city's foundries and car plants, working alongside locals and immigrants from Ireland. They brought with them cultures that would soon manifest themselves in popular music. In Smethwick, south Asian groups began to play bhangra music in Sikh temples. In Handsworth, Caribbean cafés and blues parties moved to the sound of reggae and ska. Then beyond Handsworth was the suburb of Aston, where the members of Black Sabbath rehearsed in a local hall, their raw, bluesy downtuned rock pioneering what would become known as heavy metal. Half an hour away was Coventry, the West Midlands city known for its car industry and for the label 2 Tone, whose bands, most notably The Specials and The Selecter, combined ska reggae with punk rock and a multicultural ethos. Coventry's manufacturing industries had been repurposed for the war effort, and the city centre was razed by the Luftwaffe's bombs and subsequently rebuilt as a modernist precinct.

The influence of reggae shaped the music scene in Bristol, the final city I planned to visit, with the St Paul's neighbourhood becoming home to post-war immigrants from the Caribbean, whose musical tastes were catered for by reggae clubs and an annual carnival. The Wild Bunch, a collective of rappers, DJs and graffiti artists, combined reggae with hip-hop in a night held in a basement club near the university. The music that melded together these influences, drawing on the speaker-rattling depth of dub bass and lowering the volume of rap so that it went from a triumphant bellow to an insistent whisper, was known in the music papers as trip-hop, and its major acts – Massive Attack, Tricky and Portishead – all hailed from the city.

You can only begin to remember what's already gone. The industry's sudden and dramatic decline drove a wedge between past glories and the present. The musical history of cities had quickly passed into the realm of memory, something to be recreated and reimagined, a story to be told and retold. In this, music mirrored other departed industries. It had become something historical to be imaginatively engaged with in the same way that you might coalmining or shipbuilding. You could now take guided tours around notable locations associated with bands and music scenes, to old venues and band rehearsal rooms and even to graveyards in which dead stars had been laid to rest. It was a contemporary version of a medieval pilgrimage in which saints were replaced by singers. Increasingly, blue plaques were being attached to the façades of buildings commemorating recording studios and record companies. Cities were happy to trade on their particular musical pasts while, simultaneously, venues were closing and bands were giving up their careers.

What does a city sound like? What set of influences or circumstances led to the sixties beat-pop of Liverpool, post-punk and baggy in Manchester, the electronic synth-pop of Sheffield, Bristol's trip-hop scene, and Coventry's punk-era revival of Jamaican ska? The answer would be found in the streets of those cities, and in the words of the musicians themselves. Each city's music scene appeared to vary in scale, taking in sometimes hundreds of people who knew each other, but it often could be narrowed down to a handful of people whose shared vision for pop music drew them together at a very specific time and in a very particular place: a bar, a venue, a students' union or even, in the case of Paul Heaton of The Housemartins and The Beautiful South, a terraced house on an otherwise unremarkable Hull street. Some musicians who couldn't find a scene to fit into had to start one themselves. Heaton wasn't alone. Many other musicians, managers, artists, producers and would-be record company owners did their dreaming – imagining the music, the artwork, the vision for their bands and their labels – in the poky rented bedsits and squat terraced houses of regional British cities.

The more I thought about it, the more I became convinced that my trip would involve comparing the map – the mythical one I had imagined when listening to British pop music and had only recently set down on the printed A4 sheet pinned to my wall – to the actual territory: the terraced streets and post-industrial edges of the country's regional cities. It was an exploration of the history of an industry whose rise and fall echoed, albeit in miniature, the fortunes of industries that had gone before. The journey would bring me through past dreams and current realities during a tumultuous contemporary moment in Britain's history.

1.

MANCHESTER

Contemporary Manchester seems a new city bolted atop the old. Walking through the city's streets you might turn a corner to find future and past juxtaposed starkly. Narrow cobbled lanes give way to stone-paved plazas whose design tends towards cubist abstraction. Old buildings deemed less desirable have been swept away – much as the terraced streets of Salford and Hulme were razed in the twentieth century – and replaced with an apparently weightless architecture of glass and steel, panelled in bright plastic as if they were constructed from colourful toy bricks. Elsewhere the remnants of Mancunian industry, the nineteenth-century redbrick warehouses and mills, have been repurposed for the requirements of the contemporary post-industrial city: housing, office space, retail. Many other formerly industrial cities in the North have tried to follow its example because architecturally, economically and culturally, Manchester provides a convincing answer to the question of what comes after industry.

I had arrived in Manchester to walk around the locations in which the city's musical history had unfolded, particularly those associated with Factory, a post-punk independent label that appropriated the imagery of industry for cultural purposes. As the label grew during the 1980s, funded largely by the success of New Order, the band formed by the remaining members of Joy Division after Ian Curtis's suicide, it opened a legendary nightclub and later a bar in the city centre, followed by a headquarters building some years later.

What was it about Factory that continued to fascinate? Julie Campbell, the Mancunian musician whose post-punk-influenced music, released under the moniker Lonelady, finds inspiration in Factory and its recorded output. She told me: 'I love the seriousness and high art of Factory. I love that it stands for depth and meaning. I don't find these things elitist but mysterious and lasting.' One of the reasons for its emergence in the Manchester of the late seventies, she says, was that it was 'a lucky alignment of northerners who created a moment, a movement, that had a very strong and lasting identity and sound, shaped by the Mancunian landscape and the artists, studio engineers, producers, designers and weirdos that emerged from that environment'. Factory was less a record company than a conceptual art project. Everything was given a catalogue number: records, posters, buildings, the nightclub cat, and even founder Tony Wilson's gravestone.

If you're a music fan, it's difficult to walk around the network of streets and canals near the city centre without thinking about how you could once hear the booming bass of the Haçienda bouncing off the warehouse buildings along Whitworth Street. Factory was a decisive intervention in the city's fabric, one that gestured in two directions: backwards to the industrial past and forwards to the contemporary post-industrial cultural city.

Although other regional cities look to Manchester as an example, the city is an exception rather than the rule. It's difficult to copy, not least because its sheer size dwarfs most other British cities, aside from London and Birmingham. It's a capital in all but name, the centre of the English North West and the largest city in the North. The centre of the industrial revolution in Britain, in the eighteenth and nineteenth centuries its land-scape was remade to industry's requirements as canals reached deep into the city centre and new railways suspended on brick viaducts spanned the streets. Forty miles from the coast, and without a navigable river to reach the sea, its industrialisation was driven by the harnessing of human and mechanical power on a previously unthinkable scale. Its population grew from 10,000 in the early eighteenth century to 700,000 in 1901 – two hundred years that made Manchester Britain's industrial capital and second city. Much of its new population had been drawn there from the countryside nearby or from further afield, by work in its factories and mills. Power looms driven by steam wove cloth at a far greater rate than hand looms ever could, and the industrialisation of the process yielded far greater profits for the company owners. Industrial Manchester was the city made into machine: its canals and railways and factories and even people ever-moving like cogs in a vast and complex mechanism.

Popular culture provided an escape from this determinism. You took joy where you could: on the terraces of the city's football grounds or in the smoky fug of the public house or maybe even in the pleasures of the music hall singalong. With the intensification of mass culture to an industrial scale during the interwar period, as chains of movie theatres expanded across the country, cinema-going became a means of temporary escape. After the Second World War, and the advent of the Cold War, music and cinema provided useful ways to shore up the influence of the Western powers, impressing on populations the joys of an individual freedom that was only guaranteed by the capitalist world. It's no surprise, then, that movies shaped several generations' view of culture, and that when it first arrived in Britain, rock 'n' roll was an image projected on the screen rather than heard on vinyl or seen in the flesh. You could hear the Bill Haley song 'Rock Around the Clock' blasting over the opening titles for the 1955 film *Blackboard Jungle*, or a year later see the kiss-curled thirtysomething Haley in the *Rock Around the Clock* jukebox movie.

Cinemas provided a network of venues for early rock tours: Haley's 1957 UK tour made the rounds of the regional cinemas, which included a February date at the Odeon on Manchester's Oxford Street. Opposite the Odeon was another cinema, the Gaumont, in which local amateurs took the stage between films to perform their act, which often consisted of children miming to chart hits. One of these acts was The Rattlesnakes, a five-piece skiffle group that included the three Gibb brothers – Barry, Robin and Maurice, born on the Isle of Man to Mancunian parents – who would go on to form The Bee Gees. Originally intending to mime along to a hit record, plans changed when the disc was dropped and smashed. Instead, the band took to the Gaumont stage and played several rock 'n' roll cover versions live. Several months later a new act, pared down to the trio of the Gibb brothers, performed at a working men's club in south Manchester. The Gibb family subsequently, in 1958, emigrated to Australia under the Assisted Passage Scheme. Still children – the eldest, Barry, wasn't yet a teenager when they left Britain – they had nevertheless been early participants in British rock 'n' roll.

Over time pop moved from the screen to stages and from there to the high streets of regional towns and cities. Pop culture was mimetic: something to be copied and refined. Coffee bars became a place for young people to linger, meet up and listen to the latest records on the jukebox. On Oxford Street, the Plaza Ballroom ran lunchtime dances DJed by Jimmy Savile. Soon clubs opened, often jazz clubs rebranded for a new audience, as with Manchester's Oasis on Lloyd Street, or in the former location of a coffee bar, as with the Twisted Wheel on Brazennose Street, which took over the premises of the Left Wing coffee bar. (Dean West and the Hellions, later renamed Herman's Hermits, had been the house band at the Left Wing.) In 1965 the Twisted Wheel moved to Whitworth Street. It was during this period that one can trace the beginnings of the Northern Soul phenomenon. The club's DJ, Roger Eagle, played black rhythm and blues, and his selections became increasingly obscure as the clientele demanded higher-tempo, less-well-known records that often originated from Chicago and Detroit rather than the southern American states. The Twisted Wheel didn't have an alcohol licence but drugs were plentiful, with many revellers at the club's all-nighters driven by amphetamines. The blueprint for Northern Soul – the all-nighter culture, the high-tempo music and the high-intensity dance moves – spread from the Twisted Wheel across the North.

Sixties Manchester had its beat-pop bands who followed in the wake of those emerging from Merseyside. Freddie and the Dreamers, Herman's Hermits and The Hollies all went from playing local clubs to national and international chart success. On 1 January 1964 the first episode of a new pop music chart show, *Top of the Pops*, was broadcast from the BBC studios on Dickenson Road in the Manchester suburb of Rusholme, with Jimmy Savile presenting and The Hollies appearing alongside The Beatles. After two years broadcasting from Manchester, the show moved to London – reflecting the general trajectory of musical acts from the regions to the capital. The concentration of music industry infrastructure in London – the record company offices and recording studios – meant that, if you were from a regional city, 'making it' often involved leaving home, and if you became a success it was more than likely that you would never come back.

But there were notable exceptions. The rock star trajectory wasn't the only one available to young musicians. Graham Gouldman was a Salford-born songwriter whose compositions – clever and catchy three-minute pop songs drawn from everyday life such as 'No Milk Today' and 'Bus Stop', or bewitchingly dark love songs like 'Evil Hearted You' and 'For Your Love' – were covered by Herman's Hermits, The Hollies and The Yardbirds. Looking back at this period, Gouldman would tell a story about how strange it was to stand at the BBC studios watching The Yardbirds play 'For Your Love' on *Top of the Pops*. (His own band The Mockingbirds were a regular warm-up act for the show.) Gouldman went on to become a songwriter-for-hire, moving to New York in 1969 to work for the bubblegum pop production company Super K, run by Jerry Kasenetz and Jeff Katz. Returning to Manchester, he convinced the company that he and a group of musicians could produce the kind of hits Kasenetz and Katz wanted – catchy, cheaply made throwaway pop. He had become a partner in Strawberry, a Stockport recording studio named after The Beatles' song 'Strawberry Fields Forever', and Super K agreed to Gouldman's proposal, hiring the studio for the production of new music.

The deal meant that the owners of the studio – Gouldman and his fellow musicians Eric Stewart, Lol Creme and Kevin Godley – could continue to improve its facilities. The group effectively became a house band, playing on records that included anthems for the football clubs Everton and Manchester City and the album *Space Hymns* by Ramases, who was a central heating plumber and singer from Sheffield who believed himself to be the reincarnation of the Egyptian pharaoh of the same name. The Strawberry musicians, minus Gouldman, had released an album under the band name Hotlegs in 1970 – their single 'Neanderthal Man' reached number 2 in the charts – and once Gouldman was back in the fold the project quickly evolved into the better-known 10cc.

At Strawberry they were essentially overqualified session musicians who could seemingly turn their hand to anything – bubblegum pop with American accents, falsetto girl-group backing vocals, whatever was necessary to turn around a song to a client's satisfaction as quickly as possible. When it came to releasing music under their own names with 10cc, songs tumbled out in near-deranged polyphony, with twisted falsetto vocals that sounded like the strings of an orchestra. This was evidence of a warping of identity, of playing with pop personae that was the inevitable result of years spent writing songs that would become hits for other people, or of recording hits for fictitious bands, as Gouldman did for Super K brands like Ohio Express. A new voice and style could be adopted for a single track before being discarded. It wasn't unusual for each track on a 10cc album to sound radically different from the one before, as if it was the work of a different band. Although the band were deeply rooted in Greater Manchester, 10cc's work was an escape from place. At the heart of their work was an industriousness that took as its inspiration the hit factories of the kind that Gouldman had worked for in New York.

Taking advantage of the cutting-edge studio they had constructed, 10cc recorded a series of increasingly experimental albums such as 1975's *The Original Soundtrack*, which included 'I'm Not in Love', a six-minute anti-love song accompanied by an orchestra of layered tape-loop vocals. Often the band's lyrics occupy a strange imaginary world that isn't quite the USA and isn't quite Britain – rather it's a kind of placelessness that you might experience if you spent most of your day in a recording studio drawing inspiration from wherever you found it, from old rock 'n' roll records and the latest news from troubled parts of the world. 'Rubber Bullets', released in 1973, splices jailhouse rock with the riot-control projectiles fired by British troops in Northern Ireland. The schizophrenic nature of their sound wasn't just the product of expert musical pastiche, it was a genuine reflection of a band pulling in different directions simultaneously. There was a division within 10cc between the more traditional melodic songwriting of Stewart and Gouldman and the experimental tendencies of Godley and Creme. Eventually this tension led to a split in 1977 during the recording of the *Dangerous Bends* album.

Aside from the records, many of which were wonderful and strange slices of art pop, 10cc's long-term legacy was Strawberry Studios. It was a cutting-edge facility within easy reach of Manchester and provided a relatively affordable place for local bands to make professional-sounding recordings. For Factory producer Martin Hannett, Strawberry became the studio of choice: it was where he recorded Joy Division, The Durutti Column and, later, Happy Mondays. One day I took a train there from central Manchester and walked from the station until I reached the building that once housed the studio. It's a three-storey redbrick building that might have once been a warehouse; its external walls are painted black at the ground-floor level. Above the ground-floor windows, whose sills and arches are painted white, is a sign that reads 'Strawberry Studios Stockport', with the 'A' in the first word replaced by an upside-down cartoon image of a strawberry. To the left of what appears to have been the main door is a blue plaque listing the studio's years of operation – 1968 to 1993 – and a selection of acts who recorded there: Paul McCartney, Neil Sedaka, The Stone Roses and The Syd Lawrence Orchestra. Such concision told only part of the story.

*

I took a train back to Manchester and made my way to the Radisson hotel, a relatively new building which has preserved the Italianate, pillared façade of the Free Trade Hall but little if anything of the interior. The hall had been funded by public subscription to commemorate the repeal of the Corn Laws, legislation that onerously taxed imports and had the effect of raising food prices and thus the cost of living. Opened in 1856, replacing a wooden building that had served as a temporary hall, it stood on Peter Street. The area was known as St Peter's Field, an open space regularly used as a site of protest during the early years of the nineteenth century. It was the site of the Peterloo Massacre of 1819, during which eleven people were killed and hundreds injured by troops during a protest in favour of parliamentary reform.

The Free Trade Hall served as a venue for political gatherings, and it became a regular venue for performances by the Hallé orchestra, which was formed in 1857. It suffered bomb damage during the Second World War and was rebuilt, and soon after its reopening it began to host popular music acts, including Paul Robeson and, famously, in 1966, Bob Dylan. The American folk singer's set was half-acoustic and half-electric, the latter provoking purist elements in the crowd into boos and slow handclaps.

I lingered for a moment outside the hotel, then stepped inside and approached a doorman, who was standing sentry. Daylight shone through the building from the rear, where a glass-walled area looked on to what had once been Manchester Central station and is now an exhibition centre in which political parties occasionally have their annual conference. He told me that there wasn't much left of the original building, that it had been substantially rebuilt when it became a hotel. I asked him about the room upstairs that had once been the Lesser Free Trade Hall, but it was fairly clear it was long gone.

The Lesser Free Trade played a highly symbolic part in the story of the local punk scene, hosting two Sex Pistols gigs. It was the venue in which two future members of Buzzcocks, Howard Trafford and Pete McNeish (later known as Howard Devoto and Pete Shelley), organised a Pistols gig on 4 June 1976. Although the concert was sparsely attended, it's seen as a galvanising moment for local punk, and by extension for the Manchester music scene. (It's not clear whether Tony Wilson was actually there, though he frequently claimed that he was, and the often fictional Wilson biopic *24 Hour Party People* depicts him foppishly pogoing at the front.) The Sex Pistols returned to the same venue the following month, and they played two more gigs in the city in December of that year, at the Electric Circus, an old hall in the suburb of Collyhurst frequently used for heavy metal gigs that had become a major venue for Manchester punk.

Perhaps the focus is on a single Sex Pistols gig, the first one, because it's easier to believe in a single moment that acted as a catalyst for a much larger movement. But it was the second one that appears to have been better attended and more influential. It was this one that Deborah Curtis went to with her husband Ian, who was frustrated at having missed the first gig. 'After the performance everyone seemed to move towards the door', she wrote, 'as if we had all been issued with instructions and now we were set to embark on a mission.'[1]

The scene up until then had been sustained by Buzzcocks, so it was little surprise they were the first to release a record. The independently released *Spiral Scratch* EP, issued just a month after it was recorded, demystified the record-making process by example. It was an object lesson in how a band could produce a record without following the traditional route of signing to a record label. Produced by Martin Hannett (credited on the sleeve as Martin Zero), it consisted of four tracks of high-tempo punk, each of which was between two and three minutes in length. It sped by, tripping over itself with excitement, Shelley's vocal contributions tending towards the melodic, Devoto's delivered with considerable topspin. A month after the EP was issued, Devoto left the band to start Magazine. In a short few months a handful of Manchester musicians had come up with a blueprint for independence that would be emulated by bands and small labels across the country.

The inscription on Tony Wilson's gravestone at Manchester's Southern Cemetery reads 'Anthony H. Wilson. Broadcaster. Cultural Catalyst'. It can't help but raise a laugh while simultaneously being completely serious. It's a final gesture that's peculiarly suited to Wilson, whose pretension was an essential part of his persona, and who wanted to harness the subversive potential of the French avant-garde artists the Situationist International in his cultural provocations. Yet his role in Manchester's cultural scene was undoubtedly that of an enabler and I wasn't surprised to see his image displayed, shrine-like, on a wall of Affleck's Palace market on Oldham Street. He's now widely seen as a secular saint, the pioneer who sparked Manchester's ascendance as a cultural powerhouse.

More than anything, Wilson understood myth and the role it played in music, and he knew how to fabricate context – to make it up but also how to weave it skilfully, seemingly from thin air – for the reception of work, creating an atmosphere in which the artists who recorded for his label, Factory Records, could thrive. He was the flawed ringmaster hawking Factory's three-ring circus, stirring up an audience's expectations, keeping the show on the road at all costs – and Factory's legendary profligacy meant that those costs were high.

At the time he started Factory, Wilson was a presenter for Granada Television, a northern franchise of Independent Television that had begun broadcasting from Manchester in 1956, promising, in the words of its founder Sidney Bernstein, 'a chance to start a new creative industry away from the metropolitan atmosphere of London'. Wilson, who presented current affairs programmes as well as a music show, *So It Goes*, broadcast in 1976 and 1977, seemed to take Bernstein's words to heart, believing it was possible to run a record label along the same lines, harnessing a similarly maverick vision.

Factory had begun as a club night held in the Russell Club, also known as the PSV Club, in Hulme, a working-class area south of the city centre and west of the studenty Oxford Road. At the time, Wilson and his friend Alan Erasmus were looking for a venue in which the band they managed, The Durutti Column, could play, and they found the Russell, a social club frequented by Afro-Caribbean bus drivers that was sited amid the Hulme Crescents, a curving brutalist social housing development constructed in the early seventies. The usual club nights at the Russell catered for black audiences from Hulme and nearby Moss Side, and consisted of reggae and American soul, whereas the Factory booked up-and-coming punk bands.

Wilson wanted to put together a compilation of the bands that played at the Factory, including The Durutti Column and Joy Division, and on Christmas Eve 1978 he released *A Factory Sample*, two seven-inch records in a plastic bag with a cover by the graphic designer Peter Saville. With this release Factory became a record label. Perhaps the provisional nature of the arrangement – that Factory, at this stage, was more an idea in a few people's heads than it was a tangible business – explains why the label's offices were housed for so long in a flat in Didsbury. One can't help but regard the Factory story as a stumble into greatness – a greatness they were unprepared for, and consequently never knew quite how to handle.

Factory Records consciously reflected Manchester's industrial heritage in its name, its use of industrial imagery and even in the sites it chose to occupy in the city centre. It was born of industrial decline; manufacturing became a metaphor, a promising concept to build the label around. The surroundings of industrial Manchester provided plenty of inspiration. Alan Erasmus, one of the founders of Factory, said he got the idea for the name when he saw a sign saying 'Factory for Sale' – 'I thought, "Factory, that's the name" because a factory was a place where people work and create things, and I thought to myself, these are workers who are also musicians and they'll be creative.'[2] (Inevitably, there's another version of this tale: Tony Wilson and promoter Alan Wise saw a sign saying 'Factory Clearance'; and another, told in Wilson's 2002 book *24 Hour Party People*: Erasmus saw a sign saying 'Factory Closing' and thought they could have one that read 'Factory Opening'.)

Factory didn't start out based in the network of rivers, canals and railways that marked the industrial city centre, but in the comfortable middle-class suburb of West Didsbury, in Erasmus's flat, on the first floor of a redbrick Victorian house that had been subdivided into individual units. The label was a product of the friendship between Wilson and Erasmus, the latter a softly spoken mixed-race actor who had appeared in a number of television programmes including the Liverpool-set sitcom *The Liver Birds*.

Remarkably, the label continued to be based in the flat from its inception in 1978 until 1990, when its operations moved to the wedge-shaped HQ building on the bank of the River Medlock. I had heard that Erasmus still lived in the house, and had tried to contact him through an intermediary who knew him, but had no luck – he had long been reluctant to talk to journalists, and it was obvious that I wouldn't be the one to change his mind. Nevertheless, I took a tram out to West Didsbury to see the building, strolling from the station along Palatine Road, past a layby set aside for idling buses, to the old Factory headquarters. What had once been the front garden was now covered with loose gravel that had been compacted over time by its use as a car park for the house's residents. A row of eleven wheelie bins was lined up along the garden wall, giving some idea of the number of flats within. A black Range Rover was the only vehicle I could see parked outside, and I wondered if it belonged to Erasmus. Looking at the slightly shabby grandeur of the house – three floors, arched windows with a gabled second storey – it seemed an incongruous location for a record label. A couple of months after my visit, an English Heritage blue plaque was unveiled on the front of the building by Shaun Ryder of Happy Mondays: 'Now everyone knows where Alan Erasmus lives,' he said.

Factory's longevity and reputation were built on the label's relationship with two bands who were essentially two phases of the same group: Joy Division and New Order. After frontman Ian Curtis's suicide in 1980, Joy Division, who had recorded their debut album *Unknown Pleasures* in Strawberry Studios with Martin Hannett, reconvened under the name New Order. The producer's association with New Order ended after the recording of their debut album, which was characterised by a guitar-based minimalism that recalled Joy Division, albeit with guitarist Bernard Sumner taking over vocals. The new group would stay with Factory until its end, pursuing a sound that allied a traditional rock line-up with electronic dance music, resulting in a series of classic albums throughout the 1980s. But Wilson was always on the lookout for another artist who would sell in numbers to help fund Factory's other signings – and to help to patch up any shortfall in their other projects.

One Friday evening in May 1984, the young Scottish footballer Pat Nevin arrived in Manchester. His club, Chelsea, were playing Manchester City in the Second Division, and the match was to be screened live on television. He scored a goal, Chelsea won 2–0, and he was awarded man of the match – 'it was a big moment in my career', he told me by phone. Afterwards, the Chelsea team returned to London while he lingered in Manchester, intending to visit the Haçienda, the nightclub run by Factory Records a couple of miles north of City's Maine Road ground. As a keen fan of indie and a regular reader of the music press, Nevin was drawn to the nightclub by its mystique – it was an extension of Factory, whose impeccably designed records he had collected for some time. The chance to visit the club run by one of his favourite labels was too good to pass up.

These were the early days of the Haçienda – although it had already been open for two years it didn't yet draw crowds in large numbers. That would happen a few years later, when the club became closely identified with dance music. That night in the Haçienda, Nevin says, there were only about ten people present, and other descriptions of the time support his recollection, making the club sound like it had something approximating the atmosphere and select clientele of a doomed regional arts centre. Nevin stayed at the club all night, before heading to the station in the early hours of the morning, sleeping on a bench, and catching the first train back to London.

The Haçienda was a grand gesture by Tony Wilson, a gamble that a new nightclub and venue could provide a stage for the kind of culture he and his associates imagined for Manchester. The club took its name from a utopian text about an ideal city by Ivan Chtcheglov, a member of the Lettrist International, the group that later became the Situationists. Chtcheglov's work was a deeply poetic mythologisation of an imagined city that might respond to human emotion rather than mere need, and wished for the construction of such a place. 'You'll never see the hacienda. It doesn't exist,' Chtcheglov wrote. 'The hacienda must be built.' (Factory needlessly added the cedilla to the 'C' in Haçienda – it doesn't occur in the Spanish word – because they thought 'çi' resembled '51', the Factory catalogue number they had attached to the club.)

By 1982, Rob Gretton, the manager of New Order and their predecessors Joy Division, had become a partner in Factory, and suggested that they should open a nightclub. Wilson and Gretton had spent time in New York on tour with the Factory bands New Order and A Certain Ratio, and Gretton wanted to mimic clubs like Manhattan's Danceteria, a multi-storey venue that combined dance and rock. The time spent in New York influenced New Order's music, which shifted towards electronic synth and sequencer-based dance. The Haçienda would be a club that fitted this new direction. Much of the money required for the design of the club was New Order's, and the band would continue to provide an influx of cash to keep the Haçienda running over the ensuing years.

When it opened on 21 May 1982, the club didn't resemble the beer-soaked subterranean spaces you'd habitually stumble into on a typical Mancunian night out. It was fitted out with brushed steel, concrete, granite, safety bollards on a sprung maple dance floor, a strangely positioned stage, and a bar named the Gay Traitor after the Cambridge art historian-turned-Soviet spy Anthony Blunt. It was a three-dimensional manifestation of the industrial aesthetic evident in the visual identity Peter Saville had established for Factory. (The designer responsible,

Ben Kelly, would later work on Factory's Dry bar and head-quarters building.) The cost of refitting the Haçienda building was, at the time of its opening, around £340,000 – a huge sum to carry out improvements when you consider that it was a building Factory rented and would never own. This must have eaten away at Wilson, influencing his later property dealings. Factory would henceforth own their buildings outright, refur-bishing old properties with Kelly's cutting-edge, and expensive, interior designs. But this combination of property investment and costly redecoration, along with the label's move towards paying large advances to unproven acts, would take its toll on Factory's finances.

Factory was known for its handshake deal with its artists that split earnings fifty/fifty between the artist and label, with the band retaining control of the rights to the recording and the label picking up the costs associated with recording and pro-motion. This was less about Wilson's equality and idealism than a result of his relative inexperience. The terms of the deal were pushed by Rob Gretton rather than Wilson himself. The label's deal with Joy Division for the band's debut *Unknown Pleasures* was then replicated in subsequent agreements with other acts, much to Factory's financial detriment.

When it came to making a deal with Happy Mondays, a rau-cous gang of drug-dealing Salfordians, for their second album, *Bummed,* Factory broke with precedent and drew up a contract that gave the band a royalty rate of 20 per cent and an advance of £40,000. They were the first band to be contracted to the label. While the Mondays' debut album, *Squirrel and G-Man Twenty Four Hour Party People Plastic Face Carnt Smile (White Out),* had been released by Factory under the old terms, there was a growing need on both sides for a more secure relation-ship. After their debut, the Mondays had no commitment for a second album from Factory, and needed money. Meanwhile, Nathan McGough, the band's manager, told me that the contract 'was born out of Tony's insecurity', believing that McGough 'would take the band to a major label'. (Factory's Gary Mc-Causland remembers the push for a contract and advance as coming from the band rather than the label.) The introduction of contracts benefited the band by giving them a wage of £80 a week, drawn from the advance, while the security of a contract enabled McGough to secure a publishing deal with London Records and an American deal with Elektra.[3] 'Wilson at the time was like, "Well, maybe we need to grow up,"' McCausland told me. Happy Mondays were 'his next big hope. He had lots and lots of bands that he thought would be the next big thing' that would reduce the label's reliance on New Order's earnings, lessening the influence their manager, Rob Gretton, had on Factory. Wilson 'wanted something which would give him that little bit of autonomy'.

Gary McCausland had come from Northern Ireland to study at the University of Manchester, leaving his PhD in Economics when he got a job working with Factory in 1988. He stayed with the label until the very end – the day that it declared bankruptcy in November 1992. Joining as a production assistant, he worked his way up to Production Manager, then Head of Marketing and Production, then Head of International.

The deals that Wilson had struck with Factory's artists up until 1988 meant that the label 'wasn't building up an asset base and any value', McCausland said. When Factory attempted to get mortgages to buy buildings, they didn't qualify because they had no contracts with their artists. Rob Gretton wanted to buy the Haçienda building, but Factory couldn't get a mortgage. They needed tangible assets to borrow against. 'That was really what underpinned' the introduction of contracts, said

McCausland. Although talk of tangible assets and mortgages doesn't quite fit with the utopian Factory mythology, these changes were necessary for the label's expansion. 'It's the untold story,' McCausland explained, 'that nobody realised the reason why the contracts were brought in was because the label didn't actually own anything.'

The introduction of contracts was one factor that enabled Factory to buy buildings: the property that would become Dry bar on Oldham Street, and the old textile warehouse on Princess Street that, after a significant and costly refit by Ben Kelly, would become the label's headquarters. The cost of Dry delayed the HQ building, with the label eventually relocating in September 1990. In the meantime, Factory continued to operate from Alan Erasmus's old flat on Palatine Road in West Didsbury. I asked McCausland what it was like to work from there: 'It was lean, man. It was lean. There were no overheads, there was no bank overdraft then. There were no liabilities. If you had a hit record you actually made money.'

While the Haçienda still needed the occasional injection of cash, it was beginning to draw crowds in 1988 and 1989. The Haçienda 'wasn't the drain', McCausland said. 'It was the rest of the empire' – the acquisition of Dry and the headquarters building and the cost of refurbishing them. 'The problem was that the empire, if you want to call it that – and Wilson would probably hate the fact that I used that word – had overstretched itself.'

The record label, on which all the other projects were dependent, had begun to lose money in a big way. 'The aspiration was to go from a DIY label that got lucky,' McCausland said, 'and then you have to grow up and try to be a big major independent record label. And it just totally overstretched itself. The record label was haemorrhaging money.' The introduction

of contracts was meant to usher in an era of maturity and se-
curity for the company, but it didn't quite work out that way.
Contracts entailed advances, and on a few notable occasions
Factory overpaid for artists who didn't set the world alight. For
Cath Carroll, a former journalist who signed a four-album deal
with Factory, the label paid an unusually large advance – over
£70,000 – for a relatively unknown artist whose previous band
Miaow had already been signed to the label. The recording of
Carroll's debut album at Sheffield's FON studios overran, and
cover photography and promotional videos pushed the cost for
that record to as much as £150,000, according to Carroll herself.[4] But there were other signs of Factory taking costly risks.
James Nice's book on Factory, *Shadowplayers*, reports that the
label budgeted £100,000 to include an advance and recording
for a band called The Adventure Babies, and £90,000 for the
Scottish band The Wendys. An advance usually reflects a label's
assessment of future sales for a band, as it's essentially a loan
that will be repaid by the band from royalties. By any estimation
Factory had overpaid for these artists. (At first I found these
figures difficult to believe, until someone showed me a Factory
chequebook he had retrieved when the label went under. The
cheques were in dollars – Factory's American account was held
with a New York branch of National Westminster Bank. Some
stubs remained, indicating the amount a cheque was made out
for and who it was paid to. One stub read: 'Factory transfer
Wendys Advance 165,000'.)

This profligacy could just about continue as long as New
Order and Happy Mondays continued to produce hit records.
McCausland told me that Wilson had been searching for another band to build Factory around, someone who would reduce
the label's dependence on New Order. With Happy Mondays it
seemed like he had found that act. But could they be relied upon

to produce a string of successful records, a new album every couple of years, as New Order had? During the period between 1987 and 1990 Factory released records from both bands whose sales rivalled and even outstripped majors – New Order scored their first and only number one in June 1990 with the official English football anthem 'World in Motion'. But it was risky to assume that such success would endure. The label's continuing survival would be tied to both bands' productivity.

The large advances were a sign of a deeper panic. McCausland told me that, near the end, activity at the label 'became a little bit frantic'. Factory moved from their offices on Palatine Road to the headquarters building that had cost a fortune to refurbish. The mortgage repayments for their properties were becoming difficult to repay. 'They were trying to get a mortgage off German banks using royalties from Rough Trade Germany, our licensee, because the mortgage rates were cheaper.' Advances were now being paid in monthly instalments rather than in lump sums. They were waiting for the next New Order album. 'And then the Mondays imploded.' Factory had sent them to Barbados to record the album *Yes Please!*, a disastrous excursion during which members of the band smoked crack cocaine, Bez crashed a car and broke his arm, and lead singer Shaun Ryder failed to write any lyrics. When they returned, Factory sent Ryder to Brighton 'with a load of drugs' to come up with the missing lyrics. It was becoming clear that the Mondays weren't the act that would save Factory.

But not to Wilson. McCausland says: 'I remember having a conversation with Wilson before *Yes Please!* He said to me: "We're going to do three hundred thousand, Gary," and I said: "Tony, honestly we'll be lucky if we do fifty."' The album sold around 60,000 copies, 'and that was a massive disappointment when you've spent three hundred grand [on recording]'. It was released at the end of September 1992. Factory hung on for a few weeks more before filing for bankruptcy.

McCausland told me: 'I was there on the last day when the liquidators came in and we all went to the pub.'

'Had you been expecting that?' I asked.

'Yeah, I hadn't been paid for four months. We all sort of knew.' Factory had been hoping that a deal with London Records would save them. 'But at the end of the day the only artist that had any long-term bankability was New Order. And there was no contract. There was actually nothing to buy, apart from some properties in negative equity.'

I had been wandering around the city's Northern Quarter early one evening when I decided to visit what remained of Factory's Dry. I had seen images of its heyday online, in which the room looked bright and pristine, like the kitchens area of an IKEA showroom. By the time I arrived, however, it was painted in dark colours, badly lit, and the leather sofas were worn. The place had a vague menace that was probably more an effect of the decor and low-wattage lighting rather than the clientele, and the general sense I got was that it was just about hanging on. Nevertheless, I ordered a beer and sat at the bar for a little while, watching a handful of customers come and go. A few months later the bar would close for good. Only the Factory HQ building remained open to the public, as a nightclub. (The Haçienda closed in 1997.) Yet Tony Wilson and Factory's legacy was frequently invoked in connection with the contemporary city. Wilson had posthumously ascended to the position of patron saint of post-industrial Mancunian culture, a visionary who had predicted the lofts and venues and lifestyles of its latter-day urban acceleration. The urban plaza outside the HOME arts centre was named after him, and there are plans to build another arts centre at his former workplace, Granada

Studios, that will be called the Factory. Wilson, everywhere and nowhere, had become the myth he had always aspired to.

My own relationship to Manchester's music began in my home city of Dublin. I had recently turned sixteen when my parents drove my cousin Leon and me to the Tivoli Theatre in Dublin's Liberties to see Oasis. It was early September 1994, and the band had released their debut album, *Definitely Maybe*, a couple of days before. I had only recently begun to read the music press, and I had followed Oasis's rise closely. I had bought their early singles, and so anticipated the gig with excitement.

My memories are of a dark venue: a wide room with two levels. On the higher level was a bar to the right of the stage, the lower level was the dance floor, where I saw people wandering around wearing Stone Roses T-shirts. I had some idea of how Oasis were being portrayed as part of a continuum of Manchester bands that stretched back through the Roses and Happy Mondays. In their early demos the relative lightness and sweetness of lead singer Liam Gallagher's voice recalled Tim Burgess of The Charlatans. But that was soon superseded on the records by a raucousness that recalled both Johnny Rotten of The Sex Pistols and John Lennon.

These were superficial resemblances that Oasis were keen to cultivate. Bands emerge from a specific context, and even though they might have talked about The Beatles or The Rolling Stones in their press interviews, they'd learned from the people around them, the bands they knew personally or those they looked up to who enjoyed some success, showed them what was possible. Oasis were no different. They consciously invoked the great Manchester bands of the past, such as The Smiths, whose records had been a perfect combination of lead singer Morrissey's nostalgic outsider wit and guitarist Johnny Marr's limber, melodic guitar work. Lyrically and musically Oasis lacked the subtlety of The Smiths, yet found inspiration in them – especially Marr, whom Oasis guitarist Noel Gallagher identified as a 'lad'. (By boiling the complexity of The Smiths down to blokeish relatability, by editing out the sexually ambivalent Morrissey, Gallagher was gesturing towards the classic rock chauvinism his band would ultimately pursue.)

But Oasis were more in line with, if rarely as transcendent as, The Stone Roses, a mop-topped four-piece whose self-titled debut album, released in 1989, melded the euphoria of dance music with classic rock in a way that seemed unforced. Another influence, especially lyrically, was Happy Mondays, but Oasis fell short of the consistent laugh-out-loud surrealism of Shaun Ryder's deft wordplay and lacked the Mondays' funk. Hints of the influence of dance on Oasis, admittedly primarily filtered through the Roses and the Mondays, had been evident on songs such as the early, trancelike, 'Columbia'. But by the time of their second album Oasis's work had erased most evidence of non-rock influence in favour of retro heritage rock. The barely controlled wildness of the band's early records gave way to a more self-consciously epic rock, leading to the overblown nadir of their third album *Be Here Now*. The second-hand surrealism had outlived its use, and the wall of distorted guitars, so vibrant on early songs like 'Slide Away', had lost its thrill.

The band were a throwback in other ways: they left Manchester – Noel had lived in India House, a converted warehouse on Whitworth Street not far from the Haçienda – and relocated to London. It was a reminder of the moves bands had made in the sixties. London was the location of their label, Creation, an indie whose Factory-style financial troubles had been resolved by the major label Sony investing in the company.

Ultimately, Oasis became the curators of a certain idea of

guitar music that was characterised by an hour or so of intense manual labour. The work was divided between five performers, and each had distinctive job descriptions that were essential to the overall sound. As the band continued, members were replaced, until the only original members were the Gallagher brothers, and eventually that relationship broke down too.

The rise of Oasis, despite initially trading on the sort of dance-rock that had become a feature of Manchester guitar bands, was ultimately a reaction against the increasing automation of music. The traditional organisation of workers within a band was under threat from electronic music: one or two people standing on a stage in front of a bank of synthesisers or computers, pushing buttons while a field of people on synthetic drugs have a good time. It traded on authenticity, a gritty classic rock realism that suited the members' working-class, industrial origins. It was a nostalgic reassertion of the primacy of industry in the face of post-industrial music-production techniques.

Another of the bands Oasis would sometimes mention in interviews was World of Twist, a Manchester group who had released only one album, *Quality Street*, in 1991, and subsequently broken up. One day I met Ian Rainford in Manchester's Northern Quarter. He met World of Twist early in their career, when he was on the same youth training scheme in video production as a couple of band members, going on to help to design and build sets for the band's stage show, as well as directing promotional videos for their singles. One of these videos, for 'The Storm', was filmed on the top floor of the building that housed Factory Records' Dry bar on Oldham Street. Happy Mondays had recently made the video for their 'Hallelujah' single in the same room, so there was still graffiti sprayed on the wall reading 'Call the Cops!' While taking a break from filming, they went downstairs to the bar on the ground floor, and the place was completely empty. They had unwittingly arrived just after Shaun Ryder had smashed a mirror, either by throwing a bottle or by firing a gun, depending on which account of the incident you believe.

For the second video, they built a set that was covered in fake fur with a giant clamshell for keyboard player Jules to sit in. 'We had a lock-up in Ancoats, and we built this big clamshell,' Rainford said, 'and we couldn't fit it in a van, so we had to put it on the back of a trailer, and I had to hold on to this big clamshell [all the way] to the studio in Stockport,' where the video was filmed. They made the video, and neither of the two singles was a hit, 'so the label were suddenly then like: "nah!"' The band had been signed to Circa, a subsidiary of Virgin. The Bristol group Massive Attack had signed to Circa around the same time, but the labelmates were going in markedly different directions. Massive Attack 'went off and did that video for "Unfinished Sympathy"', which was filmed in Los Angeles, and meanwhile World of Twist were 'stuck in Ancoats building a big clamshell!'

The band's lead singer, the charismatic Tony Ogden, was 'exciting to be around', Rainford told me. But he was also troubled, and a reluctant frontman. He would ensure that the band stood in a line onstage, and he would stand to one side when he performed. Ogden suffered from mental ill-health that was exacerbated by the band's lack of success. When Rainford toured with the band he shared a room with Ogden, and recalls him crying every night. When they began to record a second album, Ogden decided that he didn't want to be the singer any more – 'he wanted to be the drummer', Rainford said. 'Which is outrageous. Because he was brilliant – one of the best frontmen I've ever seen.' They auditioned singers to replace him. At a gig in the Sheffield Leadmill, local band Pulp supported World of Twist. Pulp's mainstream success and lead singer Jarvis Cocker's celebrity 'could have happened' for World of Twist, Rainford thinks. But the second album wasn't picked up by Circa, and the band fell apart.

Afterwards, Ogden moved back to his mother's house in Stockport, and continued to have mental health problems, but he returned to music and began to record again with a friend called John West under the name Bubblegum Secret Pop Explosion. Rainford had started his own band, Mum and Dad, and approached Ogden to arrange vocals for a track called 'Dawn Rider', which he did, but didn't want to sing it. When Ogden was found dead in a Stockport park, it was a shock, 'because it seemed like he was having a bit of a turnaround'.

The memory of World of Twist has been kept alive by the band's fans. After Oasis split up, lead singer Liam Gallagher formed a new band, Beady Eye, and the B-side of their debut single was a cover of World of Twist's 'Sons of the Stage'. For a 2009 public artwork in Manchester, the artist Jeremy Deller printed a banner that read 'We Miss the World Of Twist'. 'You meet people in bands and they're usually quite boring, but [Ogden] was like something else, really,' Rainford said. 'He was like a proper star. I'd never really met anyone like that.' In comparison to the complexity of World of Twist, whose songs were distinct, as if products of different bands in a similar way to the work of 10cc, Oasis kept it relatively simple and were rewarded for it.

It was time to leave Manchester. I walked east along Whitworth Street from the apartment building that stands on the site of the Haçienda nightclub. It was dark now, and the glow from a building beyond the railway arches lit up the evening. The building

I could see was called Home, a glass-clad complex containing cinemas, restaurants and theatres that stands on a plaza named Tony Wilson Place. In 1976, Manchester was in decline, much of its city centre left derelict when Britain's industrial era ended. What would happen to the empty buildings, the bulldozed sites, to the large population whose ancestors had been drawn to the city by its thriving industries? Punk inspired a generation to create something new, to put in place an independent infrastructure – venues, record labels, shops – that helped to nurture and sustain bands over the ensuing decades. Factory Records, started by a group of people that included the television presenter and impresario Tony Wilson, became an important hub of cultural endeavour, releasing records by local acts and putting on gigs in the Haçienda, an old warehouse redeployed as a music venue. Despite successful bands and a thriving venue, the label's efforts to become financially stable came to naught. Yet the legend of Factory persists, an idiosyncratic cultural endeavour built on the ruins of Manchester's old industries.

2.

LIVERPOOL

When I checked into my budget hotel on Liverpool's Dale Street I couldn't help noticing that the wall above my bed was covered in images of the *Sgt. Pepper*-era Fab Four. Their four giant heads were outlined in white on a black background. Their faces had been reduced to a haircut, eyebrows and moustache, and, in the case of John Lennon, the addition of an extra element, a pair of granny glasses. None of the hotel room Beatles had eyes or noses, meaning that the centre of their faces formed a strange inexpressive void to consider as you lay awake on the bed below. These were blank spaces that I unconsciously filled in, so familiar were the band members' features from the record sleeves, promotional photos and films I had seen them in over the years. I could picture the (invisible) ridge of John Lennon's nose that his (visible) glasses hovered on. When you try to reassemble the past you often tend towards imagining the parts of it you can't quite reach. You fill in the gaps.

I was in Liverpool to find out a little about what made this largely working-class city a byword for sixties beat music, and why it continued to produce such great bands through the punk era and up to the present day. Any scene depends on venues, record shops and labels to give local musicians a sense of community – somewhere to run into Rory Storm in the sixties or

Jayne Casey in the eighties – and to allow them opportunities to perform, record and make money. It also depends on people who are more drawn to the business side of music who can help to create the conditions in which musicians thrive, of which Liverpool has had many notable examples, including Brian Epstein, who ran a branch of his family's NEMS music shop before managing the Beatles. A few years later, in 1971, Geoff Davies opened an independent record shop, Probe, which became a Liverpool institution and a regular haunt of musicians like Julian Cope and Pete Burns. In the 1980s he started an independent label, Probe Plus, on which the Wirral surrealists Half Man Half Biscuit have released many records since their 1985 debut album *Back in the DHSS*.

When I met him in his house, a redbrick semi-detached on a leafy street in south Liverpool, Davies told me about his background. As the son of a docker, he could have easily gone into his father's profession, which was seen as a desirable job, but he chose not to. A few months before the end of his education, his school organised a trip to a local electronics factory to see if the students, who were then aged in their mid-teens, would be interested in that line of work. Davies had just seen Charlie Chaplin's film *Modern Times*, which depicts the alienation of the worker as a result of repetitive factory work, and decided it wasn't for him: 'I thought: fuck that.' Instead, he went along each side of Dale Street, the business area of the city that adjoins the Cavern Quarter, looking for work. Eventually he was taken on at the Liverpool Stock Exchange at the west end of Dale Street, not far from the docks, working as a clerk and answering phones. It was during this period that he saw The Beatles for the first time.

Davies used to go to the Cavern to see British traditional jazz acts like Humphrey Lyttelton and Kenny Ball. One night he heard a rock band who appeared just after the jazzmen and was unimpressed at their racket. It turned out to be The Beatles. But later he went with a friend to a lunchtime session at the Cavern at which The Beatles were playing and this time realised that they had something. The Cavern had been opened in January 1957 in the redbrick arches of the cellar of a fruit warehouse on Mathew Street by Alan Sytner, who had been inspired by Parisian Latin Quarter jazz clubs such as the Caveau de la Huchette. Soon jazz was joined by skiffle, a primitive acoustic version of rock 'n' roll that local band The Quarrymen played. The latter made a couple of appearances at the Cavern in the late fifties, but it was after the club was sold to Ray McFall, and Beat nights were introduced, that The Beatles became regular performers. By then they had already spent time abroad in Hamburg, playing seedy Reeperbahn nightclubs for hours at a time, perfecting their covers of rock 'n' roll standards during amphetamine-driven marathon sets.

What impressed Davies when he got to see The Beatles again was the way the band interacted while performing. They would closely watch each other, playing off what the other members were doing, and this reminded him of jazz groups. During their cover of 'Money (That's What I Want)', a tough, cynical R&B song co-written by Tamla Motown founder Berry Gordy, Lennon would sing with, Davies told me, 'complete and utter disgust', spitting out the lyrics. Lennon's was very much a dramatic performance. 'It was so mean, as though he was acting out his disgust.' Recordings from the time confirm this, with Lennon dropping in pauses and adding emphasis to heighten the drama of the song. But when it came to be recorded by the band for their second album, the darkness and drama of Lennon's vocals were considerably toned down, sanitised for the pop market.

The Beatles' gigs at the Cavern formed a key stage in their development, and the venue was where their future manager

Brian Epstein saw them for the first time. He had learned of the band through the local fortnightly music paper to which he contributed columns, *Mersey Beat*, which was edited by Bill Harry, who had been John Lennon's fellow student at Liverpool School of Art. First published in July 1961, the paper sold in huge numbers on Merseyside – where bands numbered in their hundreds – and became so closely identified with the local music scene that the Liverpool sound came to be referred to as Merseybeat. Its influence soon stretched beyond Liverpool, covering bands from other regional cities in the North. As its reach extended, Harry ran articles promoting Merseyside bands to London-based record companies. *Mersey Beat* helped to sustain an infrastructure of bands, venues and fans. When The Beatles succeeded on a national level, other Merseyside bands followed.

I was curious to know what had happened before The Beatles' ascent to local fame, to find out a little more about where they had come from. I decided to travel to the neighbourhood in which Lennon and McCartney had grown up, walking in a west-to-east direction between McCartney's terraced council house in Allerton and Lennon's aunt Mimi's semi-detached middle-class home on Menlove Avenue, a journey of just over a mile. I had a vague idea of the trajectory I would take, across a golf course that sat between my departure point and my destination, but I didn't know exactly how I would do it. Would there be a path through the golf club or would I have to dodge across the fairways?

Early in their career The Beatles became one of those phenomena that seem specific to the mass culture of the mid-twentieth century. As a child born in the late seventies and growing up in the eighties, I could still detect the glow of their aura, although they were by no means omnipresent. Perhaps that continued glow was stoked by a nostalgia for what they represented to a generation that came of age in the sixties, a nostalgia that must have been prematurely accelerated by the assassination of John Lennon in December 1980. I was two at the time of Lennon's death, so it was not part of my consciousness. But I do recall something that happened a little later: on hearing a Beatles record, I was told by my mother or father that John Lennon was dead. To me this placed the band in the distant past, more a historic event than a cultural phenomenon. When I listened to their records I was engaged in unearthing the past. My parents didn't have a huge record collection, but among some seven-inch singles I found and played on their record player was an Irish pressing of 'Help!', with the McCartney-sung B-side 'I'm Down'. The Beatles compilation we bought for my dad – which was released in October 1980, before Lennon's death, but we could well have purchased later – was frequently played on a small tape recorder, and, later on, the tape deck of our car. But that was it. I didn't know about the albums or even the films until many years later. So my primary contact with The Beatles was McCartney, with songs like 'We All Stand Together' (popularly known as 'The Frog Chorus') and 'Wonderful Christmastime'. The Beatles were a distant phenomenon, but McCartney was a proximal presence, familiar and faintly embarrassing – like a lovable uncle who broke into humorous song inopportunely. At the same time there was a warmth in his work that I'm sure other children aside from me responded to, and a sweetness and unassuming straightforwardness – I would later learn this simplicity to be an artful illusion – to The Beatles songs that he wrote and sang.

For me, McCartney and the Beatles seemed completely separate things. I couldn't quite connect them. I'm not even sure I knew he had been a member, but I recall being told this by my parents and not being able to associate the McCartney you'd see thumbing and gurning in music videos with the impassive Buster Keatonesque visage of a highly stylised McCartney in the hippyish illustration on the sleeve of *Beatles Ballads*. (Again, I'm not sure if I could picture The Beatles at this point, working with the materials I had at hand.) Later, when I was in my late teens, I was in a covers band that, in line with the Oasis-era tendency, lionised Lennon while being slightly suspicious of the work of McCartney, but I could never quite go along with it, especially when I listened to the laziness of some of Lennon's seventies work. When I walked between McCartney's house and Lennon's, and I became aware of the possibility that I was retracing their steps, it was Paul's perspective I was drawn to rather than John's.

I had arrived at Paul's house by taking a local train from Lime Street to West Allerton station, a rickety yellow-painted wooden building that looked like it probably hadn't changed too much since Paul was a child. Only the occasional train stopped there, and I assumed it was mainly used by commuters. Paul's house was a short walk away, through a small estate of three-storey redbrick flats and terraced houses, a working-class area tucked into a largely middle-class suburb. Number 20 Forthlin Road itself stands in a neat post-war redbrick terrace, with a gated passageway leading to the rear of the house to the left of the sitting room's sash window. The drain pipes are painted red, and the white front door closely matches the square-paned windows. Now owned by the National Trust, it's pristine: a time capsule of McCartney's past, while also gesturing more widely to the context that produced him, a post-war society that built new council houses in large numbers and enabled his genius to flourish. There's a tension between the exception and the rule in figures like McCartney: an exceptional talent, but one which may not have flourished in different circumstances. Post-war

investment in housing and education supplied a relatively be-
nevolent context in which he could thrive. I began to speculate.
If these houses had been larger, and privately built, it's unlikely
the McCartneys would have lived here, and the chances of The
Beatles forming would have been reduced. I felt like I was doing
sums in my head about how one could accurately predict The
Beatles, the possibilities of something going wrong, as if I was
plotting the optimum trajectory of a rocket headed for space.
I thought it ridiculous, but then considered for a moment the
kind of planning that goes into trying to foster creative cities.
Could you plan for The Beatles? And what if that plan was
slightly off? I toyed with the idea that had McCartney's house
been five hundred metres further east, his whole geographical
centre would have been shifted: instead of getting the bus to
school, the bus that was often driven by George Harrison's dad,
he might get the train, and Lennon's house might have seemed
more of a schlep, and instead he might have become an account-
ant or something.

As I walked towards the McCartney home, a guided tour dawdled into my path. Their guide gestured to the house and talked
about the family: his father Jim, his mother Mary, a nurse who
died when Paul was a teenager, and his brother Michael, later
Mike McGear of the Merseyside pranksters The Scaffold. The
small group of tourists listened intently, asking questions, while
I wandered over to look at a National Trust plaque that listed
the members of the McCartney family and gave details of how
one could access the house, which was closed at that moment
but would open for guided tours over the summer months.

I turned and walked north-eastwards, crossing Mather
Avenue, one of three dual carriageways that dig into middle-
class south Liverpool, which also include Brodie Avenue and
Menlove Avenue, on which Lennon lived with his aunt Mimi.

These three roads provided a framework for me to understand this unfamiliar territory, to get a sense of where I was when exploring The Beatles' world. Because this was recognisably the landscape of The Beatles. It seemed like a zone arranged specifically to provide the sort of relatively comfortable, happy childhood for which twenty-something rock stars who had seen the world fall at their feet might become nostalgic. Its parks, avenues and bucolic lanes opened a wormhole into the idyllic version of Englishness of the kind you could abstract from the *Sgt. Pepper* album: bandstands and hedgerows and a sense of purposeful leisure. It happened to provide a particularly reassuring imaginative landscape in which to play hide-and-seek as an escape from the profound strangeness of global stardom.

I climbed a hill, passing semi-detached houses, and stared through their windows at the Christmas decorations. It was a week until Christmas Day, three days until the shortest day of the year, and the afternoon sun was weak, watery and hung low in the sky. A mist was descending, and the fading light of the sun lent it a strange, unworldly glow. I reached a road that, although suburban, retained a bucolic charm, and heard the metallic clink of a golf ball being struck. Beyond a stone wall and a clump of trees I could see the golf course I had been seeking, on the other side of which was Lennon's house.

I've never been a huge fan of golf, even though for a while, in a short-lived teenage engagement with a stripped-down version of the sport, I played pitch and putt with my dad. While I liked the idea of large swathes of green space being kept in suburban areas, I also knew that these places were essentially private property, and thus inaccessible except to members or trespassers. Nevertheless, during my limited engagements with golf courses in England – the one I sometimes cross during a walk near my house in Sunderland, the one I went to near Ryton along the River Tyne whose grounds were on fire because of burning coal spoils beneath the fairway – I had learned that there were sometimes rights-of-way that cut across the courses.

At the entrance to Allerton Manor golf course was a gate house next to a lane leading towards the clubhouse with a barrier across it to stop unwanted vehicles. Next to the golf club's sign, which was surrounded in fairy lights in a festive gesture, was another more functional sign that indicated the rights-of-way. Confusingly, rather than showing me a single trajectory to take towards Menlove Avenue, it showed me three, one of which broke away south across the course and ended up nowhere near my destination. The other two appeared more comprehensible and useful to me, so I quickly took a photo of them with my phone, just in case I became stranded and needed guidance. I set off, following well-trodden earth that suggested a frequently used path.

As I mentioned earlier, I was beginning to think of myself as Paul McCartney making the journey by foot from his house to John Lennon's on Menlove Avenue. I'm not a religious person, but a sense of what I had unintentionally undertaken had begun to descend on me with the odd, unworldly clarity of a saint's vision, near where Cleverley Road meets Allerton Road. I'll try to explain it rationally. I hadn't eaten lunch, so my senses were affected by my flagging energy in ways I can't quite pinpoint. The oddness of the mist that hung illuminated by the strange winter light above the fairway mixed with my blurred consciousness to create a peculiar atmosphere. It fostered in me a sense that my experience was somehow slipping between Whitney and McCartney as I walked onwards, a dialectic process, a semi-dream state of faux-collaboration in which I now realise I should have co-written a song with the McCartney I had conjured up in my head.

I pushed on, wondering if McCartney would have worn these light trainers that were now soaking up the mud that had resulted from weeks of wet weather. The right-of-way took a sharp turn left past a row of trees, then right, where it became a narrow, swampy channel of sludge that in better conditions would have been a path. It cut alongside some houses, and to my right I could see the pristine fairways. I looked at the green, well-tended golf course, and cast a glance to my sponge-like trainers, squelchy now in the boggy wetness of the path. It seemed like a most un-McCartney activity, this trudging through muck, unless it was the post-Beatles, countryside-loving McCartney I was now channelling, but I'm sure he would have worn sturdier footwear.

The line of trees gave way to a hedgerow at about waist height, allowing me a view across the fairways. The light was slipping away and the view was softened by the fog, still lit in the faint evening light by a warm glow. A lone golfer was barely visible in the mist, fading away as he followed the sequence of holes around the course. Ahead of me I could see a gap in the trees, and I could hear the roar of traffic. Infected as I was with this strange sense that I was being someone else (the bass player for The Beatles, who surely followed this path around sixty years before), and that my path was being laid out for me, I went ahead.

McCartney used to check in to hotels under assumed names and enjoyed wearing disguises like false beards – you can see him don one in the opening sequences of the 1964 film *A Hard Day's Night*. It's most likely this was straightforwardly about a star's desire to remain unrecognised, to try to hold on to some kind of normal life, but I wondered if there was also in this a desire to establish an equivalence between the 'Paul' he was meant to be – the one in The Beatles, the one everyone thought they knew – and the fake identity. That the interplay between the two implied that neither was real, or that one was as real as the other. There was a long-running conspiracy theory that Paul had died and been replaced by someone else, that the Paul on *Sgt. Pepper* wasn't the same one as the Paul on *Revolver*, that the flower arrangement on the cover of the later album formed a cluster of words that read 'Paul is Dead', and it was as if general frustration at the mass mediation of human unknowability had suddenly become homicidal.

Once, at a gig by the Liverpool band Cast in the Tivoli Theatre in Dublin, I saw the actor Ian Hart standing around drinking with a group of people that included members of the headlining act. Even though I knew he was in Dublin to act in Neil Jordan's *Michael Collins*, which was being filmed at locations around the city, when I saw Hart there I thought, immediately: John Lennon. It was the mid-nineties, and at that point Hart had made his name with two uncanny performances as John Lennon in *The Hours and Times* and *Backbeat*, the first a speculative fictionalisation conjured from the fact that Lennon and Beatles manager Brian Epstein holidayed together in Barcelona, the second a raucous account of the band's Hamburg years, with a scuzzy soundtrack of rock 'n' roll covers in a Fab Four style by a group of grunge-era musicians including members of Nirvana, Soul Asylum, R.E.M. and The Afghan Whigs. It provides a seriously weird answer to a question that no one had asked: how would the early Beatles have sounded if Greg Dulli of The Afghan Whigs was John Lennon and Dave Grohl of Nirvana was Ringo Starr? Interestingly enough, the band couldn't find a McCartney to match Dulli's Lennon, and instead Dave Pirner of Soul Asylum's vocals failed to match Paul's own attempts at a Little Richard impersonation.

In cinematic portrayals of the band McCartney has often seemed peripheral, aloof and unknowable, whereas Lennon could be pinned down as an angry genius raging against the system. (Later, Hart played Lennon once more, in *Snodgrass*, a film that imagined a parallel history in which Lennon left the Beatles, lived on, and ended up on the dole in Birmingham.) Rock 'n' roll is a form founded on impersonation. Everyone's pretending to be somebody else, adopting a persona and playing out a part. I couldn't help but wonder if the enduring perception was that McCartney was a little too good at playing his part, or perhaps multiple parts, whereas Lennon couldn't sustain the role. Those cracks in the façade gave actors something to work with.

My shoes sodden from the muddy path, I walked through the gap in the hedgerow, down the steps leading to Menlove Avenue. The roar of traffic grew louder as cars sped by in the half-light of the late afternoon. This was the road on which Lennon had lived with his aunt and on which his mother died, hit by a car driven by an off-duty policeman after she stepped from the central reservation into the traffic lane on the way to the bus stop. The speed of the traffic and the lack of a safe crossing – there were no lights or pedestrian crossings visible – still made it difficult to get to the other side of the road. I waited for a gap in traffic, scampered across to the central reservation, then repeated the process, before reaching the opposite side and, after a brief walk, 251 Menlove Avenue, where John's aunt Mimi reputedly made Lennon and McCartney rehearse in the front porch. (The house is central to another cinematic portrayal of Lennon, Sam Taylor-Wood's *Nowhere Boy*.)

I continued along Menlove Avenue in the direction of the city centre, then decided to take a detour back towards West Allerton station. The light was low, and I saw to my right a funfair that had set up in a park illuminated in the dusk, while the mist hung just above the wet grass. I decided to go in and have a look, and as I stood on the marshy ground, my sodden shoes sinking into the wet turf, I watched the Ferris wheel slowly spin and remembered the final track on the first side of *Sgt. Pepper's Lonely Hearts Club Band*, 'Being for the Benefit of Mr. Kite!' The fairground appeared a gaudy mirage hovering on the horizon, a cluster of trailers and tents disguised by a combination of the fading day and its own coloured lights as something that transcended its limitations and acquired a level of unthinkable glamour. Although I would later find out in the cold light of day that it was called Santa Land UK and was by no means from another world (the operators had a business address in Wigan), at that moment it seemed to manifest the kind of wonder and transcendence I had been feeling as I retraced The Beatles' childhood world.

At school we used to have a teacher whose memorable persona I subsequently came to understand as a performance. It was an all-male, extremely Catholic school located in what seemed the middle of nowhere, a geographical situation that left me feeling stranded far from any sense of coherent or stable identity. Maybe everyone there felt the need to put up a shield, to assume a role, including the teachers. Hence the tendency towards the outsized melodrama of teacherly performance, designed to intimidate and entertain. This teacher, who was nicknamed and would frequently refer to himself as Bulldog, would often announce to the class, to prove his toughness and obstinacy, that 'I wasn't born, lads, I was quarried!' This came to mind as I walked along Quarry Road, uphill from and parallel to Menlove Avenue, where the Lennon house stands. There's a covered reservoir on the hill that lends nearby Reservoir Road its name. I could see from here towards a tree-lined hill on the horizon, which, on consulting my map, seemed to be Woolton Wood. I reached a ridge of exposed sandstone that edged, surreally, right up to a housing estate, as if it were a wildly overgrown tree root. A pathway led along the top of this ridge in the direction I wanted to go.

It's tempting to believe that The Beatles were chiselled from this landscape. Although it's well known that the band that eventually evolved into The Beatles was originally called The Quarrymen, it's worth restating here. The band took its name from the anthem of Lennon's nearby Quarry Bank grammar school, a song which finds in the metaphor of digging stone from the ground plenty to occupy it lyrically for several verses of hymn-like pep. ('Quarry of manhood! Quarry bank! Rock of the lives before us.') It had seemed to me that if the school had been named after a quarry, that quarry was probably long gone, but when I saw the exposed sandstone and began to climb the path up the hill I realised that the stone ridge I was walking along was likely to be a remnant of the hymned quarry. As I ascended, I could see to my right a hollowed-out hill that now formed sandstone cliffs that curved around a suburban road. A large, modern detached house sat incongruously at the foot of a cliff, overshadowed by a sheer wall of red stone. The stone was of an instantly recognisable colour, the colour of many buildings in Liverpool city centre, and the quarry had been the source of the red sandstone used to construct the city's Anglican cathedral.

I continued uphill along the path, which was fenced on both sides for safety's sake because of its vertiginous position atop a narrow wall of stone. At a certain point the wall of stone met a wider plinth of bedrock, and the landscape returned to normal. I passed two workmen fixing the fence where it adjoined a school playing field, and wondered if it might have been the field in which The Quarrymen played at a church fête in the summer of 1957, when Lennon first met McCartney.

The church, St Peter's, stands at what appeared to me the highest point in the area (it's also reputed to be the highest point in Liverpool), uphill from the village of Woolton, atop the sandstone cliffs that I had seen from the path. Lennon had childhood connections with the church, a short walk from his aunt Mimi's house – it was where he had attended Sunday school and sung in the church choir. When he stepped onstage at the church fête, he was sixteen, wearing a check shirt with the sleeves rolled up and his hair in a quiff, and he and his band ran through skiffle hits and their own versions of rock 'n' roll standards. In a much-reproduced photo taken on the day he stares straight into the camera, and thus gives the impression of staring straight out of the photo, his right hand blurred as he strums his acoustic guitar, while the other members of the band – a tea-chest bass player, a second guitarist, banjo player and drummer – seem oblivious to the photographer's presence. It's a tough, unblinking stare. Paul had already seen him around: 'This Ted would get on the bus. I wouldn't stare at him too hard in case he hit me.'[1] This quote makes me wonder if John's actually peering irately into the crowd at Paul McCartney, who himself, albeit unintentionally, had stared too hard for a few moments, maybe during the band's version of Lonnie Donegan's 'Puttin' on the Style'.

Nevertheless, after The Quarrymen finished their two sets and removed to the church hall, McCartney was introduced to them and took one of their guitars to perform a cover of Eddie Cochran's 'Twenty Flight Rock', followed by a version of Jerry Lee Lewis's 'Whole Lot of Shakin' Going On' on the church hall's upright piano. John sat alongside Paul, and, in a halting gesture of friendship and collaboration, leaned over to play along. Paul noted the smell of beer on his breath. Lennon agonised over bringing in a member of the band whose musical skill he thought superior to his own, but gave in and within a couple of days McCartney was a Quarryman. From the highest point in Liverpool, where can you go? 'Where we going, fellas?' John Lennon would later ask, as The Beatles made the circuit of regional dancehalls. 'To the toppermost of the poppermost, Johnny!' the band would answer.[2]

When I arrived at the church, a small group of people waited at the roadside for a funeral, two black traffic cones reserving space for the hearse. Others stood around next to the side door of the church. I felt like the tourist I was: ticking off sights before moving on somewhere else, in the process descending on a site that wasn't mine at a particularly inopportune moment. I encountered a group of tourists, a family whose language I couldn't identify, whom I had seen at another Beatles site down the road, the Strawberry Field gates. They were just leaving as I arrived, and I couldn't judge exactly where in the graveyard they had come from. Aside from St Peter's being the place where Lennon finally met McCartney, it's the site of Eleanor Rigby's gravestone. In one account of how the song was composed, McCartney said that he got the first name Eleanor from the actress Eleanor Bron, who had appeared in the film *Help!*, and the surname Rigby was taken from the name of a clothes shop.[3] If you take him at his word, the coincidence is fairly mind-boggling. Alternatively, it's possible he was dredging through memories to find a name that scanned and happened upon this one, or through a process of random combinations resulted in a name identical to the one on the gravestone that I was looking for. I considered asking the people waiting outside the church where the Eleanor Rigby grave was. But then thought about how it would look to them, waiting to bury a loved-one and friend, and how it would look to future readers of any narrative I might write about the scene, and decided not to. I got an inkling, then, of the ethics that might surround naming one of your most famous songs after a real person, and why you might deny it in any future interviews. Instead, I wandered around the graveyard in a concentric circle, trying to zone in on the text of each gravestone as I walked, like someone speed-reading a jumbled-up phonebook whose text has been somewhat eroded. Eventually I found the gravestone, not far from the entrance gate, where Eleanor Rigby, who died in 1939, was buried along with members of her family. I thought for a moment of the strange eternity she had posthumously been dragged into, simply because of the coincidence of a name on a stone near where Lennon and McCartney met. Perhaps there are worse fates.

I strolled down the hill to Woolton, a well-kept middle-class village, and waited for a bus back to the city centre. There was a short gap until the next one was due, so I turned up a side street to the Woolton Picture House, a beautifully preserved one-screen cinema opened in 1927, and as I stood outside I could clearly recall the pleading notes the young Lennon used to leave for his uncle George, the husband of his aunt Mimi: 'Dear George, will you take me to Woolton Pictures?'[4] (Mimi refused him all but a couple of trips to the cinema a year, but George was more amenable to John's demands.) Sam Taylor-Wood later filmed scenes from *Nowhere Boy* in the cinema.

Leaving the Picture House, I returned to the bus stop and jumped on the first bus that came along. I've long been convinced that there are deep connections between public transport and memory – that an old map of bus routes and train lines can conjure deeply embedded memories. This is born from my personal experience of writing about Dublin bus routes in my first book, how their trajectories embodied a certain perspective on the city, one that shaped my childhood understanding of my home and my place in it. So I was intrigued when I discovered lyrical traces of Liverpool's public transport system in The Beatles' mid-period work. Of the song 'Penny Lane', for example, Philip Norman writes that it is 'in effect, a view from the top deck of a 1950s green Liverpool Corporation bus, possibly with George's dad at the wheel, while waiting for the conductor to ring the bell for departure'.[5]

As their songwriting progressed, the relationship between The Beatles and the landscape of south Liverpool became a subject of explicit investigation. At a certain point, when incessant touring was becoming a grind, the studio began to seem a cocoon from the outside world and The Beatles' attention turned inwards, towards their own consciousnesses and their personal experiences. Specific memories became viable songwriting material. This played out in different ways among the band members, and the new direction arguably first shows itself in Lennon's songs on *Rubber Soul*, particularly the pseudo-bohemian one-night-stand shenanigans of 'Norwegian Wood (This Bird Has Flown)', and the suburban Dylan's Mr Jones-style archetype, shot through with autobiographical self-laceration, of 'Nowhere Man'. Dylan was the clearest influence on this personal turn in their work, but the muted nostalgia of 'In My Life', from its earlier drafts referencing specific Liverpool landmarks, to its finished, universalised lyrics, provided an even more durable framework for the referential and deeply personal work to come.

When you look at an early draft of Lennon's lyrics for the song, you see that it's structured around specific locations and features that he enumerates: Penny Lane, Church Road with a view of a clock tower (I assume the Church Road that intersects Penny Lane, but the street leading to St Peter's in Woolton shares the name), the circle of the Abbey cinema, Calderstones Park. He includes references to public transport: the now-tramless tramsheds, the 'Dockers Umbrella' which was an overhead railway that had run along the Mersey until its closure at the end of

1956, when Lennon was turning sixteen, and what looks like a reference to the number 5 bus. This jumble of references is dealt with uneasily by Lennon in this draft, as if he doesn't know how to manage them into a coherent song. Description isn't enough for him, or perhaps defeats him, and he instead turns, like an essayist rather than a reporter, towards his own relationship to the material, and it's there he finds the emotional core of the song. The finished version doesn't refer to Liverpool at all yet feels steeped in the city. It's universalised by its lack of specificity but remains haunted by its repressed locations.

On a BBC radio programme in November 1964 the presenter, Brian Matthew, asked the band if they ever got tired of being Beatles. What about the simpler things in life, he asked, like . . . 'riding on a bus', McCartney replied.[6] You can see this yearning for the anonymity of everyday life, the relative banality of ordinariness, dramatized in *A Hard Day's Night*, their debut film of the same year, where the band's relentless urge to escape the confines of their train compartment, dressing room or the back seat of a taxi cab represents the wider constraints of a pop career. Ringo briefly escapes, and proves ill-equipped for the outside world, ending up arrested for disturbance of the peace. Their estrangement from their pre-Beatles lives seemed complete and irreversible, and this loss became a focus for an accelerated nostalgia, eventually finding its way into their songs, initially uncomfortably with the earlier draft of 'In My Life', which the released version refined into a nostalgic, universal song of love and loss, but soon coherently and brilliantly on 'Strawberry Fields Forever'/'Penny Lane', a double-A-sided single that's kaleidoscopic in its complexity.

Two paths lead from 'In My Life'. These are illustrated by the two sides of the 'Strawberry Fields Forever' and 'Penny Lane' single. One path leads towards a deeply personal, idiosyncratic essay, and the other towards an observational, lightly fictional-ised vignette. Lennon seemed more comfortable pursuing the former, while McCartney quickly mastered the latter. As Lennon was turning his attention inwards, McCartney was looking out. Both songs are explicitly located in the same stretch of south Liverpool landscape: the territory of their childhoods filtered, perhaps distorted, by the songwriters' creative imaginations.

If McCartney's natural inclination is towards disguise, he has employed this tendency in his songs to brilliant effect, frequently embroidering them with clues to their fictional nature. The 'face' that Eleanor Rigby keeps in a jar is obviously symbolic of the brittle and brutal English middle-class urge to keep up appear-ances, and the lyric is surely a product of years of McCartney's observation of that class. From the McCartney home's position – a council house located in a largely middle-class area – to his friendship and collaboration with the well-to-do if troubled Lennon, to living on the top floor of the north London family home of his girlfriend Jane Asher, and onwards into the strat-ospheric social mobility enabled by The Beatles' success, you can't help but feel that at every step along the way Paul was taking notes while himself playing a role, adjusting to the situa-tion. Paul's subject, when in narratorial, observational mode, is invariably the peculiarly exotic aridity of middle-class lives. He's more interested in other people than himself, but those other people invariably turn out to be different versions of himself. Eleanor Rigby's face that she keeps in a jar by the door recalls Paul's own.

McCartney is a natural fiction writer, observing characters, subtly shaping their concerns and worries, and occasionally directing them like they're actors in a play. Although they're sometimes given names – Eleanor Rigby, Lovely Rita the meter maid – he's comfortable writing about types that embody deeper emotions and fears, some of which may be his own ('The Fool on the Hill', for example). Sometimes he sings in character. The voice he adopts to sing 'When I'm Sixty Four', an ostensibly personal song that's often thought of as the young McCartney wishing for future stability and comfort – a forthright Lancashire or possibly even Yorkshire accent – is not his own. (Perhaps this is a result of the wider concept of *Sgt. Pepper*, which if anything is an attempt to distil a pan-northern identity through disparate material – the brass bands, the circuses, a lyrical concern with the substandard road metalling in Blackburn – then reprocess it through acid-tinged psychedelia.) Lennon's songs, even when staging scenes of surrealist nonsense, can be quickly traced back to his own personal perspective. You always feel like the songs are being sung by the Lennon persona, while you're never quite certain which McCartney has turned up. I think this is what drives some of the suspicion of McCartney, and why Lennon, whose apparently authentic self is always present, leering at the listener, is an icon, a genius, while McCartney is frequently dismissed as a facile song-and-dance man who's most comfortable with cheesy pop and music hall pastiche. But the protean nature of McCartney's songs merely gestures towards their author's complexity.

Before I went to see Eleanor Rigby's gravestone I had walked up Penny Lane, a reasonably nondescript if fairly pleasant suburban street that passes by Dovedale Road, the location of the primary school Lennon and Harrison attended, and leads to Smithdown Place, where it meets a road that, a little further east, becomes Menlove Avenue. (Before moving to his aunt's house, Lennon had lived at 9 Newcastle Road, a short walk from Smithdown Place, with his mother, Julia.) A tall red sandstone church in which the young McCartney was a chorister overlooks the scene. The landscape feels unusually familiar from its description in 'Penny Lane' – a circle of shops surrounding a central reservation on which stands a strange building, the shelter on the roundabout described in the song, now glassed-in and converted into a restaurant named Sgt Pepper's Bistro, which has been closed since 2004 – a source of much annoyance to local people and the council. The *Liverpool Echo* described the building in 2013, unromantically, as a 'former tram ticket office and public toilet', which doesn't do justice to how it originally looked, an elegant classical building with a crescent of four pillars forming an entrance to a waiting room, ticket office and toilets.

Penny Lane's presence in a discarded early draft of 'In My Life' prompted Lennon and McCartney to return to their childhood haunts for 'Strawberry Fields Forever' and 'Penny Lane'. In the latter, McCartney uses Smithdown Place as a stage for a carefully choreographed scene that hovers somewhere between fact and fiction. The place seems real enough to identify, but the protagonists, although drawn from life, are reduced to types – the barber, the banker, the fireman, the nurse, the children – and the scenes unfold with a wind-up toy-style clockwork precision that appears to surprise even the characters. The song is warped at its edges, cheery psychedelia. The nurse who is selling poppies at the tram shelter, we're told, feels like a character in a play. It's a peculiar feature of this teeming narrative that Paul finds the room to grant her an inner life, and that she would take that moment to reflect upon the fictional nature of the world she inhabits. (Inevitably the figure recalls Paul's mother, Mary, who worked as a district nurse and died when he was fourteen.) The world of the song feels self-contained, miniature and comforting in the way of particularly warm memories of childhood. It's perhaps even reminiscent of *Trumpton*, the stop-motion animated children's television programme that debuted on 3 January

1967, the day before the second 'Penny Lane' recording session. (Here I picture Paul watching children's television at home, notebook in hand.) The programme began with Trumpton townspeople going about their business in a similar way to the barber and banker of 'Penny Lane' and featured a fire brigade who rode their fire engine around town, ending each episode playing a concert at the local bandstand, like a toytown Lonely Hearts Club Band. At certain points in 'Penny Lane' McCartney reminds the listener that it's a playful and elaborate confection, that the blue suburban skies of the chorus are somewhere far away from the south Liverpool scene that he sketches, where in fact it's raining, and that the sounds and sights McCartney experiences are a nostalgic fantasy that he skilfully orchestrates.

I walked from Smithdown Place in the direction of Strawberry Field, which is sited on an incline at the foot of the hill atop which is the churchyard where Eleanor Rigby is buried. A taxi idled next to the wrought-iron gates that marked the unused entrance to the derelict Strawberry Field, as the driver waited for his tourist passengers to snap photos of the graffitied gateposts. The lane beyond the gates was overgrown with weeds, and I imagined it trapped in time: a summer day in the fifties when Lennon was brought here by his aunt for the garden party in the grounds of what was a Salvation Army children's home, or perhaps frozen on the day of the release of the 'Strawberry Fields Forever' single in February 1967. The gates had been disused since the entrance to the home was moved in the seventies, and the home itself was closed in 2005. Nevertheless, when I walked around the immediate area while thinking of Lennon's composition, I found that the woozy atmosphere of the song still clings to the neighbourhood. Further up the hill, on Quarry Road, there's a row of gothic mansions that would look more comfortable in a rural setting rather than interspersed among the suburban fabric. The suburbs of Lennon's youth were interspersed with reminders of a deeper and darker past, and his childhood was troubled. In 'Strawberry Fields Forever' the autobiographical melds with the landscape to produce a deeply subjective and unnerving recollection of his suburban upbringing, a forbidding fairy tale drawn to the dark corners of childhood. Lennon's vocals sound faint, ghostly, like radio broadcasts from a distant past, while the lyrics, jumbled and often incoherent, sustain the claustrophobic atmosphere. The 'forever' in the title seems more a threat than a wish, an ever-repeating circle of hell, and illustrates the sinister underside of The Beatles' nostalgic turn.

In the 1964 film *A Hard Day's Night* The Beatles, chased by excited fans through the streets, take a train from what's meant to be Liverpool's Lime Street station to London to film a musical segment for a television variety show. The scenes were, in fact, filmed in London's Marylebone station, and the terminal they arrive at in the capital is also Marylebone, albeit filmed from a different angle. Thanks in no small part to the band's success, Liverpool had become a marketable brand, an essence which the band had captured and exported successfully. By the mid-sixties, from 'In My Life' onwards, the city would also become a set of memories that they could creatively explore. But London was their day-to-day reality, as they fulfilled a timetable of press duties, recording and touring. The band had transcended their regional act status and their trajectory towards stardom was one that other regional bands closely studied. Their move to London was a journey imitated by other successful acts, such as Newcastle's Animals, and this reflected a growing tendency for regional scenes to be cherry-picked for talented acts who would leave their home city for greater fame in the capital. But, as in Manchester, the independence of punk enabled the rebirth of a local scene, with Geoff Davies's Probe Records becoming a focal point. Additionally, Roger Eagle, the former DJ at Manchester's Twisted Wheel club, co-founded Eric's, on Mathew Street directly across from the old Cavern club. Although it closed in 1980 following drug raids by police, a club called Eric's Live opened under new ownership in 2011 in the same location. Across from Eric's is a reconstruction of the Cavern which attempts to replicate the experience of what it might have been like when The Beatles played the venue (the redbrick vaulted ceiling of the Cavern's cellar has been recreated), while also catering for tourists in search of a drink and some authentically local live music. I took one last walk through the Cavern Quarter on the way to my hotel. It was a strange feeling to walk down Mathew Street, past the John Lennon and Cilla Black statues and venues that claimed to represent the legendary clubs of the past. But at the same time I wondered if it was better to keep these venues, or at least recreate them, rather than erase them altogether. I was still considering this question as I travelled to Lime Street station to take the train to a city whose key sixties venues had been wiped from the map.

3.

NEWCASTLE

My train brought me back to the North East, to Newcastle. For the last couple of years, I've spent most weekdays in Newcastle city centre, working in a rented office on articles and the odd jobs that come along when you're a writer, making a living of sorts. My office is a small room in the corner of a big seventies office block that's scheduled to be knocked down to make way for a shopping precinct, or more offices, or perhaps student housing. But for the moment it hangs on, surrounded by half-empty buildings and a multi-storey car park and within view of the monument to Earl Grey that marks the centre of town. The honey-coloured sandstone buildings of the historic Georgian centre are a street or two away from the office block, which, aside from the odd preserved nineteenth-century façade, lies amid the rotting detritus of Newcastle's largely unloved twentieth-century architecture.

This, in a way, is my Newcastle – the part I've come to understand, the area that intrigues me most. It's familiar to me. This corner of the city is not a particularly comfortable place, or a beautiful place, but it holds a certain charm and plays an important part in the musical history of the city. If I walk out of the main entrance of the office block, cross Market Street East and walk one street to the east, I meet a pedestrian path between a student apartment block and some offices on which stands a tower that's a remnant of the walls of the city. Beyond that is the old site of the city jail at Carliol Square, replaced in the thirties by a telephone exchange. A little up the road, sitting opposite a Catholic church, is the decaying canopy of a defunct bus station that's now used as a car park and a base for a taxi firm. Further on, the buildings are disused, boarded up. While there's some activity in this area – a hostel, a nightclub, a coffee shop, a gym, taxis coming and going, students returning home from class – it lacks the vitality of the city centre core a couple of streets to the west. This zone is, additionally, cut off from the Tyne quayside by the Central Motorway, opened in 1973, which curves around it forming its eastern and southern boundaries.

It feels isolated from the bustle of the city, a place apart. I wondered if this strange, in-between atmosphere was a recent phenomenon or whether it existed back when, on the east side of Carliol Square, the Newcastle rhythm and blues band The Animals used to play all night at the Downbeat Club. Was there an edge-of-town feeling then, too? I suspect so. The Downbeat was located on the upper floor of a two-storey stone building that had once been a school. It stood in a streetscape that embodied working-class industrial Tyneside: next door was a brass foundry, and the surrounding streets were home to warehouses, pubs and terraced houses. To the east of the Downbeat was Manors station, whose railway lines were suspended on brick arches above the streets. Facing the club, on the site of the old jail, was Newcastle's telephone exchange. Although that building remains, much else is changed, not least by the presence of the motorway: for construction of the road, the south-east corner of the square was lopped off, and along with it went the Downbeat. I've walked down there a few times to look for the approximate location of the club, but it can't be reached unless you want to risk life and limb on the motorway below. As close as you can get in its absence is a modern office building with a wedge-shaped footprint that teeters on the brink of the sheer drop to the road's northbound lanes.

In 1961 Nik Cohn, a fifteen-year-old from Derry, arrived in Newcastle to attend the Royal Grammar School. Within a couple of years he would move to London to become a pioneer of music journalism. When he arrived in Newcastle, he found that the city could supply the forbidden glamour he had craved since he had first heard Little Richard's 'Tutti Frutti' screaming from a coffee bar's jukebox back home in Derry. While in Newcastle, he developed a taste for the city's nightlife: the nightclubs, the raucous rhythm and blues bands, the girls. Growing up an outsider in a religiously sectarian city, rock 'n' roll had seemed like a portal to another world, and Newcastle provided him with a first step into that world.

When Cohn arrived in Newcastle in the early sixties it was a tough city dominated by Tyneside's heavy industries of coalmining and shipbuilding. Although some mines were beginning to close as seams became exhausted, the city – its power stations and houses – still depended on coal for power and heat, and the smoke from countless hearths blackened Newcastle's sandstone buildings with soot. Employment in industry was largely male, creating a masculine working world that was mirrored in the social spaces of Tyneside's hundreds of pubs and working men's clubs. But there were signs of change in employment from the 1930s onwards, with trading and industrial estates providing work in lighter manufacturing industries that took on increasing numbers of women. Office and shop work provided still more employment for young men and women, giving them disposable income and greater independence. This shift in the character of employment had implications for young people's social lives, as jazz and rhythm and blues clubs opened to provide alternative spaces where people could meet and dance.

For Cohn, whose parents were intellectuals, pop music provided an escape from rationality, and he embraced it, losing himself in it. 'Self-conscious myself, I worshipped abandon in others,' he wrote.[1] In Newcastle, Cohn indulged a nascent desire for anthropological adventure in nocturnal subcultures, a tendency that would later become his journalistic trademark. 'It was Newcastle that taught me to embrace the dark,' he wrote.[2] Roaming around the bars and clubs of Tyneside, he encountered tribes who gathered in the unlikeliest haunts in Byker, Gateshead and the city centre. Later he would bring these observational skills to bear on the disco-dancing subculture of New York in his article 'Tribal Rites of the New Saturday Night', a notoriously embellished piece of reportage that was subsequently adapted into the hit film *Saturday Night Fever*. His trip through the Tyneside night was an effort to uncover these 'rebel points of light', to map the outposts of subversion in a hard-working, no-nonsense city.[3]

One of these outposts was the Downbeat Club. 'It was stuck on the top of some kind of disused warehouse,' Cohn wrote, 'down towards the docks, and the railway bridge ran right outside it, making it shake.' (A photo from the period shows an unremarkable squat stone building, yet one recognisable as the same construction as that depicted in a nineteenth-century lithograph showing the Clergy Jubilee School.) 'It was cramped, wet, ratty and music made its walls buckle. [. . .] it was a fierce atmosphere. It burned.' Here he saw The Animals for the first time, when they were still called The Alan Price Combo and they played all-nighters. 'Musically, they were quite limited but they came across angry, they hit so hard. Nothing else mattered much but the drive,' he wrote.[4]

The Animals were an assembly of local rhythm and blues musicians who had played on the scene for some time – keyboard player Alan Price had been a member of The Kon-Tors, a pop band who had recorded a demo at the Mortonsound studio, where for a small fee you could cut a record in little more than the time it took to perform a song. Eric Burdon was an industrial design student who would get up and sing with local jazz bands, although his gritty, plaintive howl seemed more suited to the blues. 'Burdon was small and round,' wrote Cohn, 'and he didn't sing in tune much but he had a wild passionate yell [. . .] he fell about the stage like some exploding doughnut.'[5]

Burdon's yell is central to The Animals' seriously limited charms. Without it, you can't imagine their brand of tightly played, skilfully arranged blues pop would have got them as far as it did. In 1964, their version of 'The House of the Rising Sun', a folk song of uncertain origin that had been included on Bob Dylan's debut album, reached the top of the British, American and French charts. The first song on their debut UK album was 'The Story of Bo Diddley', which replicated the bluesman's insistent, repetitive trademark riff over which Burdon attempted to summarise the history of rock 'n' roll in under six minutes, in the process mythologising The Beatles and The Rolling Stones (and thus placing The Animals in that lineage) and finally ending with an anecdote about the bluesman arriving at the Club A-Go-Go in Newcastle to inform the band they're terrible. But at their best, as on their hit singles 'Don't Let Me Be Misunderstood' and 'We've Gotta Get Out of This Place', both covers, the band are truly special, and Burdon's bluesy yearning ceases to function merely as a tribute to his heroes and truly comes alive.

I remember hearing 'The House of the Rising Sun' when I was a child, probably on the radio or on a sixties compilation tape, and I can recall listening to 'Don't Let Me Be Misunderstood' too. The Animals' singles didn't possess the manic thrill of a lot of my favourite songs, which were typically of the kind that would appeal to a child whose musical education consisted of the sugary end of the hit parade of twenty years before and the flashy high-concept videos of eighties commercial pop. Blues-indebted sixties singles such as theirs felt less immediate, more adult. Nik Cohn wrote that Burdon idolised Ray Charles, and certainly The Animals give every impression of attempting to tread carefully in the footsteps of their forebears, never straying too far from the blues ideal, but inevitably, as a result of their geographic origin, sounding very different from the artists they venerated. By channelling bluesmen they were essentially bypassing youth for a doleful maturity, ambivalence, regret, an appropriation that lends them a grizzled character, the Tyne becoming a previously uncharted tributary of the Mississippi. (Although 'The House of the Rising Sun' is a traditional American folk song, its name has a local resonance: the last mine on the north bank of the Tyne was Wallsend's Rising Sun colliery, where Burdon's father, who worked for the electricity board, would often check the equipment.)[6]

The members of The Animals had first become aware of the Downbeat's owner, Mike Jeffery, when they attended his University Jazz Club, which took place over the Gardeners Arms on Nelson Street, a side street adjoining the city's Market. This was Jeffery's first venture in the city, and it attracted students from the nearby King's College, which Jeffery had attended when he arrived in Newcastle in the late fifties, having recently left the army. The whole area is now known as Grainger Town, after the builder Richard Grainger, who redeveloped the centre of Newcastle in the nineteenth century into a network of broad streets of elegant stone buildings. The pub, the Gardeners Arms, had occupied what was the former Cordwainers Hall. Although the pub is gone, the 1838 frontage of the building was preserved when a vast new shopping centre expanded into Grainger Town in the seventies, taking all but one side of Grainger's Eldon Square, and taking its name too.

The University Jazz Club built on an already burgeoning jazz scene in the city. Another jazz club, the New Orleans, had been based in the Labour Club on Melbourne Street since 1954. But Jeffery's University Jazz Club was the beginning of something else: his jazz clubs soon mutated into ideal venues for rough-hewn rhythm and blues that, by the early sixties, provided an edgy alternative to the beat-pop boom. If you could identify where the sound of sixties Newcastle began, it would be in one of Jeffery's Tyneside clubs – either the Downbeat or the Club A-Go-Go.

After the University Jazz Club, Jeffery opened his own venue, a café called the Marimba, on a lane off Grey Street called High Bridge. I walked there through Bigg Market, the centre of New-castle nightlife that, at weekends, is typically the site of drunken revelry, but in the weak sunlight of a Monday afternoon ini-tially seemed to me quite placid. A middle-aged man walked unsteadily out of a busy pub carrying a black sports satchel. He hoisted it up over his shoulder and his whole body tilted under the weight. He raised a foot to try to balance, but it was no good. He collapsed to the ground in what seemed like slow motion, and lay there as a man who had been smoking outside wandered up to him, laughing and reassuring him.

I found a black and white photo online that was taken on High Bridge, apparently just in front of the Marimba, of Mike Jeffery leaning against the boot of a car in the company of two women. One of the women, sitting behind Jeffery, with short hair and caught mid-laugh, is Jenny Clarke, his girlfriend at the time. Although the building in which the café was located is gone, it's easy enough to climb the cobbled incline of High Bridge to the point where the photo was taken, where you can match the photo's background to the current streetscape. Working from my memory of the photo, which I had examined while sitting at my computer a couple of days before, I snapped a picture of the lane as it sloped down to Grey Street. A passer-by who had noticed I was taking a photo waved at me. To my left was the location of the Marimba, now part of a building that used the Georgian façade of Grey Street to mask a redbrick office block whose fire exit opened on to High Bridge. In the old photo, which must date from around the time that the Marimba opened, in 1959, Jeffery, goatee-bearded with heavy-rimmed glasses and wavy, short, dark hair, looks every bit the jazzman, hip and modern. He wears a bird's-eye-patterned jacket over a check shirt and his head is tilted slightly, making it seem like he's regarding the camera sceptically, as if he's hoping to give nothing away.

Jeffery is the most important person in the Newcastle music scene during the sixties, and he remains, if viewed in isolation, something of a dark enigma. His management of The Animals, and later Jimi Hendrix, showed him to be the kind of gangster-ish mogul common at the time, closely controlling his artists' creative decisions while, allegedly, siphoning a considerable amount of money from their earnings. Jeffery had initially co-managed Hendrix with former Animals bass player Chas Chandler, who also produced the guitarist's records, eventually buying Chandler out of his share for $300,000 before the release of *Electric Ladyland* in 1968. At the time of Hendrix's death in 1970 Jeffery was pushing the guitarist to participate in film projects while discouraging his desire to move into a more jazz-based form. Bigger bands and less commercial music, no matter how artistically satisfying they might be, weren't guaranteed to keep the cash rolling in. Unhappy with Jeffery, Hendrix reportedly began consulting lawyers about breaking from his management.[7] Hendrix died soon afterwards. (Jeffery himself died in 1973, when the plane he was travelling on was involved in a mid-air collision.)

Jeffery's most famous venture, the Club A-Go-Go, was opened on the top floor of the Handyside Arcade building on Percy Street in 1962. The club was divided into two rooms: the Jazz Lounge, licensed for the sale of alcohol, and the Young Set, an unlicensed venue where underage customers could attend concerts, tapping into the growing teenage appetite for pop music. It wasn't unusual for the same band to play two sets, one in each room. The Club A-Go-Go was a much plusher proposition than the Downbeat or the Marimba: owing to changes in the gambling laws, the Jazz Lounge was fitted out with roulette and *chemin de fer* tables.

Once a week, The Animals would play both rooms before leaving at around midnight to play the Downbeat, but mostly they were the resident band at the new club, playing one of the two rooms there. The Club A-Go-Go had an edge to it. Bryan Ferry, then a teenager in a covers band, recalled the hard men 'like gangsters' who used to go there, and Jeffery employed tough doormen and a club manager, Myer Thomas (Ferry: 'he was a great character – really scary'),[8] who would dole out cash to performers at the end of the night. The Animals went from playing the Downbeat and the Club A-Go-Go to a residency in London in a matter of months. In January 1964, they moved to the capital with Jeffery as their manager, and fame quickly ensued.

The Club A-Go-Go continued to bring rock, soul and blues music to Newcastle – The Rolling Stones, Sonny Boy Williamson,

Captain Beefheart. And in March 1967, the Jimi Hendrix Experience played two gigs at the club. But from 1964 onwards the exemplars of the Newcastle sound, The Animals, were elsewhere, touring around Britain and America. In 1965, Alan Price left, and the band continued in various incarnations until the end of the sixties. Eric Burdon, drawn to the cod-spiritualism of American psychedelia, began to pursue a solo career. In 1969, Nik Cohn believed he had lost the edge that gave his early performances such power. He had begun to preach: 'these days, his records are tracts and his interviews are gospels,' Cohn wrote. 'He sermonizes endlessly.'[9]

The building in which the Club A-Go-Go had been housed, the Handyside Arcade, was knocked down in the late eighties and replaced with an extension of the Eldon Square shopping centre, Eldon Garden, linked by an enclosed bridge across Percy Street. The arcade had, in the sixties, been a hotbed of alternative shops which included a hippy clothes store owned by The Animals' drummer John Steel. Film footage from 1967 of a 'love-in' held in the arcade shows a crowd of teenagers, some of whom are clad in sheepskin and beads in an approximation of West Coast hippydom, watching a performance by a local band whose vocalist was a young Bryan Ferry.

Ferry's Roxy Music, the band he would form at the turn of the seventies once he had relocated to London, produced a mutated, amplified, distorted, dissected and reconstituted version of the kind of shout-along bluesy chug that had been a mainstay of the Newcastle scene. Unlike The Animals, Roxy were no longer in awe of the music's Delta origins, or eager to prove authenticity, and instead took joy in the synthetic character of their strange futuristic pop noise. The bands that Ferry had performed with during his time in Newcastle provided some of the cloth from which Roxy Music would be cut: The City Blues, an R&B band,

and the seven-piece Gas Board, the band who had played at the Handyside Arcade 'love-in', who were influenced by the Stax label's brand of gritty soul. With Roxy Music these influences were jaggedly imposed on one another at awkward angles, a cubist collage, a seemingly contradictory mass of influences re-shaped into something coherent and novel. Yet you could still recognise the elements they had used to fabricate the work.

This self-conscious cut-and-paste appropriation is a product of Ferry's experience of a specific artistic milieu at Newcastle University. Ferry was from Washington, the rural Durham village that in the sixties expanded into the new town in which RCA built the record plant whose ruins I had visited. He had taken full advantage of his home's proximity to Newcastle, travelling to the city to take up part-time jobs, to buy records, musical instruments and clothes, and to go to gigs. When he left school, he got a place on the Fine Art degree course at Newcastle University and moved to the city. Ferry shows how pop music could become a means of social mobility. The music scene in many regional cities held out the opportunity for those who were good enough to 'make it' – to go beyond the relative confines of their home city and make a wider impact. This often involved, as it did in Ferry's case, a move to London, where one encountered likeminded musicians who had often come from similar backgrounds in comparable towns and cities. His father was from the rural working class, but Ferry was a grammar schoolboy drawn to music and film. As a child, Ferry would attend showings in the Carlton cinema, tucked away behind a redbrick terrace next to his father's allotment a couple of streets from the Ferry family home. It was a particularly unglamorous location, but cinema provided an escape.

In his teens he'd travel to Newcastle to a music shop that's still there, JG Windows, in the Central Arcade, an elegant tiled

79

Edwardian passageway near Grey's Monument. Here he'd pick out the latest jazz records, ask to hear them, and walk to a booth to listen to the record on a tiny speaker before deciding whether to buy it. Initially a fan of jazz and blues, he was also intrigued by the arrival of rock 'n' roll in Britain, making the short trip with his sister to see Bill Haley's tour when it arrived in Sunderland in 1957.[10] As a teenager he took a job in a Newcastle tailors' shop, Jacksons, looking through old style books when he wasn't taking down customers' measurements and advising them on suits. He grew interested in the intersection between music and fashion, and became a Mod. While in the sixth form of Washington Grammar School, Ferry started making trips to the New Orleans Jazz Club on Melbourne Street, seeing a pre-Animals Eric Burdon. He joined a rock 'n' roll covers band, The Banshees, and played local venues: working men's clubs and, eventually, the Club A-Go-Go. 'You'd go up these stairs, past all these bus drivers and bus conductors who had a tea-room or an office there, and the club was at the top,' Ferry recalled.[11]

Leaving his covers band to become a university student in 1964, Ferry encountered a Fine Art department in Newcastle University (as King's College had been renamed) in which the artist Richard Hamilton taught. Hamilton was interested in the Pop Art of Warhol and Robert Rauschenberg, in the artistic possibilities of mass production and mass culture. He had developed his ideas as a member of the Independent Group in the 1950s, a gathering of artists, architects and critics in London's Institute of Contemporary Art (ICA) who investigated the potential uses of modern methods in the construction of artworks. Central to this was a process of philosophical inquiry, of reflection on the wider post-war consumer culture, and this fed back into an art practice that utilised industrial techniques such as printing and photography, frequently resulting in the use of collage. While British teenagers were excitedly greeting rock 'n' roll from America, Hamilton's response was intellectual. A colleague of his from the ICA brought records back from America – Elvis Presley, and Bill Haley's 'Rock Around the Clock' – that Hamilton and fellow artists listened to and discussed. 'It was like a social analysis of what was going on,' he said.[12] In 1968, two years after he had left Newcastle to concentrate on his career as an artist, Hamilton designed the sleeve for The Beatles' *White Album*.

Office workers in sixties Newcastle would often spend their lunchtimes attending dances held in city centre ballrooms before returning to work. Members of Newcastle's Fine Art department would go along to watch. Rita Donagh, a student and later a demonstrator in Fine Art, was the first to attend, often alone or with another female student, but later others joined, including Hamilton. You can picture them taking notes, observing the lines of office girls dancing. But their interest in popular culture wasn't merely intellectual but also genuinely enthusiastic. Maintaining a critical perspective didn't preclude having a good time. The influence of this approach on Ferry was undeniable. It recontextualised and deepened his interest in popular culture, while the Pop Art concentration on images of American glamour extended the escapism of his days spent in the Carlton cinema in Washington. When Ferry began university, an older student, Mark Lancaster, returned from New York, where he had spent time at Warhol's Factory, and gave a lecture on his experiences. After graduating from his degree, Ferry headed to London, and a few years later started Roxy Music, a band whose approach to pop forced together the musical and artistic worlds Ferry had experienced in Newcastle, a collage of influences that generated a gloriously new and strange aesthetic. The clubs of Newcastle had offered Ferry the opportunity to develop musically, working in local tailors' shops sharpened his conception of classic style, and his time studying Fine Art at Newcastle enabled him in Roxy Music to meld a Pop Art sensibility with the warped blues of glam rock.

Visiting some of the locations of venues where The Animals and Bryan Ferry had played, I couldn't help reflecting on the changes to Newcastle that had erased these places. The fascination with the future that led in a line through the Independent Group, Hamilton and Ferry had its counterpart in a forward-thinking strain of town planning that would remodel cities according to the needs of the automobile, and cut close to their historic core. This resulted in some of the strange landscapes that I often wander around to the east of Newcastle city centre: the tangle of overhead walkways that lead from the city library towards Northumbria University, or that bring you around the back of what was until recently a Premier Inn hotel, then across the Central Motorway, circling back to Manors car park and the Tyne Bridge via a series of underpasses. Inside the sci-fi concrete megastructure of Swan House, a former British Telecom building that spans a roundabout and entrance ramp to the motorway, is a two-thirds scale reconstruction of the interior of the nineteenth-century Royal Arcade, pulled down in the sixties to make room for the new building. Plans to install a raised deck running down the main shopping thoroughfare Northumberland Street never came to fruition, but the multi-levelled city's remnants can be seen in these walkways and in the Eldon Square shopping mall, which for the most part is suspended at first-floor level, above the nineteenth-century streetscape. My lunchtime walks often bring me through Eldon Square, and past the bridge that links the shopping centre to Eldon Garden, to what was once the site of the Club A-Go-Go.

The city's rock 'n' roll heritage and this tough-minded, visionary intervention in Newcastle's urban form are inextricably linked in my mind through the coincidence of their chronologies and the fact that none of the buildings that housed Mike Jeffery's clubs has survived. The Downbeat was the first to go, swept away by the Central Motorway, but others followed, a reminder of both the huge physical changes in Newcastle during that period and the ephemeral nature of musical culture. The records have outlasted the buildings, and the places have become memories.

I had begun to think of pop music as an extractive industry comparable, at least symbolically, to mining, with the performers as the raw material. Talent was invariably removed from the place in which it originated and was processed and polished elsewhere. The Animals made it big once they went to London and met the hitmaker Mickey Most, who produced many of their songs. Bryan Ferry's ambitions took off when he moved to the capital. And, later, Wallsend-born Sting, who as a schoolboy had attended gigs in the Club A-Go-Go – including Jimi Hendrix's performance – travelled to London, returning with his band The Police to collect fifty copies of their first single, put out on an independent label, from the RCA pressing plant in Washington.[13] Historian Jonathan Watson observes that this southward migration conforms to 'a general pattern consisting of the migration of skilled labour away from the North East'.[14] This was a problem that faced the music scenes of most regional cities over the years, and it's something that has only recently been rebalanced as a result of the decline of the traditional music industry, and the high cost of living in London when set against its relatively low cost in regional cities. Although, in other high-skilled occupations the brain-drain from the regions to London persists.

*

Central to the local music scene from the late sixties onwards was Impulse Studios, set up by Dave Wood above a bingo hall on Wallsend High Street. The building itself was an old theatre, built in 1910, and the studios were on the first and second floors, accessible by stairs from a door on the street level. While the studio is of great interest to folk music fans – members of Lindisfarne recorded there at various points, and one of its labels, Rubber Records, issued countless folk records – its true glory years are linked to what was known as the New Wave of British Heavy Metal.

Impulse established a couple of imprints, Rubber and Wudwink, under which it issued records made in the studio, and in 1979 it added another label, Neat Records. The new label's metal credentials were established with their third single, the lurid 'Don't Touch Me There' from the Whitley Bay band Tygers of Pan Tang. Played with a punk energy that was arguably sharpened by the studio's technical limitations, the band established a hard, uncompromising sound and other Tyneside metal soon followed them onto Neat – Fist, Raven and Venom being the most notable. While many of the bands, including the Tygers of Pan Tang, soon left for major labels, Venom and Raven went on to record a series of albums for Neat.

Under the pseudonym Cronos, Conrad Lant fronted Venom, a trio who, in their songs at least, professed to be Satanists (the other members of the band went under the names Mantas and Abaddon). Lant was employed as a tape operator at Impulse, and had hand-drawn the rudimentary cover for Fist's 'Name, Rank and Serial Number' single. Venom underlined their interest in the dark side with their albums *Welcome to Hell*, released in 1981, and *Black Metal*, released in the following year. Both were recorded at Impulse and issued on Neat Records. It's difficult to overemphasise how important these albums are to the development of heavy metal, and particularly speed metal of the kind practised by Metallica. Powerfully welding barked guttural vocals to disciplined martial riffing, a seemingly un-sustainable double-speed tempo and an apparently sincere devotion to the dark lord, Venom's records still feel immediate and fresh, a sign perhaps of their great influence on the genre. Their sound emerged close to fully formed on their debut EP, *In League with Satan*, which incorporated virtuosic yet abbre-viated guitar solos and strange looped feedback that I assume is intended to be Satanic. An interview with *Kerrang!* magazine in 1981 indicates their devotion to perfecting their stagecraft, as they tell the journalist why they've delayed playing live: 'we've had to buy two gigs worth of bombs to test how close we can stand to them'.[15]

While it's easy to mock heavy metal and to explain away its adherents as, say, white working-class men channelling their anxiety about masculinity in a post-industrial context into heavy riffing and elaborate soloing, there's something para-doxically close to sincerity in Venom's pose, in the way their obsessive thematic Satanism combines with their pummelling music. It's a wholesale escape from the mundane everyday into a vibrant-if-derivative fantasy world. In promotional photos from around the time of the first album they cavort while waving an axe, ostensibly Satanically, on what seems likely to be a North Tyneside beach, possibly near Whitley Bay. Their mask falls en-tertainingly in that 1981 *Kerrang!* interview. When asked about black magic, the drummer says, 'I know you think we're med-dling in it, but we're not. We're just writing songs.' Which seems a dismayingly sober reflection when it comes from a member of a band whose first single loudly proclaimed that they were in league with Satan.

Neat Records was able to build on an independent infra-structure that had already been established by Impulse Studios through its other labels – largely folk, spoken word and regionally focused records. The nearby RCA record plant in Washington would press smaller runs of records, often from independent labels, in between the larger batches it pressed for RCA. So while the music Neat released was at some remove from Buzzcocks' tuneful punk, and pretty far from the guitar pop typical of 1980s indie labels, it was nonetheless a pioneering independent with a distinctive sound. Subsequently Kitchenware, formed in 1982 from a collective that ran the Soul Kitchen night in Newcastle, became a high-profile indie on which Prefab Sprout released their first six records. (The drummer on the band's debut album, *Swoon*, was Graham Lant, the brother of Venom's Cronos.) In 1992, punk rock label Slampt, drawing inspiration from American DIY labels such as K Records, put out its first records. The label was run by Pete Dale and Rachel Holborow, who also produced the *Fast Connection* fanzine. The cut-and-paste aesthetic and radical politics of the fanzine-based DIY punk scene around this time became familiar to me a little later on, through the record shops in Dublin. Prior to that, I was dimly aware that there was an underground punk scene that occasionally burst into the world of the mainstream music press, but generally kept itself to itself. One band to cross over between these two worlds was Kenickie, a four-piece from Sunderland, whose first record, an EP that squeezed an improbable eight songs onto two sides of a vinyl seven-inch, was issued by Slampt in 1995. I bought a copy in London that summer, from HMV on Oxford Street. It was the run-up to the Britpop war between Oasis and Blur, and their labels – the supposedly indie Food, an imprint of EMI, and Creation, which was by then 49 per cent owned by Sony – had reached deep into the major labels' pockets to heavily invest in poster campaigns around the city for their forthcoming singles 'Roll With It' and 'Country House'. Compared to that, the first Kenickie single seemed primitive, visually – its cover consisted of a folded piece of paper slipped into a flimsy cellophane sleeve – and, when I finally got it home to Dublin and listened to it, the record was primitive musically too. Yet it was still recognisable as pop music, it was witty and entertaining, and made by a group that was around the same age that I was. It was also an antidote to the increasingly desperate hype around Britpop.

Sunderland, where I've lived for the last five years, is a city located twelve miles south-east of Newcastle. Although economically in the shadow of Tyneside, and lacking the cultural investment of Newcastle or Gateshead, it has nevertheless produced a string of excellent artists, many of whom have adopted a staunchly independent approach to their work, playing in and producing one another's bands, opening small businesses and even building their own studios. Sunderland bands illustrate the ups and downs of a precarious creative career in a regional British city, how musicians need to diversify, to adjust their mindset from the all-or-nothing major label era towards different expectations.

Field Music are the quintessential independent Sunderland band – signed to an independent label in London but producing their own records from a self-built studio in their home city. Centred around the core of brothers David and Peter Brewis, they've perfected a brand of tightly played, jerkily funky psychedelia that recalls post-punk bands like XTC and Scritti Politti. They've been able to stay in the area – I see David occasionally at my local Metro station – and produce strong, distinctive work. Frankie and the Heartstrings, whose three albums are a muscular, soulful take on eighties-style jangly indie, opened a record shop, Pop Recs, in a former tourist office on the city's main street in 2013, staging concerts from artists like Franz Ferdinand and Gruff Rhys of Super Furry Animals while also putting on local acts and providing space for arts and community groups. Later the building was sold for student housing, and the shop moved to another, smaller premises, but it remains an important cultural hub in the city. Meanwhile another band, Lilliput, opened a coffee shop in which the members work – providing another cultural centre for creative writing groups and book clubs.

These are all great places to spend some time, but the fact is that they're surviving in defiance of the wider austerity that's evident in the boarded-up shops, short-lived businesses and defunct libraries of Sunderland, which like many regional northern cities continues to be blighted by a decline in public and private investment. Nevertheless, a recent bid for UK City of Culture, although unsuccessful, provided a cultural focus that looks likely to lead to future development. Despite these efforts, there remains the problem of getting a significant audience together in the city. Bands admit that it's easier to play Newcastle, where you can usually muster a decent crowd, than Sunderland, where live music is less well supported.

What is the relationship between music and place? In the case of folk music and traditional music there's an argument that it's an authentic expression of a regional culture. But with pop music it's not as clear-cut. Pop involved musicians adopting masks, willing themselves to be something other than the role assigned to them by society. Certain cities fixed on particular sounds and appropriated them, whether it's the blues in Newcastle or European electronica in Sheffield, transforming them into something remarkably different. Ferry's Roxy Music acknowledged that musical performance was a construction, that your stage persona and your subject matter didn't have to be determined by your origins, by a sense of being true to your roots.

Newcastle and the wider North East were relatively untouched by post-war migration from the Commonwealth. This showed itself in the music. It didn't have the reggae or bhangra influences that would shape the West Midlands scenes in Birmingham and Coventry, or the unique melding of post-punk, hip-hop and reggae that influenced Bristol's trip-hop. As an outsider living in the region who despaired of its relative insularity, especially after the EU referendum of 2016, I began to wonder about how immigrants and outsiders had made their own musical worlds in Britain, and if they had done so in Newcastle. As someone living in the country during an era of hostility to outsiders, when the rights of non-British residents were under threat, I thought about how those of us who are migrants or children of migrants fitted into the musical history of Britain.

I found an answer in Tom Caulker, who owns Newcastle's World Headquarters nightclub. The club occupies two floors of a six-storey building on Carliol Square, around the corner from the old site of the Downbeat Club. I first became aware of the location of World Headquarters when I opened an online map and saw that the building was named Curtis Mayfield House after the politically conscious American soul singer.

One overcast summer morning I went to meet Caulker in his house in Jesmond, a suburb north of Newcastle city centre. We sat at a dinner table in a room whose walls were lined with shelves filled with vinyl records, and, as he talked, my eyes were drawn to the shelves behind him, as I tried to identify some of his collection. Tom Caulker was born in Gateshead in 1964 to a father from Sierra Leone and an Irish mother from Tuam, Co. Galway. Growing up mixed race in a white region in the sixties and seventies, he and his brother suffered from racist abuse at school. 'I think the racism that I experienced has been a big driver for me to say: Well, what am I going to do about this?' he said. He found his answer in music: 'I'm going to change it one fucking record at a time.' He was a music fan from a very young age. 'My parents would always have house parties, and I would put all the records in order on the little Dansette and let them drop.' He was, in effect, DJing, a career he would later pursue in the clubs of Newcastle. As a teenager, he started to listen to Northern Soul – older boys at school would go off to Wigan or Manchester at weekends and bring back records they'd bought. Caulker would then go about trying to get these records from them, becoming a collector. 'You would hear about these mythical soul records and think: I've got to hear that, I've got to get a copy of that,' he told me. 'There would be different companies who would sell records, so you would get on their mailing lists, find something on the list you wanted and order it. I remember paying forty quid for a copy of James Coit's "Black Power" when I was about fifteen. And that was a *fortune* back then.' He continued to collect records: disco, then Hi-NRG and house. He got a job in the Trent House, a pub between the university and the St James's Park football ground, and then became the landlord. He loaded the jukebox with his rare soul records, and made it free to play. 'People would flock to the Trent to hear the jukebox, because it was just so ridiculous that all these great records were on this jukebox, and it was free.'

It wasn't all plain sailing. 'When I took over the Trent I was the youngest licensee in the city and the only black licensee in the region.' The pub's windows were smashed regularly. 'We had a nightmare of racial hassle.' It drove him to set up his 'own little culture', he told me. 'If the mainstream culture won't accept us, all right: we're outsiders. We'll be outsiders so we'll make our own little world. And everybody else who was an outsider gravitated towards us.' He had been keen to start a career as a DJ, but encountered resistance from clubs. 'It was such a racist time then that you couldn't even get into clubs, never mind play records in clubs.' But members of Newcastle's gay community knew him from the Trent House, and he began to DJ in gay clubs, doing an indie night and another night that initially consisted of black music but eventually specialised exclusively in house music. He started to bring in guest DJs, Danny Rampling from London, or Americans Robert Owens and Tony Humphries. Ecstasy arrived on the scene, and there was a 'fantastic honeymoon period', but soon there was a lot of drug-related violence as a gangster element crept in. The friendly, multicultural atmosphere that Caulker had worked hard to create inside the club was threatened. He decided to start his own club.

He was able to buy a club, Africa, down near Central station, and he closed it for six months 'to get rid of all the gangsters', reopening it as World Headquarters in 1993. It was small, holding at first only 180 people, but it was always busy, and he could play what he wanted. It was 'like a live DJ version of the Trent jukebox'. He ran it for ten years before finding out that the building needed to be knocked down to provide access for the bus station behind. After a year of looking for a new location, he found the old six-storey warehouse at Carliol Square and he's been there ever since. He decorated the club with murals that embodied his ethos. 'I wanted to be very clear – the two-hand shake on our logo', a white hand and a black hand clasped together, while the club's slogan is 'World Headquarters: Uniting All Communities'.

You could see Caulker's musical world as one that occupied ever larger spaces: the front room of his parents' house where he used to put records on their Dansette during parties, the

Trent House pub, then the first and second World Headquarters. Forced to be an outsider by the prevailing racist culture, he created a parallel world that grew bigger all the time. 'I'm not going to just sit there and go "what a shame" or move away. This is my fucking town. I live here, you know? I'm going to make it so that when my kids grow up there's less of that shit than there was when I was a kid.'

The toughness of sixties Newcastle, a city still dominated by heavy industry, was reflected in its music, most notably the rhythm and blues of The Animals. But the rise of blues and beat clubs, such as the Downbeat and the Club A-Go-Go, was a sign of wider changes in the city. The growth of light industry meant more employment for women, including young women who became active consumers of pop culture, attending dances and going to clubs. The impact of pop culture on the intellectual world was almost instant, leading artists from Newcastle University to attend lunchtime dances in the city centre. This artistic world would influence the work of Bryan Ferry, a local musician from a working-class family whose path to stardom symbolised pop music's potential for social mobility. But that social mobility necessitated a move away from Newcastle to London. The rise of independent labels and the local studio Impulse in the seventies and eighties signalled a revival of music scenes in Newcastle and its near neighbour Sunderland. Yet the latter provides an illustration of the creative possibilities and economic limitations of regional cities. Clubs and venues continued to be important as social spaces that provided an alternative to the wider culture, and in some cases, as with World Headquarters, were an outsider's response to the widespread racism of that culture.

Newcastle had illustrated how art could combine with music to create something new. In the seventies, art's influence on British

pop music would be joined by a growing political consciousness. I left Newcastle to travel to a city in which a generation
of musicians in the late seventies drew on their experience of
radical politics and critical theory to produce a unique strain of
visceral-yet-intellectual post-punk.

4.

LEEDS

When my Megabus pulled into Leeds bus station I was sitting in a window seat thinking about Marxism. Specifically, the Marxist pop that had emerged from the city in the late seventies, particularly the band Gang of Four. But first: food, and a brief exploration of the city. After checking into my budget hotel, I walked through the hangar-like extension of Kirkgate Market, passing stalls selling Yorkshire pudding wraps and Vietnamese street food. Beyond that is the main hall of the market, a vast chamber constructed using elaborately wrought iron. A 1904 expansion of a Victorian-era market, the main hall of Kirkgate is a charming jumble of newsagents, vape stores, shoe shops. Leeds had been granted city status in 1893, and the architectural response to this elevation was to construct buildings of a suitable grandeur and scale, notably the markets and arcades of the city centre.

Being greeted with these glass and iron dream houses triggered the long-dormant grocer in me. Marks & Spencer had been founded in Kirkgate in 1884. My dad had worked in the supermarket trade, and though I knew it to be a cutthroat and increasingly soulless business, I was also aware of his, and my, strange attachment to the nobility of its heritage and the idiosyncratic romance of markets and stalls. Here was commerce stripped down to its basics. Even I, a vegetarian of twenty-five years' standing, could see the beauty in a butcher's stall being washed down of blood and all detritus attendant meaty crap at the end of the working day. So, when I looked at a vape store it was through misty eyes. Ah, the nobility of the grocer's life! I thought, as a wheezy auld lad in a tracksuit stocked up on fruity-smelling cartridges of nicotine vapour.

I could also recognise my own commodity fetishism, which had gone into overdrive during the research for this book. On my travels around the country, I would call into record shops or charity shops and flick through racks of records, picking up whatever caught my eye or seemed like it might be useful in writing the book. I convinced myself that it just about qualified as research, although really I was in search of the kind of hedonistic escape some people get from buying a smart tie or a new dress – the potentially transformative thrill of shopping. I wasn't engaging in high-end glamour, merely picking out dusty seven-inch records, but I liked to imagine that I was experiencing something of the same elation the person who first bought that record must have felt when they brought their purchase home from Woolworths or Our Price.

In his book *Revolt Into Style: The Pop Arts in Britain*, a sharp and funny analysis of new cultural forms published in 1970, George Melly distinguishes between popular culture and pop. Both were working-class in origin, but whereas popular culture was unconscious, or unselfconscious in its growth and elaboration – I think of the reassuring, familiar entertainment in music halls here, sentimental but tough, reflecting the everyday lives of the audience – pop was 'the result of a deliberate search for objects, clothes, music, heroes and attitudes which could help to define a stance'.[1] Pop was instinctively adversarial towards the wider culture, and at the core was a protest '*against* a great deal, but *for* nothing'.[2] Pop was obstreperous, nihilistic, but most of all material.

As a child I was fascinated by the physicality of pop. It was communicated through objects – records or posters or magazines – things you could hold in your hand or arrange around you, creating what you fondly imagine might be a microcosm of the wider world, little realising that you were looking through the wrong end of the telescope. Taking such pleasure in the objects, the products of pop, eventually led me towards record shops: the dark, carpeted store in the middle of Tallaght Town Centre not far from my primary school, then later the industrial-chic interior of the Virgin Megastore on Dublin's Aston Quay. But as a typically cashless child, most of my pleasure was limited to browsing the displays. Purchases would come later, in my teenage years, but the joy of browsing even the most unpromising second-hand record shop hasn't yet left me.

Now products are always with us on our smartphones or computer screens – the Google ads data chasing us from site to site reminding us of our latest searches. They're shorn of the halo of the showroom and instead incessantly chip away at us until we give in and buy that – and here I must consult my search history – rubber hammer or pair of fashionable but impractical trainers. The strange, addictive thrill of encountering the peculiarly exotic and compelling object seems increasingly to belong to luxury goods, those priced beyond everyday affordability. Perhaps that was why, as I walked through the arcades of Leeds on my way to record shops and sites of musical relevance, so many of the units were now occupied by high-end brands like Harvey Nichols and Paul Smith. In an era of cheap mass production, only these products retained their aura by dint of their inaccessibility. Nevertheless, I could see the parallels between someone passing through the arcades in and around 1900, finding themselves in a world of strange glamour where unaffordable objects dangled tantalisingly behind shop windows, and my childhood adventures among the record racks, visually consuming the sleeves of a thousand records but never buying any. In both cases the viewer is forced to resort to the imagination in trying to flesh out the possibility of the object, the idea that it might be transformative in some way. You invest your imagination in the object, outsource it to a piece of plastic or a carefully sewn bit of cloth and think: That's what I need, that can change me for the better. And, speaking autobiographically, I did at one point think that records might change my life, and really I still do, although now the quest for those physical objects has been diverted somewhat by the mass availability of online streaming, foreshortening the gap between imagining what a piece of music might sound like and actually hearing it to perhaps a few seconds rather than weeks, months or even years.

The arcades were architectural products of a thriving city whose expansion had been underwritten by the wealth accrued from industry. The wool traders of Leeds had benefited greatly from the industrial era: by the time it became a city it was linked to ports on the east and west of the country by canal and to other thriving British metropolises by the railway network, which also transported coal into the city to drive its mills. The construction of the arcades in Leeds now seemed a precursor of the contemporary city, a dream space of the consumer-capitalism yet to come. The pedestrianised central streets of the city are now almost wholly devoted to the function of shopping. The Corn Exchange, a vast oval building housed beneath an iron and glass dome, had once been the thriving centre of the nineteenth-century corn trade. It was converted into a shopping centre in the late eighties, and reopened, newly gentrified, as a boutique market for independent retailers in 2013. The building was modelled on Paris's eighteenth-century Halle aux blés, which served an identical function to the Leeds building and was later converted into the French capital's stock exchange. It's clear that the city sought to emulate neoclassical Parisian grandeur in its public buildings – Leeds Town Hall, on the Headrow, was constructed in the 1850s, a few years before the Corn Exchange, and drew from architect Cuthbert Brodrick's travels in Europe, especially his observations of Parisian public buildings.

By the 1970s the city's glory years had passed, but the architecture of its industrial pomp remained. If you were a student of French history or art and wanted to walk around Leeds imagining nineteenth-century Paris, you could, and, although a couple of the arcades are gone now, you can still find monumental aspects of that metropolis replicated with varying levels of success around Leeds city centre. In 1976, the young art historian T. J. Clark arrived at the university to take up a position as the head of the department of Fine Art. Clark had briefly been a member of the left-wing French avant-garde group the Situationist International, and had begun to apply a broadly Marxist approach to art criticism, focusing on the Paris of the mid-nineteenth century, examining the work of art in relation to the economic, social and political structures of the time. (The Situationists had been an influence on Tony Wilson's Factory Records, and he had named the Haçienda nightclub after a line in one of their texts.) The Situationists had concentrated in their earlier years on the exploration of Paris, mainly by foot, in a drifting across the city they called the *dérive*. They also constructed artworks that drew from the trajectories they followed across the city, in maps, paintings and books that incorporated collages of texts and images, often cut from magazines and newspapers. Drawing from an avant-garde lineage that included the dreamlike, dark-humoured poetry of Lautréamont and the urban dream-scapes of the Surrealists, they ultimately saw the artwork merely as a vehicle for the wider subversion of capitalist society.

Could the art object do this? Was it possible to make a com-modity, the type of product you might see in the window of an arcade or perhaps on a rack of seven-inch singles in a record shop, carry the kind of subversive political possibilities that the Situationists hoped the artwork might? Could it transmit an idea or embody an approach that challenged the economic and political system into which it was delivered? To revisit and extend George Melly's formulation, could pop music channel its reflexive revolt, 'being *against* a great deal', into a constructive art-political practice?

I walked from the city centre past the Town Hall and uphill in the direction of the university. I was on my way to have a look at the Fine Art building, but I wanted first to call in on the university's refectory, an interwar redbrick building that for the most part housed the university's students' union. A blue plaque fixed next to the entrance informed me that this was where The Who's *Live at Leeds* album had been recorded. Once inside, having passed counters at which canteen staff dished out hot food and salad, I found a large, dimly lit hall with a parquet wooden floor whose blocks were arranged in a herringbone pattern. Students were sitting at tables, eating dinner, and I felt slightly confused that the building had functioned as a venue for what had been, in 1970, one of the biggest rock bands in Britain. I sat for a while, looking up at the balconies above, watching the comings and goings of diners. It was certainly shaped like a venue, but I guessed that these tables were swept away for performances. After a little while I decided this wasn't going to suffice, so I turned back in the direction of a set of barriers that ran across the middle of the room, blocking off another section of seating that I hadn't previously seen. On this side of the barriers the room opened up. Rows of seats swept towards a low stage in front of a huge bay window that I was sure I could vaguely recognise from photos of The Who's gig. Along the walls were posters listing the bands who had played there by academic year: 1976–77 included Irish traditional band The Chieftains, AC/DC, Sly and the Family Stone, and former members of The Byrds.

Live at Leeds was The Who's reassertion of their primal rock credentials after a period spent indulging in the experimental rock opera *Tommy*, released as an album the year before. As a break with the Superpop of The Who's early years, the kind of thrilling throwaway pop beloved of critic Nik Cohn, *Tommy* represented a risk, a change in direction from what might have been expected of the band. (Cohn was a huge fan of The Who, but was indifferent to *Tommy* when they played him its songs, so they promised to include a new song about pinball to placate him, the song ending up being 'Pinball Wizard'.) Although the band later returned to the rock opera with *Quadrophenia*, the decision to go back to basics with *Live at Leeds* expressed the tension between rock and art in their work. The post-*Sgt. Pepper* turn towards pop music as art led bands towards progressive rock. You could hear elements of prog in Roxy Music, especially their second album *For Your Pleasure*, but they and The Who at least preserved recognisable elements of pop music, if not necessarily in the three-minute form you'd come to expect. Elsewhere, prog bands turned towards a rapt post-hippydom spirituality and a tendency towards the long-form display of prodigious musical skill over the course of extended-play double-albums and overlong concerts. The reaction against this perceived bloatedness and overaccomplishment, when it finally came in the form of punk, was a reassertion of the primacy of rock 'n' roll twelve-bar blues. This was a return to the basics of rock 'n' roll, and allied to the negation that Melly identified as a key feature of the pop culture attitude. 'No future' was that negation amped up and directed towards the pre-Thatcher Britain of the late seventies. It has been much remarked that what emerged from punk was more interesting and enduring than punk itself. Post-punk was an intellectualisation of punk, as it attempted to turn punk's primal rock urge to ideas drawn from art, but also to radical politics.

Roxy Music and The Who had an art school education in common, something that's true of several of the more interesting groups of the time. Many of the key bands who formed and played in Leeds in the late seventies were educated in art schools: Gang of Four, The Mekons, Scritti Politti and Soft Cell. Leaving the refectory, I located the University of Leeds Fine Art building on a map on my phone, and followed the trajectory on my screen, along a small service road running parallel to the main pedestrian route through campus. Although I hadn't been aware of it, the Fine Art department had recently moved to the old Geography building, now refurbished, in a shuffle of buildings that was typical of the obsession with efficient use of space of the contemporary British university.

Taking their cue from their studies, Gang of Four attempted to investigate the possibilities of melding a stripped-down funky art pop to a radical political analysis of everyday life, in the process creating a brilliant and hugely influential oeuvre. The band included two students from the Leeds Fine Art department, Jon King and Andy Gill, and they directly trace their application of radical politics to pop music to their time in the university, where they were influenced by lecturers such as T. J. Clark and feminist art historian Griselda Pollock. (While King and Gill were art students at Leeds, drummer Hugo Burnham studied English literature.) Gill credits his research interest in Édouard Manet – he completed his undergraduate dissertation on the French impressionist painter – to the influence of Clark, who would later publish a book about the artist, *The Painter of Modern Life*. Although the band formed in Leeds and performed their early gigs in the city, King and Gill had moved there for university. They were friends who came from Sevenoaks in Kent, where their fellow students at the private Sevenoaks School included three future members of The Mekons and filmmakers Paul Greengrass and Adam Curtis. King recalls an early musical memory of running into three of The Beatles as they emerged from the Sevenoaks antique shop in which John Lennon had bought the poster that would inspire the song 'Being for the Benefit of Mr Kite!'. The Beatles were in Sevenoaks to film footage that would be used to promote the 'Strawberry Fields Forever/ Penny Lane' single.[3] Initially drawn to study at Newcastle, in part because it housed Richard Hamilton's reconstruction of Marcel Duchamp's 'The Large Glass', King eventually chose Leeds, as did Andy Gill the following year.[4]

The possibility of Gang of Four having become a Newcastle band, an heir to Roxy Music, is worth considering, because both bands diverge in their interpretations of art and mass production. Bryan Ferry was influenced by the celebration of the possibilities of consumer culture and the potential for the melding of art and commerce through industrial design. Gang of Four, although drawing on American culture through their love of soul and abstract expressionism, to take two examples, were also drawing from a broadly Marxist perspective that sought to critique consumer capitalism, as well as from a wider context of countercultural disputation with the dominant culture. In Leeds, the artistic perspective King and Gill had developed in Sevenoaks was hardened by the radical politics of the seminar room and the street. Leeds in 1976 was a radically different context from Newcastle in 1964. Art pop had become explicitly political.

Leaving the university campus, I travelled west, crossing Moorland Road to walk along the path leading through Woodhouse Moor, to which many residents of the city had removed during the plague of 1644, living there until the disease abated a year later. Much of the university had been built on the moor, while the land that remained became a city park. Geographically, sitting slightly elevated on the side of a hill above the city, the university felt to me quite separate from Leeds, an illusion encouraged by the motorway that ran between it and the centre. As I walked through Woodhouse Moor, and subsequently read a little about its history, I could see that this area's separateness from the city had once provided a refuge for those fearing death. I knew from studying other cities that fringe spaces that were later incorporated into the city as suburbs often had dark histories. People were sent there by necessity – disease or war – hundreds of years before others moved there out of choice, or were impelled there by poverty.

My walk was taking me in the direction of the Brudenell Social Club, a thriving live music venue a mile or so from the university. The road sloped downhill and I passed a group of students standing and chatting on a corner. Mainly redbrick townhouses gave way to smaller terraces once I passed the Brudenell, set back from the road between the Abu Bakr Asian supermarket and a barber's shop. The Brudenell was initially a working men's club, and still holds community events, but since the Clark family took it over in 1992 it has become an increasingly cutting-edge music venue. Now run by Nathan Clark, the venue is a thriving mainstay on the national circuit, attracting both international and local artists.

I had read about England's back-to-back housing – the construction of terraces in which each house shares party walls on three of its four sides, meaning that only the side of the house that faced the street had ventilation. But I had assumed most of these houses, if not all, had been knocked down. Despite legislation introduced to stop the construction of back-to-backs in the late nineteenth and early twentieth century, Leeds had chosen to continue to build the houses, initially intended as cheap housing for the working classes. So when, not far from the Brudenell, and barely a mile from the university, I passed terraces of inhabited back-to-backs I was a little bit surprised. They felt like a hangover from the industrial past, the B-side to the monumental grandeur of the city centre. The student population was much less visible around here, and instead the people I passed were mostly Asian or white working class. This juxtaposition of the relatively privileged space of the university against the comparative poverty of the adjoining neighbourhoods is far from unique to Leeds, but it did lead me to reflect on what I had read about the relationship between radical politics and the city. Was it just a university thing, I wondered, and how representative were the left-wing bands I had chosen to focus on – all of whom had come to the city from elsewhere and many of whom would later move to London?

Such class-guilt handwringing was par for the course in the Brexit era. Mainstream liberal opinion had reacted against its pre-referendum self, adjusting to the new reality. It was time to listen to the voices of the working classes that had been silenced before the vote. Except that the way I saw it those voices were increasingly well catered for, or, at least, ventriloquised by a media that enabled, unwittingly or in some cases by design, the debate to be dragged rightwards, and instead EU migrants, lacking the vote that would have secured their future in the country, were almost entirely unheard throughout the campaign. Later that night I would return to my hotel and switch on the television to a news channel, seeing that an agreement had been concluded between Britain and the EU on a variety of issues, including the rights of EU citizens and the nature of a post-Brexit border between Northern Ireland and the Republic of Ireland. But nothing felt definitive any more; everything felt temporary and unstable, liable to change at short notice.

The rhetoric before and after the vote had profoundly reconfigured the way I felt about the connection between place and culture. It sounds strange, but in the days after the referendum I mused with considerable anger on the naivety of much English psychogeography, the faux-magical connections forged with questionable logic between blood and soil. While I believed that there were many reasons why a city might influence the sound of a record, I didn't think there was anything inevitable about the connection between a sound and a city. I began to see almost everyone as a migrant, and their supposed connection to a place as far from eternal.

When she was a child, my mother travelled from her home in Drogheda, on the east coast of Ireland, to Elland, near Leeds, to visit her aunt, who had moved there to work in a factory. It wouldn't be that difficult to conjure a plausible alternative history in which my mother moved there too, or her mother before her. I shudder at the thought before realising that as I write this I'm sitting in my house in northern England, and that rather than her I was the one who eventually made the move. Such is the history of the Irish diaspora. My move came in the aftermath of the Irish economic crash, which sent many of my generation, and younger, around the world. I can remember uncles leaving for work in England and America throughout the eighties, and friends of mine, older and younger, live in France, Austria,

Germany and Hong Kong. This is not really a boast about cosmopolitanism, but instead an observation about the forces that drive emigration and how common it is for Irish people, and I suspect for a lot of other nations too. It's not the experience just of my generation, but of those who have gone before and come after. So, for me the notion of identity is complex, fraught with alternative paths, by the possibility that things might have been different. And I hope that the effect of this acknowledgement of alternatives, of how one's own identity is contingent on chance, is to open up a degree of empathy for people and cultures other than my own. Much of the most interesting pop music is the result of someone trying imaginatively to transcend their given place in the world. It takes a huge effort of the will to do this; it's not an inevitable outcome or a natural career path. Migrants to a city don't necessarily adjust themselves to the dominant culture, and instead reshape that culture in their own image. For this reason, I was more drawn to those sounds that were the result of some interaction between migrant cultures, and not necessarily inherently rooted in that place. Frequently these sounds are the result of a chance intersection of ideas and approaches that are nearly always carried by migrants. The history of Britain is deeply intertwined with migration, and that has a cultural impact. The industrial revolution drew large numbers of workers from the countryside to the city. The requirements of British industry, particularly in the post-war era, drew migrants from Ireland, and the Commonwealth, to British cities. Later, universities were an agent of this change, as young people relocated to unfamiliar cities for three or four years, forming bands and investigating ideas that may not have come across had they stayed where they were. Leeds is a clear example of this. The cultural climate in which pop music thrived was in large part a result of the presence of a number of institutions: the University of Leeds, the Leeds School of Art, and Leeds Polytechnic, and the Marxist academics working in those institutions. In practical terms, this attracted many young people to the city who latched on to existing countercultural currents and created something different and new.

I walked back to the city, in the direction of Leeds School of Art, where Green Gartside of Scritti Politti had studied. Gartside had arrived in Leeds with an existing commitment to radical politics. Growing up on the edge of the South Wales new town of Cwmbran as the son of Conservative-voting working-class parents, he had formed a branch of the Young Communist League in his school. The notoriety led to his being physically attacked and estranged from his politically right-wing parents.[5] In conversation with music writer Simon Reynolds, Gartside remarked upon the new town's 'fairly broad mix of people' at school: his friend Niall Jinks had moved to Cwmbran from Kent, and his father was a member of the Communist Party, influences that undoubtedly played a part in the development of Gartside's politics.[6] The town had been established in 1949 to help provide new opportunities in the South Wales coalfield, and there Gartside found plenty of evidence of inequality to drive his Marxist critique of capital, while at the same time acknowledging that his Communism had allowed room for more artistic pursuits.[7] Having studied for a foundation art degree in Newport Art College, he moved to Leeds to take up a place at the School of Art, which had become part of the new Leeds Polytechnic in 1970. Although polytechnics were intended to provide an applied education that would equip students for industry, it appears that Leeds Poly's art department remained untamed for the time being, sustaining an avant-garde reputation. While at Leeds Gartside's focus shifted away from painting and towards writing, a process that was hastened by his critical consideration of his own production of art in that particular context.[8] (Gartside's thinking was influenced by the ideas of the Art & Language group – that the artwork should emerge from critical debate and essentially be an intervention in that debate. Prefiguring Gartside's shift towards writing, the group's critical focus moved over the course of the seventies away from visual art and sculpture towards textual forms. Founding member of Art & Language Terry Atkinson worked in the university Fine Art department.) Given his focus, it's perhaps unsurprising that when the staff of the Poly found themselves unable to judge the artistic validity of Gartside's writing – did writing qualify as art? – they called on T. J. Clark to adjudicate.[9] Gartside had been worried about being kicked off the course, but he credits Clark's intervention with retaining his place. Scritti Politti formed during this period, after Gartside saw the Sex Pistols Anarchy Tour at Leeds Poly on 10 December 1976, a tour that included as support The Clash, New York punk band The Heartbreakers and The Damned. A few days before the Leeds gig, the Pistols had appeared on Bill Grundy's *Today* programme and sworn on prime-time television, triggering outraged tabloid headlines and the cancellation of many of their tour dates. Gartside reacted in the same way those who saw the Pistols' Manchester gigs earlier in the year did: he formed a band. (Jon King of Gang of Four was also there.)

A couple of hours after writing that last paragraph, I took a train into Newcastle city centre to see a concert by Public Image Limited, the band Johnny Rotten (John Lydon) formed after the Sex Pistols broke up. Between songs he swore at the audience in a sort of punk pantomime. It appeared that both he and the crowd were in on the joke but felt mutually compelled to perform in this way. It wasn't really about the content of the badinage thrown back and forth between audience and Lydon

– instead it seemed to be about mutual acknowledgement: an audience member swore at him, he swore back, the audience member felt like he'd got his money's worth. Meanwhile his band were extremely polished and professional – as was he. I wondered if the early days of the Pistols were actually like this: theatrically shambolic but also ruthlessly professional and effective, delivering a carefully packaged anarchy through the mainstream media to a general audience unprepared for such an attack. It was revolt as style, the oldest trick in the brief history of pop music, but at maximum volume. It generated a moral outrage similar to that stirred up by Elvis or even Bill Haley. It was important most of all because of the way it was interpreted by its audience, especially those who took what they could from punk and allied it with other influences: most frequently a political position or an independent ethos that was markedly different from the Pistols' take-the-money-and-run attitude, and taking inspiration from a range of musical forms that frequently included dub reggae. Indeed, Lydon's post-Pistols group PiL, although lacking the radical politics that others would bring to bear on post-punk musical forms, showed the clear influence of the booming bass of dub and an experimental attitude to lyrical content – the Pistols-style provocation was still there, but it was more carefully directed, the defiance tempered with personal vulnerability. If Lydon could move on, everyone else could too. The need to move beyond punk was obvious to many of those who had seen the Pistols in '76 – people on the Manchester scene and in Leeds.

In a move that recalled Mark Lancaster's grant-funded re-search trip from Newcastle to New York to hang out at Andy Warhol's Factory in the sixties, future members of Gang of Four Jon King and Andy Gill had travelled to Manhattan, researching at the Whitney Museum of American Art and MoMA during the day, and going to punk club CBGB at night. They stayed with journalist and future film director Mary Harron at her St Mark's Place loft. Here, in the East Village, they were at the epicentre of a scene that included Television, Blondie and The Ramones. King and Gill were impressed by the openness of the bands, the fact that there was little division between them and the audience, that you could have conversations with them.[10] The experience of this scene convinced King and Gill that they should follow a musical path. Not long afterwards, the Pistols played Leeds Poly. While King attended, Gill went to a film instead. The object lesson many took from the Pistols and from other punk bands was that anyone could pick up an instrument and be in a band, but for King and Gill the question was how to effectively meld their interests in art theory with the practice of pop music, and New York showed the way.

I walked from the School of Art back towards the Headrow, the wide street on which the Town Hall stands. Later Gang of Four would reproduce an image of the imposing Victorian building on the sleeve of their 'Outside the Trains Don't Run On Time' single. It brought me back to my arrival earlier that day, when I had first set eyes on the city's markets and arcades. Turning off the Headrow, I passed along a shopping street from which a number of arcades branched off. But it was late, and the shops were closed, and for the first time I could see that the arcades had gates that were locked at night. On the other side of the street, up an alley, was the City Varieties, a music hall built in 1865 by architect George Smith for the local entrepreneur Charles Thornton, who in 1877 also commissioned Smith to complete Thornton's Arcade, the first built in the city.

The City Varieties, its long auditorium, cast-iron pillars and balconies, was familiar to me from watching re-enactments of music hall variety shows on television. Between 1953 and

1983 the programme *The Good Old Days* was broadcast on BBC television. What I know of it is drawn from the repeats that often fill gaps in BBC4's schedule. It's a deeply nostalgic programme, a throwback to a pre-war era – before the First World War rather than the Second. During the show, comedians, singers and actors, some of them well-known television person-alities, would take to the stage in period costume to re-enact the entertainment of a bygone era. It's sobering to think that while pop music was outraging and innovating, while careers came and went, while Elvis had his first hit, joined the army, and died, *The Good Old Days* continued its run of 245 episodes, each one ending with a knees-up and a singalong to the standard 'Down at the Old Bull and Bush', the audience, who were also dressed in costume, apparently enjoying themselves.

For those of you who haven't already detected my scepticism about all of this, I confess that I find watching even a few minutes of these programmes extremely jarring. My mind rebels against the idea that people were dressing up in Victorian gear in 1983 and catching the train from, say, Bradford to Leeds to sing along to the misty-eyed lyrics of songs that predated their birth. It seems even more ridiculous to me than punks wearing bin liners or the androgyny of glam or the New Romantics. Although all these movements in their own way have fallen prey to nostalgia, it seems that music hall got there first and had a TV show to prove it. If you narrow your eyes enough you can still see the influence of music hall on the British Saturday night TV variety show, in the way it combines music and comedy to banal effect, playing to the expectations of the audience. It's comforting, I suppose, this extension of a community of shared values and expectations, one that once existed in countless small theatres around the country, to the television screen in your front room.

Maybe the experience of music hall wasn't so different from

punk music, though. Watching John Lydon harangue the crowd at a PiL gig, I could see how an initial attempt at avant-garde alienation, at making the crowd uncomfortable – if that's what the Sex Pistols really were – could also become an expected part of a night out. It reminded me of a stand-up gig where the crowd trigger cruel put-downs with their heckling, and cheer joyfully the comedian's withering comeback, shorn of any shock value that it might once have had. Ultimately, though, the transgressive power of punk and the political potential of post-punk continue to fascinate. Punk's do-it-yourself ethos still provides a blueprint for independent cultural endeavour. Its style remains strange and otherworldly, and the unrestrained anger of its music hasn't faded over time. Post-punk was serious, intellectual, sardonic – punk's bigger brother. It significantly expanded on punk's possibilities, broadening the musical palette to include dub reggae, electronic music and even progressive rock. Politically, post-punk moved on from the essentially apolitical provocations of punk into a variety of political positions, most notably the radical left-wing politics espoused by the Leeds bands.

In 1978 the Leeds bands released their first records. First came a single from The Mekons, a collective whose anarchic gigs attempted to break down the division between audience and performer and who were close friends with the members of Gang of Four and the band Delta 5. The record was the first to be issued by the Fast Product label, a highly influential Edinburgh-based independent that was the product of a small group of likeminded people, including Bob Last and Hilary Morrison, and that later issued the first single by Sheffield synth-pop band The Human League. The Mekons single, 'I've Never Been in a Riot', was a satirical response to The Clash's 'White Riot', and set the tone for a long-running career that continues to this day.

By the summer of 1978 Green Gartside had moved to a squat in Camden Town in London, and formed Scritti Politti with his Cwmbran schoolfriend Niall Jinks. They recorded the unwieldy and brilliant *Skank Bloc Bologna* EP and released it on their own label in September 1978. It was obviously influenced by dub reggae and notable for both the complex, allusive and surreal lyrics and the polished vocals from Gartside, foreshadowing the group's later move into smooth eighties pop. A month or so later, Gang of Four followed their friends The Mekons onto Fast Product, with an EP that included the songs 'Damaged Goods', 'Love Like Anthrax' and 'Armalite Rifle'. Here were three examples of the approach that they would perfect the following year with their EMI LP *Entertainment!*, namely a stripped-down sound notable for the intensity of Andy Gill's clipped, metallic guitar and the tightly funky, jerky rhythm section underpinning a lyrical concern with unveiling the contradictions of everyday life. On *Entertainment!* the band zone in on the alienated spaces of contemporary leisure, the economy of the disco floor, the banal domestic life momentarily invigorated by cultural consumption in 'At Home He's a Tourist', and in 'Natural's Not In It' questioning whether leisure time can genuinely satisfy human desire, sketching an alienation from satisfaction in both work and play. In their songs Gang of Four provided an intentional illustration of the idea that the artwork inevitably embodies the political and social contexts of its time, and therefore should be explicit about that relationship, something that had been implicit in T. J. Clark's work and a key idea in the Art & Language group.

In the summer of 1981, *Sounds* journalist Betty Page (the pseudonym of writer Beverley Glick) visited a flat 'that appears to have been built on top of a slag heap' in central Leeds. Greeted by the diminutive Marc Almond, clad in black and wearing chains around his neck, the journalist followed him upstairs, where he and his bandmate Dave Ball regaled her with gritty urban detail. A few weeks before the interview, riots took place in nearby Chapeltown. Almond tells Page about the visible glow on the horizon during the riots, and how a car outside their flat was petrol-bombed in the middle of the night. In this context of urban strife, the glamour of Soft Cell represented an escape – especially Almond's bedroom, which was filled with vintage comic books, jewellery and clothes. On the bedroom wall, gold spray-painted graffiti read 'A non-stop erotic cabaret', which would become the title of the band's debut album.[11] While Gang of Four and Scritti Politti were outlining their theoretical approaches to pop music, Almond and Ball were developing an approach that owed more to cabaret than to Marxist theory, one that was nonetheless steeped in a distinctively northern pop: from the Kraftwerk-like synth-based sounds emerging from Sheffield, to Northern Soul.

Both had moved to Leeds from seaside towns: Almond from Southport, on Merseyside, and Ball from a few miles up the coast in Blackpool. Ball had seen Almond, who was in the year above him, doing performance art at the Poly: 'His main piece was called Mirror Fucking,' Ball told the *Guardian*. 'He'd be naked in front of a full-length mirror, smearing himself with cat food and shagging himself. It provoked quite a reaction.'[12] They began to collaborate, at first Ball providing an electronic soundtrack for Almond's performances, but eventually this evolved into something that was recognisable as pop music. Their early songs were described by Ball in another interview with Page as 'very mechanical [. . .] all about hackneyed things like modern living, modern-cliches like "Tupperware Party" and "The Fondue Set", about housewives'.[13] Ball was keen to draw a distinction between

Soft Cell's approach to music and other artists' darker electronica: 'they weren't bleak or industrial though, it was all danceable sort of pop music', although years later Almond would call Soft Cell 'an experimental electro band more in keeping with Suicide or Throbbing Gristle than the Top 40'.[14]

The truth was that Soft Cell were perfectly suited to the Top 40 – their noir pop was wrapped in melodies whose minor key wasn't exactly sunny, but was certainly catchy, and you could dance to it. They mixed minimalist electronica with transgressive sleaze to produce sharp, witty pop music. Their first record, the *Mutant Moments* EP, had been self-released in October 1980, which happened to be at the tail-end of the brutal attacks and murders of women in West Yorkshire, especially Leeds, that were carried out by Peter Sutcliffe, who up until his capture and identification was known only as the Yorkshire Ripper. The effect on the atmosphere in Leeds was profound – local feminist groups organised Reclaim the Night marches as a response to a curfew imposed on women by police, and in solidarity with prostitutes, who had been disproportionately targeted by the attacker. It was in this atmosphere of fear and defiance that Soft Cell's first record was released. When I listened to the first track, 'Potential', I thought: wow, what a strangely upbeat tune. But the concept of potential emerges with a double-edge: the idea that you could *be* anything is logically accompanied by the idea that you could also *do* anything. Potential is empowering, sure, but also deeply terrifying. Almond's observations of people going about their everyday business – on a bus, playing in a playground – are undercut by hints of something dark at work. If we could *do* anything, then maybe we're capable of murder; if we could *be* anyone then maybe we, or someone we know, could be the Ripper? The song ends with an exhortation to look again at a man, in case he could be recognisable, as if an

identikit image is being waved in front of your face. This dark sleaziness was later generalised into a Soho-like landscape of nightclubs, neon and sadomasochism, but I feel that Soft Cell distilled something dark and compelling from their place and time, channelling it into glamorous yet chilling pop.

Making the specific universal in this way, tapping into the atmosphere of a city to create a piece of music with wider resonance, is one way in which location makes itself known in pop. With 'In My Life', The Beatles had already wrestled with the question of how to channel specific memories of Liverpool into a song that would appeal to the general listener. But the specific context of a city can make itself known in pop music in other ways. In the post-war era the expansion of education meant that more young people were going to university than ever before, and many of them moved to new cities far from home to study. The University of Leeds played a part in the city's music scene as an important venue for touring acts, most famously The Who. In a comparable way to Bryan Ferry's education at Newcastle, members of the Fine Art department at Leeds exercised a conceptual influence on Gang of Four, whose Marxist post-punk deconstructed the conventions of pop music and society. There was a practical element to this too: grants primarily intended to fund research into art history enabled band members to visit New York, where they experienced that city's influential punk scene. Elsewhere in Leeds, Soft Cell were experimenting with the fusion of visual art, performance and electronic music. The growing interest in using new technology – synthesisers and sequencers – to produce pop music was evident elsewhere, in the South Yorkshire city of Sheffield, where a small number of influential bands were producing music that ranged from experimental noise to chart-bound pop.

5.

SHEFFIELD

The Megabus from Leeds dropped me at the windswept Meadowhall bus station, next to the shopping centre of the same name on the suburban edge of Sheffield. It was the early afternoon of an overcast early December day. I was on a low budget in a country whose rail fares were often costly. The meagre price of the bus journey came at the cost of being dumped in a far-flung corner of the city. But, as I climbed aboard a Supertram and passed through the formerly industrial landscape of factories and canals I wondered whether what it did provide, this abbreviated point-to-point journey that left you some miles from your destination, was an insight into a place that you wouldn't necessarily have got had you arrived at the relatively grand Sheffield station. As it happened, I had come to Sheffield the year before, during the summer months, when I found the city to be warm and welcoming. Back then I was in the city for that rare thing: an enjoyable academic conference. This time, the city was cold and grey, and I had no appointments to keep. I checked into the same hotel I had stayed in the previous year, down a side street next to the Crucible Theatre. It was named after the Cutlers, the guild responsible for the city's cutlery and metalworking industries, whose headquarters are just around the corner on Church Street.

I lay on the bed for an hour or so puzzling over the question that had been on my mind for some time: what does a city sound like? By which I mean: how would you characterise a city's sound? I had already thought about this in connection to the post-punk of Manchester, the beat-pop of Liverpool, the rhythm and blues of Newcastle and the critical theory-derived post-punk of Leeds. But what about Sheffield? How do The Human League, Def Leppard and Pulp fit together? At first I thought they didn't, but as I began to piece things together it became clear that it was almost impossible for musicians in regional cities, especially if they were contemporaries, not to know each other. The unlikeliest combinations of bands played together at early stages in their careers, and musicians who remained in a city often became important enablers of younger acts, by building studios or starting record labels.

But back to the sound of a city. Primarily it's a subjective question: what music do you think of when you think of Sheffield? I'm sure I wouldn't be alone in thinking of the synth-pop that emerged from the city as characteristic of its sound – The Human League, ABC, or the experimental electronica of Cabaret Voltaire. New technology demanded a different kind of musician, one of great technical ability whose skills tended towards the practical requirements of an engineer. It entailed a new approach to musical production, one that would become increasingly influential during the eighties. Synths were at the centre of Sheffield pop. Singular though Jarvis Cocker's Pulp were, their use of synths and their love of a 4/4 Europop beat marked them out as a defiantly pop band during the guitar-heavy Britpop era, and connected them to the earlier electronic bands from the city.

There are other characters to take note of in Sheffield, not least the club-promoter-turned-sleaze-merchant Peter Stringfellow,

brought up in the Pitsmoor district, who turned to putting on concerts after being convicted for selling stolen carpets. At first, he rented out local church halls for club nights, then promoted a Beatles gig in the city, before moving into clubs. (During this time local act Dave Berry began to reach the charts with songs like 'Little Things' and 'Mama'.) Stringfellow's King Mojo club in Pitsmoor became a local centre for Northern Soul, and he opened clubs in the city centre before moving to Leeds, then Manchester, in the process slowly discarding live music in favour of DJs spinning records and cabaret, eventually leading to his table-dancing London clubs and a degree of national celebrity. In the sixties, every regional city had the equivalent of Peter Stringfellow, but his genius, if you can call it that, had been to diversify into discotheques, cabaret and strip clubs.

I recalled Stringfellow as I walked out of my hotel and turned up High Street, following the tram line in the direction of the university. Across the road was a building that had once housed a shoe shop beneath which Stringfellow opened his Down Broadway club. It was a cramped city centre location that, judging by the comments I found on an online message board about it, didn't much appeal to the blues and soul fans that had previously attended the suburban King Mojo club. In Down Broadway Stringfellow began to experiment with differently themed nights – prog, soul, rock – to target different audiences, and this was in part the source of King Mojo regulars' alienation.

A little further up the street was the Santander bank, in a building that had housed the Crazy Daisy nightclub, where, legend has it, Phil Oakey of The Human League spotted Susan Ann Sulley and Joanne Catherall dancing together and asked them to join the band, kicking off the second phase of the group's career. When I visited there was little sign of nightlife in the area around High Street – it was predominantly used for shopping and got very quiet at night – but a little further uphill, just past the Cathedral, the commercial district gave way to what was obviously a centre for nightlife. It was the late afternoon, and dark, and large student pubs advertising discounted drinks were just then beginning to open for the evening's trade. I stood outside a Chinese restaurant and consulted the A4 sheet of paper on which I had scribbled the address of an old nightclub. The restaurant was housed in a modern redbrick and glass apartment block that had been built on the site of a row of separate buildings. It made identifying a specific address almost impossible. Apartment buildings now had addresses like 45–53 High Street, spanning several residences. I was looking for The Limit, one of those classic sticky-floored clubs stocked with cheap beer in which bands like The Human League and Cabaret Voltaire had played. It had stood at 55 High Street. Somewhere around here, I thought, as I idled outside the U Buffet restaurant.

The Limit had been granted its licence in 1978 on condition that The Sex Pistols never play there, but it did stage gigs by Siouxsie and the Banshees, U2, and Adam and the Ants, as well as being the location in which Jarvis Cocker appeared onstage in 1986 in a wheelchair having recently thrown himself out of a window to impress a girl. Interviewed at the time by journalist Jon Wilde for *Sounds*, Cocker said he was 'ten times more Sheffield' than other, harder, industrial-funk bands like Chakk or Hula. 'Just because it's from Sheffield, why does it have to sound like a steel factory?' Cocker said. 'You go to Grimsby, you don't expect fish-slapping, or the noise of trawlers.'[1] The driving, relentless industrial funk emerging from Sheffield at that time was clearly something Cocker felt compelled to kick against. Music could be a reaction against the determinism of place, a stubborn choice to pursue a different path.

Around the corner from where The Limit had been, tucked

away behind the City Hall in Holly Street, is an ornate stone building dating from 1899, in which from 1972 onwards an avant-garde, experimental youth project called Meatwhistle was based. Founded by the playwright Christopher Wilkinson and his wife, the artist Veronica Wilkinson, and funded by the city council, Meatwhistle had started out as a summer school held in the Crucible Theatre which attracted young people who included Martyn Ware and Ian Craig Marsh, later of The Human League, and Glenn Gregory, who would later join with Ware to form Heaven 17.[2] The building was large and the project was clearly well funded, with musical instruments and video cameras available to participants. Bands formed and rehearsed in the many empty rooms of the building, and shows were put on every Sunday by members – music, comedy, theatre. Participants would cook and eat communally, and word got around, attracting outsiders to come and see what was going on in the former teacher training building. Ware had been a trainee manager at a Co-op supermarket when his friend Paul Bowers invited him to come along and see what was happening at Meatwhistle.[3]

During the same period, and intersecting slightly with the experimental collective at Holly Street, Cabaret Voltaire were making their first forays into electronic noise. Former art student Richard H. Kirk, telephone engineer Chris Watson and their friend Stephen Mallinder would meet on Tuesday and Thursday nights in Watson's attic and improvise music onto tape, using tape loops, a basic drum machine, and a bass, organ and clarinet that were heavily distorted using effects.[4] At this point the idea of making records seemed far from their minds, and instead they drove around playing tape loops or brought their recordings into pubs and played them. Their art was an intentional provocation, and was true to their name, which had been taken from the nightclub in Zurich that was central to the formation of the Dada movement. Their debut gig, in May 1975, during which the band used a recording of a steam hammer as percussion, triggered a stage invasion.[5] Cabaret Voltaire's urge towards provocation was proto-punk.

I was intrigued by the connection between synth music and Sheffield. It's tempting to directly link the sound of the city's electronic music with what once was the constant sonic accompaniment of Sheffield's heavy industry. The thump of a hammer from a steel mill or the roar of a furnace served as an audible reminder of the machinery that underpinned the everyday existence of the city. You can certainly trace the found sounds of Cabaret Voltaire in this way: the rhythm of the steam hammer could become a beat to be electronically manipulated. I think that Cabaret Voltaire, through their longevity and influence, provided a model for electronic music that other bands could adapt for their own ends. So, through a process of refinement, the external environment was integrated into the core DNA of Sheffield electronica, becoming a building block for future bands. The jerky rhythm of a steam hammer recorded by Cabaret Voltaire could then worm its way into the work of another band, who would attempt to reproduce the rhythm electronically, processing it and smoothing it out. The noises of industry could be reproduced, manipulated and distorted by sampling and synthesising. Even when the specific sample was lost, the steam hammer rhythm remained, a ghostly reminder of its industrial origin. To work with sequencers and synths didn't necessarily require musical genius, or any particular musical talent at all. But what was important in electronic music was the technical ability of the people involved. Because of the nature of Chris Watson's work at the telephone company he was able to wire together effects that Cabaret Voltaire could use. During the seventies a surprising number of musicians read

Practical Electronics magazine seeking tips on how to solder together their own synthesiser, as commercially available synths were unaffordable. But, later in the decade, synths became less expensive and more within the reach of musicians.

Mainstream pop music was increasingly integrating electronic elements – warm burbles of synths on the edges of the sound mix of an otherwise traditional guitar-based record, or, in the case of the German band Kraftwerk, becoming wholly electronic, providing a blueprint for what successful synth-pop might sound like. Having initially built their own synth, and found it to be cumbersome and difficult to use, Martyn Ware and Ian Craig Marsh eventually invested in two commercially available synths, first the Korg Minikorg 700S and then the Roland System 100, which was more advanced and expensive than the Korg and could be expanded to include a sequencer and mixer. When the system was up and running it would look like this: two sets of control panels sat above a music keyboard, and from them sprouted a tangle of wires, each connecting one socket to another. The control panels bore sliders and knobs that could be adjusted to create sounds, blips and beats that could be sequenced so that they became loops of throbbing bass, sheets of white noise, or ersatz drum tracks. These sounds could be modified, distorted, sped up or slowed down. You could do all of this without touching a key of the keyboard, in a series of actions that each appeared as simple as tuning a radio. Although rudimentary, the synth was capable of creating music simultaneously familiar and strange.

Ware and Marsh had begun to perform together under the name The Future, elaborately generating sounds – bass lines, drums – on the Roland while playing melodies on the Korg. A third member of The Future, Adi Newton, lived in Devonshire Lane, among the network of streets near the station, and that address soon came to serve as a studio for the band.[6] At first all the band members shared vocal duties, but it was eventually decided that they needed a singer. Newton left, afterwards forming Clock DVA, and the remaining members of The Future recruited Phil Oakey a hospital porter whose trademark lopsided hairstyle was already in place. Oakey had previously worked in a university bookshop where he had become a devoted reader of the science-fiction work of Philip K. Dick and J. G. Ballard. Oakey would go on to channel his interest in sci-fi into his complex, dark and often hilarious lyrics, but first The Future became The Human League, taken from the name of an interstellar state in the science-fiction board game Star Force: Alpha Centauri.

The science-fiction influence on Sheffield bands is notable: many were fascinated by Stanley Kubrick's adaptation of Anthony Burgess's novel *A Clockwork Orange*, some of its scenes of dystopian violence filmed in the starkly contemporary brutalist housing of the new London suburb of Thamesmead. (The film was released in Britain in 1972 but withdrawn by the director the following year in response to a supposed spate of copycat violence.) Such a landscape would have been comparable to certain sections of Sheffield: the concrete zig-zag of the Park Hill flats sitting on the ridge above the station, the hexagonal towers of Sheffield University's Geography building sitting like a space station on the road out of town, the banal brutalist city centre office blocks, or the dull pedestrian underpasses beneath the ring road, the alienating non-places of post-war planning that thrummed with an atmosphere of threat, one amplified by popular fictional works such as Kubrick's film. The Human League's *The Dignity of Labour* EP is named after a mural in *A Clockwork Orange*, the bands Heaven 17 and Clock DVA also drew their names from the film, and, later on, the band Moloko, formed by ex-Chakk member Mark Brydon and vocalist Róisín Murphy, took their name from an amphetamine-laced milk drink favoured by Alex and his gang.[7] Wendy Carlos's soundtrack for the film brought a suitably odd, processed modernity to bear on classical compositions such as Beethoven's 'Ode to Joy', the sounds channelled through the Moog synthesiser. Carlos's soundtrack seemed peculiarly suited to the forbidding concrete spaces of the film. For those already thinking in terms of the relationship between a future-oriented electronica and their everyday lives, it must have seemed a blueprint. (When The Future came up with a random lyric composition program, they named it CARLOS.)[8] The analogy between the dystopia of Kubrick's film and the modernist spaces of Sheffield was far from direct, but the rubbing up of one against the other, of the Kubrick/Carlos vision – trying to capture the world they conjured from the architecture and how it maps onto Sheffield. Science fiction provided a framework of atmospheres and idiosyncrasies that complemented the experimental nature of electronic music.

While The Future had drawn on progressive rock, The Human League for the most part distilled their ideas into the short, sharp shock of the three-minute pop song. There was still room for more experimental extended work in their album tracks and the instrumental EP *The Dignity of Labour*, but the melding of the technical ability of Ware and Marsh with the startling lyrical perspectives of Phil Oakey hastened a shift into pop. As The Future, Ware and Marsh had cultivated major record labels by sending dot-matrix printed brochures pitching the band. Those efforts drew some interest, and had motivated them to find a singer, so when it was time to promote The Human League, it wasn't a surprise that they repeated them: a demo sent to Bob Last's Fast Product label included a computer printout manifesto that appealed to Last's high-concept, low-budget aesthetic. Last signed the band on the strength of that demo, which included the song 'Being Boiled', consisting of a fat bass synth riff over which Oakey's lyrics focus on the moral implications of sericulture – both silkworm breeding and the production of silk. The song could be read either as an earnest, microscopic manifestation of animal rights, or, conversely, a parody of that position. But most of all what emerges from the song is the feeling that it's fictional: an exhortation narrated by a character created and voiced by Oakey, an experiment in finding a new perspective from which a pop song can be delivered. Fast Product decided to put out 'Being Boiled' as a seven-inch single, with on the B-side 'Circus of Death', another song demonstrating Oakey's pulp and sci-fi-inflected imagination: the Steve McGarrett character from TV show *Hawaii-Five-O* arrives at Heathrow Airport to attempt to solve the particularly bizarre case of a murderous circus run by a clown who draws his power from a drug called 'dominion'. Oakey's spoken-word introduction suggests that verses of the song were drawn from a 1962 *Guardian* article and that the final couplet is a shortwave radio message from the last surviving man on earth. This is compound weirdness from Oakey, a fantastical framing of fiction as fact, a straight-faced delivery of ludicrousness, and ultimately another experiment in pushing a pop song beyond its traditional boundaries. Fast Product released the single at the end of June 1978.

The Human League's first gig took place that same month, in Psalter Lane Art School. Soon after, the band began to perform live against a visual backdrop of slide projections, provided by new member Adrian Wright, incorporating images of celebrities, landscapes and cities, a Pop Art-style exercise in creating a suitable atmosphere in which the music could be presented and received. A 1979 performance from a German TV show illustrates what this staging would evolve into: during the song 'Only After Dark', a cover of a Mick Ronson song that appeared on the band's second album *Travelogue*, Wright projects images onto three screens, mostly stills from the Hitchcock film *Psycho*, casting the lyrics' theme of night-time escape in a murderous context. The slides' transitions create a visual rhythm that intersects with the tempo of the song while casting light or shadow on the lyrical content. The effect is very different from the literal or figurative pyrotechnics of a rock concert, and actively courts the alienation of the audience from emotional involvement with the show. At times during the performance Oakey appears to turn towards one of the screens to watch what's being displayed. They had incorporated slides in their performances for the first time at The Limit club on 25 July 1978, which Marsh calls 'our first really successful show'.[9]

This date, which happens to be the day I was born, triggers a timeline that isn't merely drawn from a pile of records and some books about the subject, but is instead taken from the fringes of my memory: witnessing the glamorous pop sheen of the later Human League on *Top of the Pops* as they mimed their way through 'Don't You Want Me'. The transformation of the band from their early days of slide projectors and peculiar, darkly funny songs to performing a kitchen-sink melodrama against a sleek Eurodisco backing, punctuated by stabs of horn-like synths, wasn't such a shock. As with the earlier songs, Oakey had drawn on popular culture – a photo story he read in a magazine – to write a song narrated from multiple perspectives: the male narrator, wounded and darkly threatening, and the female narrator (Susan Ann Sulley, whom he had recruited at the Crazy Daisy) voicing a competing perspective. Oakey's interest in relatively complex pop songs persisted in the structure and dark undertow of 'Don't You Want Me'. By this point, Martyn Ware and Ian Craig Marsh had departed to form Heaven 17, and Oakey was in full control of the group. With producer Martin Rushent and multi-instrumentalist Ian Burden, Oakey was able to create a widescreen version of the earlier iteration of The Human League, preserving the synth backing but applying a mainstream pop polish – the minimalism of the early records was transformed into something richer. Their art pop vision was intact, but now refined into a form that would conquer the charts. (The album *Dare*, released in October 1981, soon reached number one in the UK, and 'Don't You Want Me', released as the fifth single from the album, was the Christmas number one, in the process probably making it notable to my three-year-old self.)

But back to 1978 for a moment. The Human League played a few more gigs and recorded a Peel Session in London before returning to The Limit in September, this time supported by Def Leppard, a teenage heavy metal band who had been gigging around working men's clubs in the city. Later that year, in November, they would record and self-release their first EP, three songs of furiously and brilliantly played heavy metal with titles like 'Getcha Rocks Off', which lead singer Joe Elliott handed to John Peel during the DJ's set at Sheffield University. Peel then played the record on his BBC radio show, and it reached the lower reaches of the charts. Onstage, they were a remarkably different prospect to The Human League in a way that makes you applaud the scattershot booking policy at The Limit. According to Dave Haslam's *Life After Dark*, Elliott took to the stage 'stripped to the waist, with skin-tight loon pants and a huge wooden black cross hanging around his neck'.[10] While The Human League were imagining a new type of pop music, Def Leppard were re-energising a persistent form: heavy rock. It was a brief and peculiar crossing of paths. (Ian Burden of Graph, the band that went onstage between Def Leppard and The Human League, later became a key member of the latter.)

Ware and Marsh's post-Human League band, Heaven 17, were a side project of a larger entity, the British Electric Foundation. Aside from their work on the Heaven 17 records, the duo produced other albums using the BEF moniker and bringing in a string of guest vocalists – Tina Turner, Sandie Shaw, Bernie Nolan – to sing on them. The idea of a larger organisation underpinning the activities of a band was perfectly compatible with the approach of Bob Last's Fast Product, a DIY label that engaged in vaguely parodic corporate shadow throwing in a manner and style that influenced Factory Records. Last had become The Human League's manager and, after the split occurred, suggested that Ware form the production company. Last became the manager of both groups, a fortuitous situation when you consider that it was by no means guaranteed that The Human League would survive the break-up or that Ware and Marsh would form a new group. (Phil Oakey believes that Last engineered the split, that 'Bob thought myself and Martyn [Ware] shouldn't be in one group. And I think he was probably right.')[11] Last became a 'shareholder' in the corporation-style BEF, describing his duties to the group as being responsible for strategy. He clearly regarded music as both a subversive art project and a hugely lucrative business.

In recruiting a singer, Ware and Marsh approached former Meatwhistle friend Glenn Gregory, and brought in a talented young black musician to play bass and guitar, John Wilson, whom Gregory had met while working backstage at the Crucible Theatre. They set about recording their first album, *Penthouse and Pavement*, in Sheffield, in the same studio space where The Human League were simultaneously making *Dare*. Much of the work on the album was completed in a few short weeks of intense, highly competitive activity, as Ware was determined to prove himself. Heaven 17 are harder and faster than The Human League ever were, and Wilson's hyperactive funk bass lines added urgency to the sound. While the album was recorded in Sheffield, it took as its subject the wider world of global capitalism, focusing particularly on London. Within a couple of years they had relocated to the capital, a city more suited to their lyrical and conceptual interests: the simmering inequalities of urban life, the gleaming surfaces of the city, how the logic of debts and deals come to shape everyday interactions. The sleeve of the *Penthouse and Pavement* album resembled a slick brochure that a company in search of new business might distribute: glass-walled office buildings in the background, pony-tailed besuited band members shaking hands in the foreground. Elsewhere on the cover there was a mixing desk, a reel-to-reel tape recorder, and Martyn Ware sitting concentratedly at a keyboard, pen in hand, notating a musical score. This made transparent the idea of pop as business, simultaneously unveiling it and celebrating it: the pop band working hard to improve the listener's experience, making deals, performing the tasks that are usually hidden away in a back room rather than reproduced on an album sleeve. A peppy corporate slogan reinforced the concept – 'B.E.F. The New Partnership that's opening doors all over the world' – while beneath the band name were listed its cities of operation: Sheffield, Edinburgh, London.

The movement of bands like Heaven 17 and The Human League from the fringes to the centre came to be referred to as New Pop, and was seen as the application of the political strategy of Entryism – the Trotskyist idea that a small group of people can join and subvert the aims of a larger organisation. At around the same time, Last began to manage Scritti Politti, who made a perhaps even more striking journey from punk dub independently released from their Camden squat to reaching the charts with smooth, radio-friendly soul-derived pop. But was it possible for formerly post-punk bands to shift to the mainstream without compromise? Heaven 17 swerved that question for the time being: as part of the deal for forgoing The Human League name, they were given a percentage of the sales of the band's next album, which sold in such quantities that Ware and Marsh were able to fund new studio equipment and take their time with future records. The result was the 1983 album *The Luxury Gap*, which sold in greater numbers than their debut.

In Heaven 17's satirical appropriation of the style of big business there's a palpable sense that for them there was no alternative but the mainstream. This is where New Pop becomes difficult to untangle from the wider context of the time. Superficially it was all too easy to interpret *Penthouse and Pavement* as an endorsement of the culture it set out to satirise. (Martyn Ware has spoken of encountering ex-stock traders who had received the album in this way.) If you weren't going to operate independently, and thus either risk or actively choose to remain on the periphery, one question was how to take major label largesse and channel it into a sustainable structure that would help you to create future work. Heaven 17 showed a way, and others would follow.

One of The Human League's many gigs in 1978 was at Sheffield University. A young local journalist, Andy Gill (no relation to the Gang of Four guitarist), covered it for the *NME*. He contrasted The Human League, who performed 'competently', to the support act, a band called Vice Versa, whose singer looked like 'he spends more time combing his hair than playing the guitar'.[12] The singer was Stephen Singleton, who had been childhood friends with Def Leppard's Joe Elliott and who published his own fanzine, *Steve's Papers*, which the reviewer also rubbished. Later, after they had formed their own label to release Vice Versa records and an EP of local synth acts that included Clock DVA, and after they had added another fanzine writer, Martin Fry, as keyboard player, Vice Versa became ABC. Fry was from Stockport in Greater Manchester but came to Sheffield as a student (his brother Jamie would join an early, Sheffield-based line-up of World of Twist). The band's move from synth-pop to slick, orchestral pop came via the rawer funk sound of their debut single 'Tears Are Not Enough', which reached the UK Top 20 and was later remixed for their debut album *Lexicon of Love*. The differences between the two versions of the track indicate the level of the band's ambition. The second one was slicker, engineered towards radio play: their eyes were on success. Bringing in producer Trevor Horn and a group of musicians, including arranger Anne Dudley, that would subsequently become the basis of the band Art of Noise and the label ZTT, ABC realised a deeply ambitious vision: lyrics deconstructing the love song while never fully giving in to cynicism about the need for the transcendence of love, set against sweeping strings and a slick, commercial funk. More chart success ensued. ABC's success was a result of the melding of the new synth-pop with a modern iteration of the old-school hit factory: the album was recorded at Trevor Horn's studio, using a combination of the band, session musicians and high-tech sequencing that was a world away from the synths available to Vice Versa. In a few short years, Sheffield electronic music had gone from sticky-floored basement nightclubs to the heart of British pop.

In fact, there were two pathways for Sheffield's electronic music. One led straight to the centre of the music industry, which frequently meant a move to London and yielded a series of truly great pop albums from The Human League, Heaven 17 and ABC. The other was a more independent route, which in many ways reflected the cultural infrastructure – particularly an organisation such as Meatwhistle – that had created the kind of conditions from which bands like The Human League emerged. Taking advantage of the relatively high availability of empty warehouse space in the city, Cabaret Voltaire – by now tangentially associated with the punk movement although they predated it by many years – set up a studio in a disused building, Western Works, on Portobello Street, not far from The Limit's premises on West Street. The building had been a cutlery factory, but just before the band moved in in 1977 it had been used as the headquarters of the Sheffield Federation of Young Socialists.[13] They soon acquired a mixing desk and multitrack tape machine after getting an advance from Rough Trade records. Having their own studio afforded them a huge degree of freedom that they took full advantage of, recording four studio albums for the label between 1978 and 1982, in a period of intense productivity that would probably have been impossible without their foresightedness in investing the advance in this way. Aside from Cabaret Voltaire the studio played host to New Order as they recorded demos a few months after Joy Division singer Ian Curtis's suicide, then local bands such as Clock DVA, Hula and Chakk.

Chakk were an industrial band who combined sampling with funk in a manner that showed the influence of Cabaret Voltaire, and whose first single was produced by Richard H. Kirk and Stephen Mallinder at Western Works. Seen as a commercial prospect by MCA Records, in 1985 they received a big advance, rumoured to be as much as £100,000, to sign with the label. Realising that it would probably cost that much to record their album in a commercial studio in London, they chose to invest the money in building their own FON Studios (FON stood for

Fuck Off Nazis). As with Cabaret Voltaire's decision to invest their Rough Trade advance in Western Works, this was a far-sighted plan that yielded long-term results, not merely in terms of attracting commercial clients such as Yazz, David Bowie and Take That to the studios, but also in terms of creating a platform for cultural activity. Over time, FON opened a record store of the same name, which was later taken over by Steve Beckett and Rob Mitchell and renamed Warp. With producer Robert Gordon, they formed Warp Records, a label that built on Sheffield's tradition of electronic experimentation while also reflecting the growing hunger for techno music in Britain's post-industrial cities. Warp Records' first release was The Forge-masters' 'Track With No Name', a slice of minimalist techno by Robert Gordon whose five hundred copies were funded with an Enterprise Allowance Grant, a scheme started by the Thatcher government that provided small grants to help young unem-ployed people start businesses. Other records followed, from Leeds DJ George Evelyn under the name Nightmares on Wax and from LFO, whose eponymous single reached number 12 in the UK chart in the summer of 1990. Built on a network of people who travelled to record shops and 'all-dayers' across Leeds, Bradford, Huddersfield, Sheffield, Manchester and Not-tingham, what came to be known as bleep techno drew on hip-hop and Detroit and Chicago house, or in Robert Gordon's case the space and depth of dub reggae. It earned its moniker because its records invariably employed a ghostly, analogue-sounding tone (as if a telephone line, left to its own devices long enough and become frustrated by the monotony of its dial tone, had begun to compose a rudimentary tune) to pick out the tracks' main melody against a minimalist backing of clean, precise beats, deep Roland 808 bass lines, and phased synth. The connections between Warp and the older scene were made explicit by the release of 'Testone' by Sweet Exorcist, a duo consisting of Cabaret Voltaire's Richard T. Kirk and DJ Parrot (Richard Barrett). If the bleep scene stretched across Yorkshire and into Manchester and Nottingham, Warp was at its centre. Sheffield DJ Winston Hazel, whom Beckett and Mitchell employed as the Warp shop's import buyer, told *Resident Advisor*'s Matt Anniss that the records reflected 'the industrial devastation and the climate in Sheffield at the time [. . .] it had the sound of the city that I grew up in imprinted within the track'.[14] Fiercely contemporary and cutting-edge, Sheffield's techno scene was an unforeseen beneficiary of the city's cultural infrastructure that had been built by independently minded bands such as Cabaret Voltaire and Chakk.

The next morning, I walked from my hotel through the centre of town and down the hill in the direction of the station. These streets, which surround Sheffield Hallam University, form a combination of business district (tall office blocks vacated after five as commuters rush downhill to the station) and, to the south, a cultural quarter in which small businesses are housed in reconditioned redbrick buildings and converted factories. I strolled down one street towards a building that consisted of four large steel drums each resembling a curling stone (it was around the time of the Winter Olympics and curling, the Zen-like ice-based version of lawn bowls, was on my mind). An air vent funnelled out of the top of each of the squat steel drums, and as I walked past I could see that there were offices in the basement of the building. Now the site of the Sheffield Hallam University students' union, the building had been one of New Labour's millennium projects, the National Centre for Popular Music, part-funded by National Lottery money and opened in March 1999. It didn't last long, getting through the Y2K celebrations before closing in June 2000, the numbers of visitors to its exhibitions significantly lower than expected. Each of the drums contained a chamber that was used for different purposes – one housed a soundscape created by Heaven 17's Martyn Ware – and afterwards the building was briefly used for concerts before being sold to the university. I went inside and wandered around for a little while. The peculiar shape of the building had been awkwardly adapted into a kind of anytown students' union: tables in the hall for societies to use, a coffee shop on one side, SU merchandise for sale on the other.

Nevertheless, the building is a reminder of a certain era, when popular culture was appropriated by mainstream political power – often willingly supported by musicians. By the mid-nineties, much indie music hadn't really been independent for a while. Instead, 'indie' became a style that suggested four white guys with guitars playing vaguely androgynous music derived from glam (Pulp or Suede) or meat and potatoes 4/4 stuff that was the result of half-listening to The Beatles (Oasis or Cast). Some of these records are excellent, and stand the test of time, but many are not. Marketing budgets went up because major labels were by now seriously involved, acquiring some of the bigger indies such as Creation, or launching new imprints to deal with many of the indie-type bands, in the process securing larger audiences and greater media coverage. These new, generally young audiences were either voting age or on the cusp of it, and they were substantial in size and reflexively anti-Conservative, engaged as they were in the mainstream recreation of the independent music culture of the eighties, which in general had been oppositional to the wider culture and either explicitly or implicitly left-wing.

It was in this context that Tony Blair's New Labour met mainstream indie, in the process riding the wave of what became known as Cool Britannia – a movement that combined a vaguely

Pop Art version of British nationalism with the overdriven guitar and sixties revivalism of some of the worst bands of the nineties, and eventually led to commemoration in such failed cultural tombstones as the former Museum of Popular Music. The building's architect, Nigel Coates, had been responsible for an interconnected cluster of four inflatable silver-coloured pods that served as pavilions for the 1998 Powerhouse::uk showcase of new British technology, science and fashion talent. Sited in Horse Guards Parade off Whitehall in London, and thus close to the symbolic centres of government and monarchy, it was emblematic of the Blair-era cultural rebrand of the United Kingdom, the employment of an apparently playful subversion in the service of power. Viewed from the air, the four inflatable drums closely resembled the steel drums of Coates's Sheffield museum, which would open a year later. Transferring the idea to Sheffield wasn't necessarily a bad one: the building was a suitably ultramodern tribute to both the bygone futurism of the city's electronic acts and the steel industry. Now it's a strangely upmarket and possibly less than ideal students' union. The assumptions underpinning the museum – that cultural histories should be converted into heritage, and that arts and cultural funding should be directed into supporting that process – continue to characterise funding policy, especially those resources channelled into the regions.

The Britpop-era movement of indie music from the cultural fringes to the centre was embodied most completely by Jarvis Cocker of Pulp. Cocker had been a figure on Sheffield's music scene since the late seventies, when he formed an early line-up of the band, bringing in some friends and his sister Saskia, as well as long-serving member Russell Senior. During the 1980s, the band recorded sessions for John Peel's show and released sporadic EPs and a couple of albums of melodic, scuffed pop, going through a few independent labels before releasing the single 'O.U.' on Gift Recordings, an imprint of Warp. This single, on which the band's new, high-tempo, euphoric Europop sound combined with Cocker's wry, observational lyrics, was picked up by the music press, leading to the band signing to Island Records. In part the band had released the single with Gift because of frustration at their previous label, Fire, delaying the release of *Separations*, an album they had recorded a couple of years before. The material recorded for Gift formed the basis of a new sound that would come to fruition on *His 'n' Hers* (1993) and *Different Class* (1995). Between those two albums Pulp, and particularly Cocker, began an ascent towards celebrity that would ultimately derail the band but supply him with a decent post-Pulp career as a broadcaster. I saw them play in Dublin's SFX centre at the end of the UK and Ireland *Different Class* tour, and by then the band were locked into a cycle of touring that would last for a full year.

There wouldn't be another album until 1998's *This Is Hardcore*, a dark, cynical and compelling work that didn't quite have the mainstream appeal of the earlier albums. *This Is Hardcore* was in many ways a downbeat companion to the pre-Island, sardonic-yet-euphoric 'Sheffield: Sex City', which consisted of keyboard player Candida Doyle reading from *My Secret Garden* by Nancy Friday, and Cocker narrating his quest for sex on a long summer night in the city, naming landmarks like the Park Hill flats, underpinned by the band's loose approximation of a techno backing: four-on-the-floor minimalism recast for guitar, bass, drums, synths and a violin. Pulp were never quite the same after their success – *This Is Hardcore* was in part a classic burnt-out rock star's lament – and after another album they broke up. Cocker moved to Paris, recorded a couple of solo albums and made the move into broadcasting. Like many other bands of the era, they've reformed from time to time for lucrative nostalgia gigs.

If I was to point to their influence in Sheffield, I'd pick the Arctic Monkeys, whose droll lyrics at times recall Cocker, and Richard Hawley, the former Longpigs guitarist who actually served as a member of Pulp for a few years near the end, and whose deeply nostalgic records are explicitly named after Sheffield places. He's the opposite of the future-oriented synth-pop that once characterised the city, instead harking back to a crooned and soothing rock 'n' roll and the image of a thriving industrial metropolis that predates his birth. You can listen to his often-excellent records and believe that they date from a time before punk rock or synths or Thatcher, when the factories were open and everyone knew everyone. It's a fantasy, of course, but one that has become remarkably common lately.

I walked down the hill from the city centre to the station. I was on my way to East Yorkshire, to a port city that had attracted an array of maverick musicians, from avant-garde experimentalists to chart-bound classic pop.

6.

HULL

The diesel railcar chugged across Yorkshire at a moderate speed, stopping for a few minutes in a large stretch of waste ground outside Doncaster before continuing in the direction of Hull. It passed the disused site of Hatfield Colliery, closed in 2015 after operating for ninety-nine years. The motionless winding-wheels of the mine shaft were just visible above the railway embankment as the train passed by. In 2013 a landslide of coal waste closed the railway line for five months. It was rare to see many visible remnants of coalmining, and I wondered how long it would be before the site was buried and the equipment removed. For the post-industrial cities of the North, culture had become a way of both celebrating local heritage and plotting a path towards the future. But culture on its own wasn't sufficient to bring a former factory town back from near death, and the jobs that filled the void left by heavy industry were often low-paid and under threat from automation.

I was travelling in the first week of December, and Hull would be the UK's City of Culture for another three and a half weeks. The following day, Hull's successor, which would hold the title in 2021, would be announced live on the BBC's desperately upbeat pan-regional magazine programme *The One Show*. At the same time as I was travelling, representatives from each of the nominated cities – Coventry, Paisley (not a city, but nominated nonetheless), Sunderland, Stoke-on-Trent and Swansea – were also making their way to Hull. Right now, it was all about winners and losers. The night before, I lay on my hotel bed and watched as the Turner Prize was awarded to the artist Lubaina Himid, whose work was on show along with that of the other nominees in Hull's Ferens Art Gallery.

Inevitably, when you visit different cities to investigate their musical heritage, you end up thinking more broadly about the place of culture, how it's used to mask all manner of problems that are by no means the fault of the city in question – the decline of industry, the lack of investment in public services, low education and attainment levels – but have come to define the place for residents, visitors and those who'll never set foot there but are content to caricature it. Living in one of the nominated cities, Sunderland, I came to see that while few people believed the award might be dramatically transformative, they did think it would be a huge step in the right direction – while others were indifferent. These opinions are pretty standard even in residents of cities that do become cities of culture. While the city of culture award would no doubt be welcomed by the victorious city, it was scant recompense in an era of regional decline hastened by government austerity.

The train swept me under the Humber Bridge. Passing beneath the bridge gave me the sense of arrival that I crave on reaching somewhere I've never been before: a signal to tell you you're there, or thereabouts. It was the end of the line: Hull's Paragon station, opened in 1847 to accommodate traffic arriving along the York and North Midland railway. As I stepped from the train, I could see that it was in the process of being renovated: wooden hoardings hid from view whatever building work was happening, and made the walk to the exit fairly circuitous.

After checking into my hotel, I walked in the direction of the city centre, past a karaoke bar where it sounded like the party was just getting started. The centre of Hull is a mostly unremarkable pedestrianised zone of shops large and small. But there's a grandeur to the buildings clustered around Queen Victoria Square, where many of the city's cultural institutions are located: the City Hall and New Theatre, the Maritime Museum, and the Ferens Art Gallery. A short walk up King Edward Street is a huge mosaic mural of three ships on the corner of what had been the Co-op building. It later became a BHS department store, but fell into disuse after the collapse of the company. Now homeless people sat in their sleeping bags in the doorway beneath the entrance canopy. The doors and windows of the entrance were covered with huge photos of the city's cultural attractions: the angular architecture of The Deep aquarium and a photograph of the interior of the Ferens gallery. Above the door was a message: 'WELCOME TO HULL – UK CITY OF CULTURE 2017'.

Derelict department stores like this one could be found in many regional cities, but few had a feature as striking as the Co-op mural, which sought to capture the city's maritime history in a single, abstract image. Three ships, their masts resembling lower-case Ts, or Christian crosses, bob atop a sea made up of shapes – waves, or perhaps fish – that look like sheets of paper blowing in the wind. Three straight, fat lines plunge directly down from the ships into the depths, either nets or reflections of the masts. Woven through the waves, faintly visible, is the Latin motto 'res per industriam prosperae': the success of industry.

It was late afternoon, the light was fading, and Christmas shoppers were making their way home through the streets. I turned down King Edward Street and could see the glow of the Ferens ahead of me, surrounded by other public buildings in one corner of the broad and grand public space of Queen Victoria Square. In the foyer of the gallery, I was met by a team of friendly greeters, who handed me a floor plan of the building that pointed out where I could find the exhibits. In early January 1973, the Hull art pranksters COUM Transmissions, who would later become the industrial band Throbbing Gristle, set up a desk, chairs and a filing cabinet in the Ferens' foyer. This was the 'Ministry of Antisocial Insecurity', a parody of the bureaucracy of both the welfare system and the Arts Council, and the group's contribution to the Fanfare for Europe, Hull's festival celebrating Britain joining the European Economic Community. The city hoped that increased trade with Europe would result from membership, reviving docks dependent on a fishing industry that was in decline following Iceland's extension of its fishing exclusion zone. Bringing in a wild avant-garde art group to celebrate this momentous event seems a little odd in hindsight, but it was a sign of COUM's relative respectability in the city's art scene at that point. Still, it felt peculiar to think about the reversal that had happened since: the way the nostalgia for the fishing industry was mobilised in the Brexit campaign, how the trade they hoped for in 1973 hadn't happened, and how Hull, along with a clear majority of regional towns and cities, had overwhelmingly voted Leave. The UK City of Culture had been established to build on Liverpool's success as 2008 European Capital of Culture – the only British city to hold the title since Glasgow in 1990 – providing a domestic award that would complement the European-wide title. Yet since June 2016 the context had changed significantly: Leeds's hopes of bidding to be the 2023 European Capital of Culture were dashed when the European Commission announced that the title couldn't be awarded to a non-EU country, as the Commission assumed Britain would become by then. Instead of being a domestic counterpart to the European award, one that would be fought for among smaller and mid-sized regional cities, the UK City of Culture would now be the only title available, which seemed to me cruelly symbolic of a country that had turned resolutely and foolishly inwards, and symptomatic of the wider loss of the European funds on which regional cities depended.

I spent perhaps an hour in the busy Ferens Art Gallery looking at the Turner nominees and then left the building to walk in the direction of the city's docks. On the way, I passed a cluster of robotic arms that were part of a public art installation, but at that moment they didn't seem to be working. (The following day I saw workmen trying to fix the problem.) I turned southwards, along the cobbled quay. Moored boats bobbed with the tide. It was dark by now, just before the end of the working day, and I followed the quay southwards, passing restaurants preparing for the post-work trade and offices that looked like they were about to finish up for the day. I crossed a busy road that divided the old town from the docks, and continued south, past a hip-looking street of restaurants and bars until I reached a run-down street along which were a few cleared sites on which buildings had once stood – some were fenced off while others were used as car parks. It was around here that the warehouse building COUM had lived and worked in had stood until its recent demolition.

COUM had been formed by a former student at the University of Hull who went by the name of Genesis P-Orridge. He had been born Neil Andrew Megson, the son of a travelling salesman whose line of work ensured that the family were peripatetic: P-Orridge was born in Manchester, and attended schools in Essex, Stockport and Solihull in the West Midlands, where the local newspaper covered the teenager's efforts to turn the town on to haiku writing by means of a 'happening' held on 1 June 1968 in Mell Square.[1] This was an early sign that P-Orridge had a talent for publicity that he would later employ to outrageous effect. That September he travelled to Hull to begin a degree in Social Administration and Philosophy. Disliking the course, and his efforts to switch to an English degree frustrated, he channelled his energies into producing a controversial student magazine called *Worm*, which was published between 1968 and 1970. Its third issue included instructions for making a Molotov cocktail, while the Student Union refused to print the fourth issue on grounds of obscenity. This resulted in coverage in the official Student Union magazine and an outraged reply from P-Orridge citing freedom of speech.[2]

In a crossing of the paths of two very different Hull cultural luminaries, in 1969 P-Orridge won a student poetry competition judged by Philip Larkin, who was the university's chief librarian. While P-Orridge's academic and literary talents were obvious, by the summer of 1969 he had dropped out of university and moved to London, where he joined the performance art group Transmedia Explorations, who lived in a commune in Islington. Focused on 'happenings' that broke down the boundaries between audience and performers, Transmedia Explorations sought to bring art together with everyday life, to make the two indistinguishable. Their happenings included aspects of theatre, dance and musical performance, and their art practice involved the collection of objects found on the street. Life in the commune involved breaking down conventional behaviour: members could not sleep in the same place on consecutive nights, money was held in a central fund, and every morning a member would wear different clothes from the day before, changing their role or persona to suit the new costume, as if they were stage clothes and life was a piece of theatre.[3] So the breaking down of theatrical convention went both ways: theatre would become more like everyday life while everyday life would become more theatrical. P-Orridge stayed for three months, subsequently returning to his parents' house and experiencing a vision during which he heard the words 'COUM Transmissions' and visualised the band's symbol of a semi-erect penis bearing the letters COUM beneath which was the phrase 'YOUR LOCAL DIRTY BANNED'.[4] Under the COUM banner, the group began to perform in pubs around Hull around the end of 1969.

In December 1969 P-Orridge's friend John Krivine took a lease on the old fruit warehouse at 17 Wellington Street. It's now a car park whose uneven ground consists of the compacted rubble of the old building. A Google Streetview image taken before the building was knocked down shows a four-storey warehouse with a rusted roller shutter that reads 'KEEP CLEAR AT ALL TIMES' and a sign above the entrance door bearing the building's name, 'WELLINGTON HOUSE'. This was the building that had been rechristened by P-Orridge and his fellow residents the Ha Ha Funhouse. Visible from the top floor of the building was the pier from which ferries departed across the Humber to New Holland in Lincolnshire, while Humber Street, directly to the north, was the site of Hull's fruit markets. By this time P-Orridge had met a local teenager at a party: Christine Carol Newby, who later renamed herself Cosey Fanni Tutti. She began a relationship with P-Orridge and moved into the building. Subsisting on food they were able to scavenge from the fruit markets and steal from shops, the group sold underground magazines, communicated with other artists across the world using mail art, made their own clothes and performed street theatre around the city centre, before moving towards happenings which often involved musical performance. The group would often fetch up in front of the Ferens and proselytise in the manner of a religious sect, with one member dressed in a gas mask representing the 'alien brain'. Their activities began to generate publicity in local newspapers, and drew the attention of the local Hell's Angels, who broke into the Funhouse. Soon after, the lease ran out on the building and the group's activities shifted to a terraced Georgian house on a narrow, cobbled street a little further north.

The neighbourhood around the old Funhouse site is one in transition – modern office buildings overlook derelict sites, and beyond those sits the jagged outline of the Terry Farrell-designed steel and glass aquarium named The Deep, projecting like a ship's prow into the river. It was one of those reasonably rare things: a genuinely successful millennium project in a regional city, attracting several million visitors since its opening. The following evening, the BBC would announce the next UK City of Culture from outside the building.

I walked north, following the sinisterly named Dagger Lane (not far away were Sewer Street and Fish Street) then turning onto the narrow Prince Street, which curved towards an archway leading to Trinity Square and the Holy Trinity Church. At numbers 8 and 9 Prince Street were two houses that were now the very model of respectability – Grade II-listed, no less – but in an earlier and more decrepit state had become the headquarters of COUM once they left the Funhouse in 1971. The buildings, which at that time were partially knocked into one unit, had previously been used by a sauce and pickle manufacturer. The top floor was uninhabitable, while there was a huge hole in the floor of one of the rooms in the rear extension, and there was a toilet but no bathroom. Lacking any heating aside from coal fires on the upper floors, the pipes would freeze on the coldest winter days.[5] The group treated the building – which they also

named the Alien Brain – like an artwork, or a gallery, and decorated the interior with Day-Glo paint and created tunnels using
black plastic sheeting, defamiliarising the environment while
also distracting from the house's rotten state. Rooms were filled
with tailor's dummies, drum kits and a multiplicity of found objects and ephemera. 'The house is my latest and evolving work',
P-Orridge told a local reporter.[6]

Perhaps better than any other group, COUM and Throbbing Gristle bridge the gap between the collective experiments
of hippydom and the provocation of punk rock. As they grew
in renown for their artistic practice, they performed more frequently, making the short but significant step from outside the
Ferens Art Gallery to inside, for example. But as time went by it
became clear that they couldn't remain in Hull for much longer.
The local police, who believed that COUM were associating
with local criminals and street gangs, pressured them to leave
the city. Members of the group were frequently harassed by the
local constabulary, and a number of their friends were jailed. A
gangster who often hung out at the squat at Prince Street was
arrested and sentenced to eighteen months for handling stolen
goods, and police suspected COUM of involvement. By that
point P-Orridge was making frequent trips away to visit artist
friends, and when, in June 1973, they heard about a studio space
that had become available in London, they took the opportunity
to leave. 'Proud as I was of being born in Hull, I no longer loved
it there and Hull didn't appear to love me,' Tutti wrote. 'It was
time to go.'[7] Their move took them to Hackney, east London,
where they worked in a studio space and lived in a nearby squat,
re-establishing the communal existence they had begun around
the docks and old town of Hull. They founded their own label,
Industrial Records, and began to tape their performances –
squalls of white noise and screams at first, but later, with their

album *20 Jazz Funk Greats*, a haunting slice of dark electronica that's probably the band's most accessible work.

The story of COUM and Throbbing Gristle isn't a particularly happy one – recently Cosey Fanni Tutti's memoir *Art Sex Music* alleged that she'd suffered psychological abuse and manipulation at the hands of P-Orridge (allegations that have been denied) and that the group's collective ideals were challenged by his authoritarianism. COUM sounded at times closer to a cult than a utopian and egalitarian alternative society. After Throbbing Gristle broke up in 1981, Cosey began a relationship with Chris Carter, a sound engineer who had become a member of the band. They went on to record their own albums as Chris & Cosey and continue to perform in various guises.

From the old COUM house on Prince Street I walked under the archway that led to Trinity Square, a pretty, paved public space on one side of which a redbrick and sandstone market building stands. Ahead of me, at the centre of the square, was Holy Trinity church, parts of which date back to the fourteenth century, and in which the Turner Prize announcement had been held the night before. The excitement of the previous night was over. The space had been filled with tables at which art-world folk sat in the glare of the lights and cameras as the result was broadcast live on television, but now the church was dark inside and the square was quiet. On the south side of the square stood a statue of the poet Andrew Marvell. The poet's father had been a clergyman at Holy Trinity church, and Marvell had attended Hull Grammar School, which was once located in the redbrick building directly behind his statue. I made my way through the winding streets of Hull's old town back towards the city centre in search of something to eat. The night had drawn in and there was a cold wind blowing in from the river, so I decided to return to the old town the next morning and travel from there around the city.

The next morning I walked in the direction of Holy Trinity church, retracing my steps around Trinity Square and passing through the halls of the market. I turned a corner and reached a narrow L-shaped nineteenth-century arcade that led behind a row of buildings. This was Hepworth Arcade, named after Joseph Hepworth, the man who developed it in 1897. I then passed Dinsdale's joke shop – 'We sell laughter – keep smiling!' – before emerging on the street. The lanes and streets of Hull's old town are particularly pretty, and are interspersed with official-looking, near-monumental buildings that serve as reminders of the city's seafaring past: Trinity House, for example, a white stucco-fronted building with a pediment above its entrance bearing a coat of arms decorated in gold leaf. It was constructed on the site of an earlier building in 1753, and had been established years before, in the fourteenth century, as a charity to help needy seafarers, later incorporating a school to train young sailors. Elsewhere, the building housing the city's Guildhall, civic offices and courts sweeps imposingly along Alfred Gelder Street, and a huge statue of Britannia points her trident towards the river from the roof of the building's west end, linking the city's maritime success with the nation's achievements.

I navigated using Britannia as my lodestar, turning around the corner to the park in which I had read that guitarist Mick Ronson used to cut the grass when he worked for the city council. I had gathered a pile of books that linked pop trivia to geographical locations, and at times I would leaf through them to see what I could turn up. I'd open Pete Frame's *Rockin' Around Britain*, in which whole music careers are often distilled into a single line of lapidary prose, and read about Ashton-under-Lyne, or

Glossop, or Hull: 'the birthplace of Mick Ronson, 26.5.46, who left Maybury High School at 15 with no qualifications. In the late Sixties, he lived in a flat in Alva Avenue. Between stints as a council grass cutter, he played in various local groups [. . .] Ronson died in April '93 and is buried here.'[8]

Ronson had been a member of several Hull bands, including The Crestas and The Rats, who recorded their own psyche-delic epic 'The Rise and Fall of Bernie Gripplestone' at Hull's Fairview Studios in 1967. On that track Ronson showed his mastery of a minimalist heavy rock style similar to The Who's Pete Townshend while also adding a venomous proto-heavy metal solo. Recorded by Keith Herd, who would later produce Def Leppard's debut EP in the same studio, it showcased Ronson's ability to switch comfortably between styles, and provides a snapshot of a distinctive guitar stylist's development. Herd met the amiable Ronson hanging around Cornell's music shop, and noted the guitarist's wide musical palate: he was interested in chart pop and heavy rock. Those tastes came through in his playing, and would later serve him well in his work with David Bowie.[9] But by 1969 there was a sense that he was stagnating in Hull. It wasn't the first time Ronson had felt this way. In 1966 he had become frustrated with his day job working as a van assistant for the Co-op, and with the limited ambition of The Crestas, so he decided to move to London. While in the capital Ronson took a job in a garage and eventually joined a group, The Voice, who lived in a big house in Park Lane which turned out to be the headquarters of a religious cult founded by disgruntled ex-Scientologists called The Process. After a few unsatisfactory months he returned home to Hull.[10] An aimlessness set in. He got a job with the council's parks department and began playing with his first professional band, The Rats, who were regarded as the best band in the city at the time. But local scenes can be difficult to break out of, especially in somewhere as relatively geographically isolated as Hull. Although they were never short of gigs in the city, they struggled to get any work elsewhere, except for a month-long stint in the Golf-Drouot nightclub in Paris, a commitment that left Ronson broke. When the guitarist returned to Hull, his father, exasperated at his son's apparent fecklessness, kicked him out of the family home.

It's not immediately obvious why Bowie chose to recruit a group of Hull musicians to form The Spiders from Mars. He had no clear personal connection with the place – no childhood holidays in Hull to look back on fondly, for example. Bowie was a suburban south Londoner who had been attempting to become a pop star since his mid-teens with not much success until the last months of the sixties. He had begun to study mime and to push his work in an increasingly artistic direction. One would have expected him to find a band from within those geographic and artistic circles. Yet London, as we have seen, drew musicians from the regions, mirroring the migration of skilled workers – even the largely self-sufficient COUM/Throbbing Gristle could only function for so long before being drawn into its art and music scene.

There were multiple connections between Ronson and Bowie. Ronson had been recruited by Rick Kemp to play on *Fully Qualified Survivor*, Hull-based singer-songwriter Michael Chapman's second album, released in 1970. Kemp, who had played bass on Chapman's first album, *Rainmaker*, was a local musician who managed the music section of Hammond's department store. He had got to know Ronson when they were both members of R&B covers band The Mariners, and met Chapman through the shop, in which local musicians would often while away their spare time. 'If you were a professional musician, you used to go there on weekday afternoons because nobody had any money and there was nothing to do,' Chapman recalled, 'so we'd go and play the guitars that we couldn't afford.'[11]

The producer of *Fully Qualified Survivor* was Gus Dudgeon, who had fulfilled the same role on Bowie's 'Space Oddity' single of 1969. Dudgeon resisted Chapman's suggestion to use Hull musicians and instead proposed London-based session players. But Chapman held his ground, wanting to use Kemp as bass player again and having been impressed with what he had seen of Ronson at a Rats gig. Kemp asked Ronson if he was interested. 'On my way home I saw Mick mowing the grass on the centre verge of the main dual carriageway from Hull to Hessle,' Kemp recalled. Kemp stopped his car, and asked Ronson who agreed. Kemp remembers his slightly disbelieving response: 'What, a real record – one that's in the shops?'[12] At the recording sessions, Ronson played brilliantly, making an impression on both Dudgeon and Chapman. Clearly pleased with how he had performed and keen to take advantage of the opportunity, Ronson asked the producer about potential session work.

There were still more connections between Bowie and Ronson's networks, connections strengthened by Hull musicians who had moved to the capital. John Cambridge, the drummer of Ronson's band The Rats, had left to join the London-based Junior's Eyes, led by Hull guitarist Mick Wayne. While Junior's Eyes went on to record their debut single with Bowie's producer Tony Visconti, drummer Mick 'Woody' Woodmansey replaced Cambridge in The Rats. In 1969, Junior's Eyes began to serve as a backing band for Bowie (Wayne played guitar on the breakthrough single 'Space Oddity'). By early 1970, however, the band were on the verge of splitting – the guitarist had become increasingly unreliable because of drug problems, and Cambridge suggested recruiting Ronson as an alternative. Bowie was scheduled for a BBC 'In Concert' session on 5 February, so time was of the essence. Cambridge convinced Ronson to come to a Bowie concert at London's Marquee on 3 February, after which he returned to Bowie's house to audition. Two days later he was backing Bowie at the BBC's Paris Theatre on Regent Street, with Tony Visconti on bass.

Although in this case it's clear that extenuating circumstances informed Bowie's decision to change musical back-up, a precedent was being set. Bowie was in the process of moving towards being a mercurial, capricious solo artist who recruits and dismisses as he sees fit according to the whims of his ever-changing musical direction. This hierarchy would be asserted periodically, his shifts in image and musical style often being accompanied by his sacking musicians. Listening to the sessions at the BBC, it's immediately apparent that Ronson's tough and heavy but melodic guitar lines gave a greater form and weight to Bowie's songs. The discipline of his playing strikes you immediately. Conversely, Bowie's approach provided a challenge for the extremely talented Ronson at exactly the right time: in Hull, he had peaked; with Bowie, another world opened up. At the conclusion of 'The Width of a Circle', which showcased Ronson's playing excellently – adding heft and fluidity to Bowie's acoustic guitar – presenter John Peel asked Bowie if he would be touring soon. Bowie confessed that he had only recently met 'Michael', his new guitarist, when he came down from Hull two days before, but that they did have plans to go on the road.[13] Within a couple of months, Woodmansey was recruited to replace Cambridge as drummer and Bowie's backing band, now named The Hype, began work on Bowie's next album, *The Man Who Sold the World*. Ronson proved that his worth stretched beyond mastery of guitar, writing many of the instrumental arrangements, as he and bass player Visconti dominated the production. But because of changes at their label Philips, the release was delayed, and the band fragmented, with Ronson and Woodmansey returning to Hull, recruiting the former Rats singer Benny Marshall and another Hull musician, bassist Trevor Bolder, for their new band Ronno. During this period Bowie, who had previously been thought of as flaky and uncommitted, applied himself to song-writing. The eventual result was the album *Hunky Dory*, which was issued by his new label, RCA, in 1971, by which point The Spiders from Mars line-up of Ronson, Bolder and Woodmansey was in place.

I left the park and wandered along the back streets on the edge of the city centre, behind the empty BHS building and then out across the usual aggregation of ring roads and industrial units that typically marks the boundary between an English city centre and its suburbs. I had earlier plotted a trajectory that would bring me in the direction of the university along Beverley Road, a run-down main thoroughfare of two- and three-storey redbrick houses, off-licences, takeaways (Al Pacino's Pizza!), pound shops, churches and pubs, interspersed with more suburban features like a Lidl or a KFC each set in its own car park, stretching northwards from its junction with the dual carriageway of Ferensway all the way into rural East Yorkshire.

The journey towards the university was bringing me into bedsit land, an area of big houses subdivided into flats and smaller houses rented by students. I passed under an old railway bridge and reached a stretch of shops and an old cinema, the Mayfair, that had been converted into apartments, directly across the road from a pub named The Bevvy. I turned down Grafton Street, a road of terraced houses, each with two wheelie bins, black and blue, parked outside on the pavement. A cluster of signs indicated that there were many properties for rent.

While most houses on Grafton Street are yellow or red brick with an arched front porch and a bay window opening from the front room on to the street, some had been modified, such as number 70, where the bay window had been removed, and a broader aperture had been knocked into the brickwork and filled with a standard rectangular window. Such adjustments seemed to me primarily motivated by the cost of maintenance rather than any aesthetic consideration – the work of a landlord. The house had all the signs of being a rental property, as it was when Paul Heaton of The Housemartins and The Beautiful South lived there during his time in Hull. Heaton, born in Cheshire and brought up in Sheffield and Surrey, had hitchhiked across Europe a couple of years before coming to Hull. His aim in doing so was to meet as many nationalities as he could and to test whether British stereotypes were true or false. He found them to be false, drinking with amiable Green Party members in the village of Dietkirchen in Germany – who kept an open house so that anyone could wander in and out, which he saw as 'socialism working in practice' – and talking politics and culture with people he met in France.[14]

Heaton was looking for somewhere he could live cheaply, and during a trip around Britain in the summer of 1983 with his German friends, he chose Hull, and he and his friend Ray 'Trotsky' Barry put down a deposit on the house in Grafton Street. But why Hull? He looked back fondly on his time living in Sheffield, and warmed to the idea of living in Yorkshire again, while Trotsky wanted to live near the sea, so Hull it was. Heaton moved in with his girlfriend, Susan, Trotsky, and another friend, Matthew. They found themselves in a sort of bedsit bohemia, surrounded by pubs, near the university. The mother of future Fine Young Cannibals singer Roland Gift ran a second-hand clothes shop at one end of Grafton Street. It was a milieu particularly suited to

Heaton's vision of working-class solidarity and droll bar-room observation. And the house on Grafton Street gave him the opportunity to try to replicate the communal atmosphere he had found in Germany: the door was always open and anyone could wander in. When you couldn't afford to go to one of the nearby pubs, you could buy a pint from Nick Hotham's Good Beer Shop off-licence, almost directly across the street at number 55, which had two hand pumps stocked with cask ale from which customers could have their own pint glasses filled.[15] Drinks thus acquired, Heaton and his flatmates would sit out on their front wall talking to neighbours and passers-by.

After a few months signing on, during which time Paul and Trotsky published their own fanzine, Heaton decided to try to form a band. As a teenager in Redhill, Surrey, he had been a member of various bands, one of which included Quentin (later Norman) Cook, who would go on to become the bass player of The Housemartins. Those bands had been formed by groups of friends from school, but now Heaton had to advertise for bandmates. He put up notices ('Trombonist seeks street musicians') in a local pub, the university, and the front window of number 70 Grafton Street. Eventually, bespectacled guitarist Stan Cullimore stormed through the open front door demanding to speak to whoever had left the ad in the window. They began to collaborate: first on another fanzine, then they both ran in the council elections in April 1984 for the Put Hull Back In Yorkshire party, getting a handful of votes for their troubles. This was during the miners' strike of 1984, a reaction to the pit closures and job losses imposed on the mining industry, and the war waged against its union, the NUM, by the Thatcher government. Paul would travel to Hatfield Colliery, which I had passed on my train journey to Hull, meeting people on the picket lines. He became consumed by the strike, and the band began to play benefits around the country for the NUM. These gigs were foundational for The Housemartins in defining their political stance, which in turn shaped their lyrical concerns and their stage act, styled by the band as left-wing gospel. Heaton would address the audience between songs, speaking about his political beliefs and discussing the state of the nation.

The band, which was still a duo, began to release some of their songs on cassette, and played support to bigger acts, including The Smiths. They returned to Surrey to record a demo with Heaton's former bandmates Norman Cook on bass and Chris Lang on drums. But they needed to recruit musicians locally to have any chance of sustaining the band, so they spent time watching groups at the New Adelphi Club, a venue at the end of a row of terraced houses two streets south of Grafton Street. The Adelphi is still there, on DeGrey Street, a bunker-like building that had been converted from a residence into the Victory Club in 1923, and becoming the Civil Service Club, an industrial laundry, the Adelphi Club in 1978 and the New Adelphi in the early 1980s. In 1984 Paul Jackson became the owner and began to stage a mix of local bands and indie touring acts, as well as a gay cabaret that was held on Sunday nights. It was a combination of the extraordinary – bands such as Radiohead and My Bloody Valentine played gigs there – and the ordinary: one visitor recalled that she 'walked into the front bar and there was an old bloke sitting there with his dog and his shopping'.[16] Through regular trips to the Adelphi, Heaton and Cullimore recruited two members of The Gargoyles, bassist Ted Key and drummer Hugh Whitaker. In June 1984 the band signed a record deal with the indie label Go! Discs on the stage of the Adelphi for a fee of £3000 plus three sets of football strips for the local youth team Dane Villa, run by Heaton's next-door neighbour, which was suitably renamed Housemartins AFC. *The Old Grey*

Whistle Test Housemartins special, broadcast in 1986 after the success of their debut album *London 0 Hull 4*, showed them miming to their own songs in the front room of the Grafton Street house, kicking a football around with local children and receiving an award for sponsoring Housemartins AFC. By this point Norman Cook had joined the band as bass player, and in the spare room of number 70 he showcased the DJing skills he would later put to work as Fatboy Slim. While the band willingly played along with the camera crew to stage these scenes, in which they presented a slightly exaggerated version of their lives in Hull, it's difficult to argue that it was unrepresentative of their everyday existence – bracingly normal, socially conscious and deeply embedded in Grafton Street and its immediate environs. When The Housemartins broke up, the decision was made by Paul and Stan, sitting on a climbing frame they called 'The Magic Tower' in a playground behind Grafton Street, where they often went to discuss important band business. When Paul's next band The Beautiful South went to number one in the charts in October 1990 with their single 'A Little Time', he celebrated with friends and neighbours in the Grafton pub, a flat-roofed, redbrick post-war building set back from the street a few doors down from Heaton's house.

I passed the Grafton, then turned onto Newland Avenue and walked in the direction of the university. On the fringes of the city, the University of Hull was founded in 1927, opening to students a year later. In the post-war era, the institution remained a work in progress. Philip Larkin, who had joined the university in 1955, was tasked in his role as University Librarian with helping to oversee the construction of the new university library, the Brynmor Jones, named after the university's vice-chancellor. I had taken advantage of an online booking system to gain access to the library, so once I had approached the neat, redbrick campus I located the library building, its three-storey brick façade only slightly obscuring the five-storey modernist cube plonked atop. I picked up an access card at the front desk and took a lift to the top floor to browse the music section, before descending again to find a suitable reading space.

As head librarian, Larkin could indulge his interests. A fan of African-American music, he amassed a huge collection of books about theology and jazz on the fifth and sixth floors of the library. Author Stuart Cosgrove, a student at Hull in the early 1970s, credits this collection of material with expanding his interest in black American music and culture, his academic investigations paralleling his exploration of the thriving Northern Soul scene: 'I scoured the shelves tirelessly for three years, reading anything and everything about the music and social conditions of black America.'[17] Genesis P-Orridge had been drawn to study in Hull by his assumption that it was 'the most ordinary, non-elitist, working-class, red brick university', but soon found his course uninspiring.[18] Nevertheless, the institution continued to draw teenagers with musical interests and ambitions to Hull.

During his first eighteen years in the city, Larkin had lived in a flat overlooking the Victorian splendour of Pearson Park. In 1983, journalists descended on a bedsit next to Pearson Park to interview a young couple, Tracey Thorn and Ben Watt, who had begun to release records under the name Everything But The Girl, taken from a shop sign in Hull. Both had arrived as students in Hull and met on their first day there. They had a common connection, being both separately signed to the same record label. Thorn had experienced indie success with the post-punk Marine Girls, and Watt's father was a jazz musician from Glasgow, a background that would influence the sophisticated jazz pop their band would produce. Visiting journalists found a vast flat filled with records and books, in Thorn's words, 'a shrine to everything we loved'.[19] Their gas fire, and the need to keep the meter fed with ten pence pieces, gave reporters enough colour to paint a picture that made them seem like students subsisting in a bedsit – which is exactly what they were, their first album being recorded, and their first single being released, while they were still students at the university. Their names on the door bell were in newsprint, having been cut from an article about the band. The impression given by these early pieces is of a band who've developed in solitude, that the bedsit was a laboratory for a mutant, unexpectedly mainstream form of jazz pop developed by two people on the periphery of the musical scene. In her memoir, Thorn mentions that few bands came to Hull. The city's geographical isolation – and the university's relative unfashionability – gave them a blank canvas, as it had COUM and Paul Heaton. There was no scene to fit into. And because there was no scene, you had to create your own. Thorn and Watt considered starting a jazz night similar to Vic Godard's Club Left, a London-based club which they had attended when it visited Manchester, but, judging that Hull might not be fertile ground for such a club night, decided instead to withdraw to the flat and to 'plan to take over the world with our stark jazz minimalism'.[20] Their first album, *Eden*, was recorded in London and released in June 1984. Soon after graduating, the couple relocated to the capital.

After sitting at a desk in the Brynmor Jones library for a couple of hours, I decided to make my way back in the direction of the city centre. I strolled through the campus towards the main road, through a car park, and waited a few minutes for a bus to come. The bus brought me back along the road I had taken to the university, past the end of Grafton Street and onwards past

Pearson Park into the city centre. I still had a couple of hours before I had to catch my train, so I wandered back towards the Ferens Art Gallery to see if there was anybody from one of the prospective cities of culture hanging around. To my surprise, all I could find was a London taxi that had been painted with a mural depicting Coventry's cultural history, beside which stood some representatives of the city's bid who were being interviewed by BBC Radio Coventry. When I reached the station, I walked over to the Hull City of Culture information stand, at which visitors could pick up a map of the city and get advice from volunteers about what to see. I talked for a little while to the three women who manned the stand, as they enthused about the cultural highlights of the year. I said that I hadn't in fact come from Ireland, but lived in Sunderland, and I was interested to see what was going on in Hull. We talked for a little while about who might win the next city of culture, and they had a feeling that it might be Coventry. I said I thought they might be right. I said my goodbyes and walked over to the concourse to wait for the train. I was a little early, and it turned out that the train was late. A statue of Philip Larkin stands in the centre of the concourse, clutching a sheaf of papers under his arm. It's Larkin in action: walking towards the platform, on his way out of Hull. On the wall behind was a big screen on which a virtual William Wilberforce, a leading abolitionist of the slave trade who was born in Hull and served as an MP for the city as a young man, guided viewers through his biography and the significance of what he had achieved. Slavery had been abolished in most of the British Empire by 1833, the year of Wilberforce's death. At the same time, I couldn't help but think of Zachariah Pearson's attempts to break the blockade of the southern United States during the Civil War in the hope of bringing back bales of raw cotton that would ensure the survival of Hull's cotton mills, a move that essentially turned a blind eye to the Confederacy's slavery. What was unacceptable at home could be tolerated abroad under the banner of economic necessity. The path of history is rarely as morally straightforward as we'd like it to be.

When the next city of culture was announced, I was on a Transpennine Express train somewhere between Leeds and Newcastle. My mobile phone's battery had run out, and there were no power points to recharge it on the train, so instead I thought for a little while about the cities nominated for the award. Recently, I had been visiting English cities that were for the most part identified with white working-class culture, and this was reflected in the music that emerged from those places in the sixties, seventies and even eighties. But as a migrant living in Britain, I was increasingly drawn towards other stories of migration, other voices that came to change the direction of British pop music, ones that might even reject the monolithic idea of British pop, led instead by alternative nationalisms or a different cultural identity. Of the cities on the list, Coventry seemed to best reflect a multiplicity of voices from various cultures and was a city that in terms of pop culture had punched significantly above its weight. The current political climate advocated listening to the concerns of the white working classes who, the story went, had been left behind by the middle-class cosmopolitanism that prioritised multiculturalism and big city life and who had been adversely affected by the influx of migrants to the country. I thought it was therefore possible that a relatively monocultural city such as Sunderland or Stoke might win. Anyway, my phone remained off, and I didn't know who had won until I arrived home, when my wife told me that Coventry would be the UK City of Culture 2023. It was December 2017, so they had plenty of time to prepare.

*

What does a musician do without any scene to fit into? The answer for many Hull-based musicians was to start their own scene. The avant-garde art group COUM Transmissions made their dockside and old town squats the centre of their artistic activities, maintaining an uneasy relationship with local people and police as their reputation in the art world grew. Paul Heaton came to the city hoping to create the kind of community he remembered from his childhood in Sheffield, an idea that had been sharpened in his mind by trips to Germany and France. The terraced house he rented on Grafton Street became the testing ground for this communal ideal. Heaton lived there while his bands The Housemartins and The Beautiful South made records that became chart hits, and he would often bring journalists and camera crews to the street as if to emphasise how entwined his music was with this specific place. Tracey Thorn and Ben Watt's band Everything But The Girl was formed in Hull when they were students at the university, and although they considered starting clubs in the city their main outlet was the band. After graduation and the success of their first record they relocated to London. In the sixties Mick Ronson, after several false starts, had made a similar move. A brilliant musician in a successful local band, he had experienced difficulties in extending that success beyond the city and seemed in danger of stagnating. His accomplishment as a guitarist and his contacts with a network of Hull musicians, some of whom had moved to the capital, brought him into contact with David Bowie, and he became a key member of The Spiders from Mars. The relative isolation of Hull enabled artists to develop away from the spotlight, to create their own worlds. But the city also illustrates the difficulties faced by regional music scenes. Self-sufficiency was difficult, if not impossible. Even if they enjoyed local success, bands needed to move away if they were to make careers in the industry.

The bigger the city, the more likely it was that it could sustain a thriving music scene. The growth of local independent labels, record shops and venues was key to making this happen. Such a city also needed a student population and relatively low rents. The city that perhaps best met these criteria was Glasgow, where I would travel next.

7.
GLASGOW

When I walk around Glasgow I hear music in my head. Rather than consciously thinking about a certain record or a certain band, the music instead comes to me involuntarily, as if my mind is shuffling through the songs from the city that it has absorbed over time. This music comes from a very specific era, the mid-to-late nineties. The urge to hear this music and to understand where it came from is born of my own nostalgia. When I visit Glasgow I often find myself walking past a bar, and that simple action triggers a chain of thought. Who played there? Perhaps Mogwai or Urusei Yatsura or The Delgados, or later, Franz Ferdinand? Or I walk down the Byres Road towards Dumbarton Road, casting a glance to my right, up the hilly side streets lined with sandstone tenements. In this network of streets is a bar run by a former member of Bis, who I remember from their visits to Dublin in the mid-nineties when they were teenagers playing fizzy, excitable indie pop.

As I've advanced in age I've come to find other aspects of the city's musical history to investigate. Now, the whole West End seems to me suffused by the sweeping jazz-inflected music of The Blue Nile. There's an enduring sense of romance to Glasgow that The Blue Nile were able to distil, and that's evident in so much of the city's pop music.

Glasgow combines this romantic spirit with toughness, and that comes through in both the sound of its music and the determined independence of its acts, record labels and venues. It feels like a city that's culturally self-sufficient. This cultural independence is a product of both its distance from London, which is over four hundred miles away, and the growing desire for political autonomy, which has been strengthened in some quarters by the failure to secure Scottish independence in 2014, a campaign energised political discussion and focused minds on the future of the country. There's an enduring sense of political possibility, and this sense of possibility is one shared by the city's music scene. I find in much of the music from Glasgow an independence, and a desire for beauty that's underpinned by a fundamental optimism, one that endures in the face of sadness, regret or deep anxiety about what the future might hold.

When you arrive at Hillhead subway station having disembarked from one of the dinky orange underground trains that run in a circle beneath the city, you're greeted by a pastel-coloured mural on the wall by the Glaswegian writer and artist Alasdair Gray. (I credit Gray with the mural's authorship, although it was produced by him and a team of artists.) It's an idiosyncratic, sweeping vision of the landscape of the West End, including the University of Glasgow, the Hillhead High School and Hillhead station itself. The mural's perspective resembles what one might see from a hovering hot air balloon somewhere west of Byres Road. To the left, stretching from the Great Western Road, a rainbow arcs towards Great George Street, where it meets dark clouds and the horizon switches from day to night. The moon hangs low over Kelvingrove Art Gallery and Museum: Gray has helpfully tagged the landmarks so that viewers can orient themselves. On the roofs of some buildings Gray has noted their date of construction and any change of use. By consulting the mural you can find out that the Kelvinside Free Church, built in 1863 at the intersection of Great Western Road and Byres Road, became the Botanic Church of Scotland in 1929, a Bible College in 1980, and the Orán Mór arts centre in 2003. Elsewhere there's a mural within the mural: on the side wall of the Western Baths is a depiction in miniature of a huge street art image of the baths, one that really exists, hidden down Burgh Lane surrounded by wheelie bins. On either side of the streetscape, a handful of Glaswegians, each one a couple of feet tall and towering over the buildings, stand or sit: a street sweeper admires the vista, and a member of the Strathclyde Partnership for Transport who commissioned the mural gestures towards the scene. At the very edges of the map, Gray engages in identifying animal equivalents for the archetypes that populate the West End: Literary Squirrels, for example, or Urban Foxes. The title of the mural is 'All Kinds of People', but the focus, I feel, is on the buildings rather than the denizens of the area. The effect of the pastel-shaded depiction of the West End streetscape and the compression of perspectives results in a kind of fairy-tale enchantment of the local landscape, an urban romanticism. I'm reminded, when I look of it, of the peculiarly weightless feeling that I get when listening to The Blue Nile's 'A Walk Across The Rooftops'. The band are associated with the area: its members attended the university, and their lead singer, Paul Buchanan, has long been a resident of the locality.

When it emerged in the early 1980s, The Blue Nile's minimalist electronica quickly transcended synth-pop and headed instead towards somewhere near the middle of the road: crooned, deeply emotional songs of love and guilt set in an austere-yet-expansive sonic landscape. The band's reputation was made by their first two albums, *A Walk Across the Rooftops*, released in 1984, and *Hats*, which followed in 1989. The Blue Nile's three core members, Buchanan, Paul Moore and Robert Bell, met while undergraduates at the University of Glasgow. They named an early line-up of the band McIntyre, after the sandstone John McIntyre building in the university – just visible next to the university gate in Gray's mural – and rehearsed in Moore's student flat at 99 Otago Street, on the fringes of the campus, tucked away somewhere behind the round McMillan reading room on the Hillhead mural. McIntyre was very much a student band that evolved into a bohemian post-university project, The Blue Nile, its members lingering well into their twenties in the same streets that had been familiar to them during their studies. Influenced by the smooth West Coast soul and the jazz-inflected Steely Dan, McIntyre recorded a handful of demos, including 'Undercover', a sunny, upbeat tune whose busyness – funkily hyperactive bass and driving drums – stands in marked contrast to the chiaroscuro mid-tempo moodiness of The Blue Nile. The band were savvy enough to organise a showcase gig for A&R representatives from London in Glasgow's Saints and Sinners, a club on St Vincent Street that would later become King Tut's Wah Wah Hut. Chrysalis Records sponsored some demo recordings but ultimately passed on the band, and McIntyre soon became The Blue Nile.[1]

An important element in the group's shift in sound and approach was their decision to turn their attention away from the London-based music business and to find a Scottish studio to record in. They planned to record two songs, 'I Love This Life' and 'The Second Act', and issue them as a single on their own label, which they named Peppermint Records. Their search for a suitable studio brought them to Castlesound, run by producer Calum Malcolm from a converted Victorian schoolhouse in the village of Pencaitland, twelve miles south of Edinburgh. Malcolm had been a member of the band The Headboys, who had been signed to the record label RSO. The label kept in touch with him to see if he had recorded any interesting bands, and when he recommended McIntyre they offered to fund the band's single. Plans for Peppermint Records were shelved. The funding was enough to help them complete the recording, and they chose the new band name on the day the single was pressed.[2] The single was relatively high-tempo and ostensibly similar to commercial synth-pop, especially when compared to the band's later work. RSO clearly believed that they were tapping into a trend that included The Human League and Soft Cell. But before their expectations could be dashed the label folded. Nevertheless, The Blue Nile had got some radio play from the release, and the working relationship with Malcolm was clearly a creative one. He also provided industry connections that had secured their first record deal and would lead to their next.

Linn Records was far from a typical label. It was an imprint of Linn Products, a manufacturer of high-end hi-fi equipment based near Glasgow, and run by Ivan Tiefenbrun, the son of a Polish father who settled in the city as a refugee during the Second World War. It cultivated a reputation for quality based on its Sondek LP2 turntable, which was introduced in 1972. The perfectionism of the company led it, around the time The Blue Nile were making demo recordings for an album, to develop its own cutting lathe for creating a lacquer disc from which vinyl records could be duplicated. Linn's engineers were dissatisfied with the records they had been using to test their turntables, which could be off-centre or have imperfections, and thought they could do better. After The Blue Nile's RSO single had been released, the band had retreated to the studio to record new songs, so when Tiefenbrun approached producer Malcolm to supply some audio tapes of sufficiently high quality to test Linn's new lathe, the producer provided a handful of recordings that included a master tape by The Blue Nile, incorporating new songs 'Tinseltown in the Rain' and 'Heatwave'. This was enough to get the attention of Linn, who had been looking for acts to sign to the new label the company had recently set up. These were the very earliest years of the rise of the compact disc, but Linn, as a manufacturer of high-end audio equipment, was resistant, and was committed to emphasising the superiority of vinyl. The label acted as a demonstration of this faith. Once the band signed to Linn, their recording sessions at Castlesound were funded by the label. The finished LP, *A Walk Across the Rooftops*, issued in 1984, would be Linn's first release. The band, increasingly allergic to the trappings of the music industry, were happy with the relatively hands-off attitude of the company. This agreeable situation no doubt contributed to the gap of five years between their debut and their second album, *Hats*.[3]

At the heart of The Blue Nile's sound was Paul Buchanan: his yearning voice, and his by turns obliquely poetic and anxiously heartfelt lyrics. The title track of *A Walk Across the Rooftops*, which opens the album, was written when the singer lived in Parkgrove Terrace near Kelvingrove Park. Its lyrics are infused with small topographic details that communicate the atmosphere of the place – the red sandstone tenement buildings, the university, the church bells, the parklands – and create the daydream illusion of weightlessness, of floating above the streets below, that staring out of a window across the city can stir in you. So, when I stood in Hillhead station and looked at Alasdair Gray's mural I found that The Blue Nile's music was playing on a loop in my head. I had heard that Buchanan could sometimes be seen out and about on Byres Road, but that day I didn't spot him. The Blue Nile are, or were, a singular band – they appear to have gone their separate ways not long after the release of their fourth album, *High*, in 2004. While their comparatively leisurely work rate is not one that most bands would be advised to emulate, their musical influence can be detected in the melancholy pop of major-label Glasgow bands like Deacon Blue. But The Blue Nile were too particular and too idiosyncratic to be the pioneers of a scene. How could you follow them?

At the centre of the Glasgow School of Art's campus, perched among the grid of streets behind Sauchiehall Street and up the sudden incline of Garnethill, is the institution's original building, an architectural masterpiece designed by Charles Rennie Mackintosh that at time of writing is little more than a ruin of heat-warped stone. When I visited the city in the summer of 2017, the building was being restored after much of it had been destroyed by fire three years earlier and on course to reopen. But a year after my visit it was engulfed by flames again, and this time the damage was much more extensive. The fire spread to adjoining buildings, destroying the O2 Academy, one of the main venues for touring bands in the city. Between the two fires the GSoA continued to function from its campus of surrounding buildings, including the Haldane, a red sandstone former drill hall further up Garnethill, which is where the band Orange Juice played their first official gig on 20 April 1979 – although as Simon Goddard points out in his lively history of Postcard Records, *Simply Thrilled*, they had already played a 'less formal and low-key' lunchtime concert the month before in the Victoria Café – the Vic – also part of the art school on Scott Street, in a building directly across from Mackintosh's.[4]

The rickety and short-lived independent label Postcard became an enduring blueprint for the Glasgow sound. It was founded in 1979 by the nineteen-year-old botany student Alan Horne and run from his second-floor tenement flat at 185 West Princes Street, a short walk from the Art School. Horne had come to Glasgow from Saltcoats, a resort town on the Ayrshire coast, and, through writing a combative fanzine, *Swankers*, that he distributed around record shops, met a group of friends from the Glasgow suburb of Bearsden who were in the process of forming Orange Juice. The music press had played a role in their formation: the band's lead singer Edwyn Collins was perusing the *NME* on the school bus when he first met the drummer Steven Daly, who was reading the *Melody Maker*. With fellow student James Kirk they began to publish a fanzine, *No Variety*, in 1977, which led to meeting fellow fanzine writer Horne. While *No Variety* contained political pieces and admiring articles about The Troggs and The Velvet Underground, *Swankers* was more interested in character assassination and provocation, a tone that was completely in keeping with Horne's arch and spiky persona ('a morose kid in transparent-framed spectacles . . . angry all his waking life', as Paul Morley described him in an early *NME* piece).[5] After seeing The Slits and Subway Sect on The Clash's White Riot tour which visited the city's Playhouse in May 1977, and identifying the American band Television as an influence, Collins, Kirk and Daly formed Orange Juice. Horne, who was not a musician but wanted to be involved in some way, became their manager and formed Postcard to release their records.

Horne fetishised the seven-inch single, keeping a selection of those he thought of as the best examples in a chest in his room. These included 'September Gurls' by Big Star, The Kinks' EPs, 'Here Come The Nice' by The Small Faces, 'Different Drum' by Linda Ronstadt's band The Stone Poneys, and anything with Motown, Stax or Elektra labels. Horne's alternative pop canon had all the appearances of having been rescued from the bargain bins of the West End record stores he frequented. When a television camera crew visited Horne's flat he appeared at the door dressed in a red bowtie and sensible-looking woollen tank top. Inviting them inside, he opened his teak wardrobe and claimed that the piece of furniture actually *was* Postcard Records. As evidence of his claim, he threw a folder of 'Orange Juice fan mail' on the floor and flicked through a hardback book of 'accounts'. His message, if satirical, was clear: this was a DIY operation that engaged in make-believe but was nonetheless still a record label, of sorts. The presentation of such apparent amateurishness seemed like a strategy to disarm music aficionados, a provocation consistent with Horne's use of *Swankers* to pick fights with his flatmate Brian Superstar. According to Steven Daly, 'he didn't want to join any organisation. He just wanted to spoil it for everyone else.'[6]

Onstage, Orange Juice would affect a campness that was in some ways calculated to provoke those audiences who didn't expect masculine norms of rock – or even of punk – to be transgressed in such a way. Collins, his long blond fringe shielding his eyes, would wear a Davy Crockett hat and cavalry boots. He recalled that the audience would break into a chant of 'Poofs! Poofs! Poofs!'[7] Such reactions would later be experienced by other bands who followed in Postcard's slipstream by combining gently melodic sixties-derived rock with archly fey stagecraft, such as BMX Bandits. Author Richard King rightly points out that there was 'something confrontational about Postcard and Orange Juice's gaucheness', an impression that was reinforced by their combative and cutting stage repartee.[8]

The band's debut record was also Postcard's first: 'Falling and Laughing', released in February 1980, bearing a sleeve image of Collins holding a guitar above his bandmates' heads. On the record label itself was the image of a drumming cat that had originally been drawn by Louis Wain, an English artist who specialised in anthropomorphised felines – cats playing golf, cats sledding – and whose later psychedelic feline portraits mirrored his distressed psychological state. Horne's vision for Postcard included the slogan 'The Sound of Young Scotland' – which cheekily repurposed Motown's 'The Sound of Young America'. Artwork for subsequent releases incorporated clichéd images of Scottishness that you might indeed find on a postcard – the liberal inclusion of tartan, illustrations of men in kilts – accompanied by an exhaustive array of cartoon cats, led always by Louis Wain's drumming kitten.

Orange Juice's second single, 'Blue Boy', was released in August 1980, and had been recorded in Calum Malcolm's Castlesound studio, in which The Blue Nile would soon record their debut single. Postcard lasted for only a year after that, during which it released singles by Aztec Camera, Australian band The Go-Betweens, and Edinburgh band Josef K. Orange Juice's final single for the label, 'Poor Old Soul', was released in January 1981, while the final Postcard single was Aztec Camera's 'Mattress of Wire', the work of East Kilbride songwriter Roddy Frame, then aged sixteen. Orange Juice moved on to join Polydor, reaching number 8 in the UK charts with 'Rip It Up' in 1983. Aztec Camera, who had made two singles for Postcard, continued on to Rough Trade, who had been Postcard's distributor, and enjoyed mainstream success in the mid-to-late eighties. Postcard was relatively short-lived but is notable for its artistic coherence in both its musical output and its visual presentation. Many indie labels with one great band sought to supplement their success with another great act, while Postcard had four. And its influence was huge.

The formerly industrial town of Bellshill sits ten miles to the south-east of Glasgow. In 1999 the DJ John Peel visited the town while presenting an episode of the Channel 4 music documentary series *Sound of the Suburbs*. So numerous were the bands to emerge from that otherwise unremarkable place that he dubbed their sound 'the Bellshill Beat'. (The singer Sheena Easton is also from Bellshill, and in his documentary Peel, guided by Sean Dickson of The Soup Dragons and The High Fidelity, visited her old home and the hospital where she was born.) Duglas Stewart of BMX Bandits and Norman Blake of Teenage Fanclub attended the same Bellshill school and connected through a love of Postcard's short-lived but memorable output in different ways. BMX Bandits records channelled the humour, camp provocation and anarchic DIY aesthetic of Postcard while Teenage Fanclub drew inspiration from Orange Juice's sixties pop influences, and their early records melded the melodic sensibility of West Coast harmony-driven rock such as The Byrds with the overdriven grunge of Dinosaur Jr. In the beginning BMX Bandits and Teenage Fanclub undeniably shared a certain sound, and as their careers progressed – both bands continue to release records – they have each tended towards classic pop. But how did the so-called Bellshill Beat come about?

I went to Duglas Stewart's flat on Glasgow's southside to meet him. He greeted me at the front door in stockinged feet, his socks resembling cartoon foxes, and he made me a cup of tea before telling me about meeting Norman Blake. 'I remember him in the art class, [saying] that he'd bought the single "Blue Boy" by Orange Juice. And it was almost like there was tumbleweed in the room, and then I was like: "I think I prefer the first single, 'Falling and Laughing'." And suddenly it was like: someone else has heard of this!' Stewart, though shy – 'I'm not very comfortable in a lot of social settings' – was a natural performer: at primary school, he 'would get sent around the classes putting on little one-man shows that I had spent my evenings writing.' He cut a singular figure at school: 'I would go to smoker's corner with a Sherlock Holmes pipe and deerstalker hoping that this would anger all these tough guys at school.' When asked his name he would say 'Nancy', in a move that recalled Orange Juice's use of camp as provocation in a tough, masculine context. Blake and Stewart would record music together on a tape recorder, making 'sometimes an album in an afternoon, of mostly quite silly songs'. They formed a group, The Pretty Flowers, with Sean Dickson and Frances McKee, later of The Vaselines. 'We'd do things like go up the main street in Bellshill and give out flyers to pretty girls that we saw, saying that we were going to do a concert in the local park, and it would just be Norman and Sean with acoustic guitars and me kind of dancing around and singing songs that we'd made up.'

I asked Stewart what Bellshill was like. 'It's a post-industrial, post-mining kind of town, where initially, I think, it was a couple of small farms, and then the mining industry and steel industry came in and grew. And it had been a quite heartening and pros-perous place. And then somewhere in the seventies all of that began to fall apart. And it became quite a depressed place.' He remembers people losing their jobs – his own father lost his job but found another fairly quickly. But other families split up or found themselves homeless. Suicides increased, he said, 'because I guess that generation of working men, a lot of them were so defined by their working life'. I feel that you have to consider the emergence of the sunny guitar pop of bands like Teenage Fanclub and BMX Bandits in this context – as an escape, as an effort to create a different world.

They set their sights beyond Bellshill. 'We don't want to be big in Bellshill. We want people to know us,' Stewart said. On Saturdays they would go into Glasgow, visiting independent record shops to buy records that couldn't be found in Bellshill, such as those issued by Postcard. 'It was a really different city [to now] – all the buildings were pretty much soot-black. It felt kind of dark and slightly foreboding and threatening.' During these Saturday trips into the city the group began to busk on Argyle Street, meeting resistance from local hecklers. 'But I think I was quite good at handling that,' Stewart said – he would put the heckler down and win the crowd's support. Over time, they built up an audience: 'new people, but also regular faces, people starting to ask for certain songs'. Another group of buskers plied their trade on Buchanan Street, which intersects with Argyle Street, including Jim McCulloch, later of The Soup Dragons, and Joe McAlinden, who would go on to release solo records under the name Superstar. They were students at Our Lady's High School in Motherwell, an institution with 'a quite strong tradition of music', according to Stewart, with a big band and a music department. This gave the Motherwell contingent a formal training that the Bellshill group lacked. McAlinden could play not just guitar, but also keyboards, saxophone and violin. For Stewart, whose ambitions stretched beyond the standard indie line-up of rudimentary guitar, bass and drums, meeting the Motherwell buskers brought 'a whole range of colours': musicians who could push his songs to a different level.

In 1985 Stewart was present on the inaugural night of Splash One, a new indie club held every second Sunday in Daddy Warbuck's disco on West George Street in Glasgow's city centre. The club was organised by a collective of music fans that included Bobby Gillespie, later a member of both The Jesus and Mary Chain and Primal Scream, and his girlfriend Karen Parker, whose candid photography provides a valuable document of the Glasgow scene, and who sang the haunting backing vocals on the Mary Chain's 'Just Like Honey'. The nights included a live band – Sonic Youth played their first Scottish show there, and Wire and Felt played too – and a support act that was often a local band. But arguably the main attraction were meeting other likeminded people – 'it was like it was a bigger, stronger force of weirdos', Stewart said – and hearing the C90 compilation tapes that Splash One made its trademark. Instead of a DJ, the organisers would each put together a mixtape of favourite songs to play over the course of the night. Most of the people who gathered at Splash One found out about interesting music through listening to their friends' record collections or hearing mixtapes they'd made. So it seemed natural that Splash One would make this DIY mixtape culture central to their club, in the process extending social circles and adding to the palette of musical influences. Stewart heard Big Star's 'September Gurls' for the first time on a Splash One mixtape. The band, a fairly obscure American seventies act who specialised in melodic, chiming rock, would go on to become a huge influence on the Glasgow scene. As a teenager, lead singer Alex Chilton had chalked up a soulful number one record in the US, The Box Tops' 'The Letter', but Big Star set their sights instead on an uneasy combination of countrified rock and the kind of high-kicking cock rock that would later be perfected by Cheap Trick. The former style found more favour among Glasgow bands.

Bobby Gillespie had grown up in the Mount Florida area of Glasgow's southside, making friends with a red-headed punk fan, Alan McGee, whose job at British Rail enabled him to transfer to London, where he started a club called The Living Room. Through this connection, Gillespie was able to book bands who had played at The Living Room for Splash One. By this time McGee had started a record label, Creation, that would play an important part in the careers of many of the bands who had formed around Splash One. Two of these bands were The Boy Hairdressers and BMX Bandits, which were formed by the musicians from Bellshill and Motherwell who had met while busking in Glasgow. A sixteen-year-old drummer from Motherwell, Francis Macdonald, had been invited by a fellow member of the Motherwell District Concert Band, Joe McAlinden, to join both The Boy Hairdressers and BMX Bandits. The Boy Hairdressers became Teenage Fanclub, and Macdonald played drums on their first album, *A Catholic Education*, before dropping out to go to university. (Later he returned to the band and has recorded and toured with them since their 2005 album *Man-Made*.) I met him upstairs in the Little Italy café on Byres Road on a July morning.

'I was a few years younger than the rest,' he told me. He didn't have the same reference points as his older bandmates, so didn't make their acquaintance through 'buying the same records and going to the same gigs. I turned up for my first rehearsal of BMX Bandits and The Boy Hairdressers wearing a Squeeze T-shirt.' The bands' reaction was, he said, 'What's he doing? We'll have to educate him.' Their tastes included The Velvet Underground, sixties bands and contemporary indie, which 'wasn't on my radar. So, I was always playing catch-up with them. They'd talk about the Splash One club, which I'd never been to and was too young for. And I was actually a wee bit cynical.' When the bands toured, he found they attracted audiences who would 'turn up with three-button tweed jackets or black leather coats [with] similar badges and all looking kind of similar. And nodding about the same bands.' He thought it was a bit uniform, 'like punk'.

The Boy Hairdressers had recorded a demo and were about to play their first gig when he joined, while BMX Bandits needed a drummer to record a B-side for their debut single, which was to be released with the new Glasgow-based indie 53rd and 3rd, run by Stephen McRobbie of The Pastels, David Keegan of The Shop Assistants and Sandy McLean, who had worked with Bob

Last and Hilary Morrison of the Edinburgh punk label Fast Product. As if two bands weren't already enough, Macdonald also found himself playing drums for McAlinden's Groovy Little Numbers. 'Almost immediately I was involved in three bands who were all very much "indie schmindie",' putting out records and playing concerts in unfamiliar venues. He played a few gigs with The Boy Hairdressers, they put out a single, 'Golden Shower', also on 53rd and 3rd, then he left to concentrate on his studies at Strathclyde University. He remained a member of BMX Bandits because it 'seemed a more fun band to play with. Less uptight in a way.' After releasing the single, The Boy Hairdressers became Teenage Fanclub, and members Norman Blake and Raymond McGinley recruited bassist Gerry Love, with Macdonald rejoining them briefly to record songs for their debut album before continuing with university. Soon after *A Catholic Education* was released with Paperhouse, an imprint of the indie Fire Records, the band signed to Alan McGee's Creation label, recruited a new drummer, Brendan O'Hare, and set about recording their second album, *Bandwagonesque*. The latter album was issued in America by Nirvana's label Geffen, and its messy melodicism and crunchy guitar sound meant it fitted perfectly with the grunge craze. In 1991 the US alt-rock bible *Spin* magazine made it their album of the year (Nirvana's *Nevermind* was in third place) and the record went on to spend a month on the Billboard 200 chart, selling well in the US and UK.

Meanwhile, Macdonald continued his studies. 'So, I'm watching Teenage Fanclub get signed to Creation and get signed to Geffen and put out *Bandwagonesque* and tour the world, and I'm thinking: maybe I've made the wrong decision.' He finished university and continued to work with Duglas Stewart and BMX Bandits, and in the mid-nineties started his own indie label, Shoeshine Records. He recorded singles under a variety of pseudonyms – Frank Blake, Astro Chimp – with members of Teenage Fanclub and The Vaselines. He began to license American artists for release in the UK, including country singer Laura Cantrell. In founding Shoeshine, Macdonald was consciously emulating great indie labels.

'I was too young for Postcard, but I was aware of the shadow Postcard cast – not shadow, the influence it had on people just a few years older than me, like Norman and Duglas and Joe McAlinden and Eugene Kelly,' Macdonald said. He gave the singles a uniform visual identity – a burgundy and silver sleeve with the record's label printed in white and silver. Initially, he saw Shoeshine as a way of putting out records that he had played a part in making as a musician, but later he wanted to 'find great music I liked and could support. I suppose being around Creation was an influence.' During BMX Bandits' time on Creation, the band had visited the label's London offices 'to see all the people, to see what they do and see how things work'. Creation 'were an enabler', Macdonald said, and Alan McGee 'is such a charismatic person that he inspires loyalty. He's had to create opportunities and be his own cheerleader.' When I visited Duglas Stewart, he recalled the same trip to Creation's London offices that Macdonald had described: 'Alan was genuinely amazing. You'd go down to the office and I'd bring in a new recording, and he'd call everybody into the office and say: "Listen to this." And he'd play it and go: "I want everybody totally a hundred per cent behind this, because I think people really need to hear this."'

McGee had continued his support for the band in the face of indifference and even hostility towards it from the music press, who saw in their DIY aesthetic merely rank amateurism, and who harboured deep hostility towards their studied feyness.

Meanwhile, Teenage Fanclub, with their classic rock references and guitar solos, got a free pass from journalists. 'The music press always really hated us,' Stewart said. When high hopes for the single 'Serious Drugs' were dashed by BBC Radio 1 banning it – misinterpreting a song about antidepressants as one about recreational drugs – it seemed their big chance might have passed. 'I think he really believed that BMX Bandits were going to be Creation's next big act,' Stewart said of McGee. Meanwhile, the band took as tour support the unknown Oasis, a young Manchester group that McGee had signed after a gig at Glasgow's King Tut's Wah Wah Hut. Oasis were to define Creation's later years, as the major-label funding McGee enjoyed from Sony was channelled into the Gallagher brothers' band. Suddenly Creation bands were sucked into the mainstream, or dropped: Scouse psychedelic band The Boo Radleys recorded a pop album and enjoyed several chart hits; Teenage Fanclub got significant play on mainstream UK radio for the singles from their *Grand Prix* and *Songs from Northern Britain* albums. But BMX Bandits' 1996 album *Theme Park* was their last for Creation. This was the period in which Macdonald started his label. A few years later, after a disagreement about songwriting with Stewart, he left BMX Bandits. He continued his work with Shoeshine, began to record his own songs, and made a move into band management, looking after the Glasgow band Camera Obscura, led by the brilliant singer-songwriter Tracyanne Campbell. 'When I crossed paths with Camera Obscura and there was an opportunity to be the manager I felt I could help,' Macdonald told me. 'I was applying all the stuff I learned being an artist and also running a label to them, helping them.'

One of the reasons I'm interested in the music industry is because I spent a couple of years in the mid-nineties studying to be a music manager on a diploma course at a suburban Dublin college. What was obvious about that period in Dublin was that U2 remained the model for a band's trajectory court UK major labels and, if the stars are aligned, a mainstream career will result. In Dublin there were a couple of independent labels, a lo-fi scene, a dance music scene and a quite separate hardcore punk scene, but few bands had ambitions beyond playing local bars and meeting likeminded folk. What intrigues me about the Glasgow scene is that it was both resolutely local and reflexively independent while at the same time having an impact beyond its geographical location. It's also striking that a lot of the labels and venues that were around in the nineties are still there in some form. Bands didn't follow London-based musical fashion – offhand, I can't think of any Britpop bands from Glasgow – and its venues and labels were able to develop over time, largely on their own terms. Postcard Records, 53rd and 3rd, Francis Macdonald's Shoeshine Records, Chemikal Underground and now Mogwai's Rock Action Records have provided an independent infrastructure for music making. Venues like Nice n' Sleazy's, 13th Note, Stereo and Mono have given band members jobs, somewhere to hang out and somewhere to put on gigs.

I wanted to talk to someone about how this informal infrastructure had developed. I was staying with my wife in a hotel room that looked across a graveyard towards the shiny black vitrolite of the old *Glasgow Herald* offices, now converted to luxury apartments, in an area that had become known as the Merchant City. Around the corner was a hip coffee shop where I arranged to meet John Williamson. I had come across Williamson's name in a book about the Glasgow art scene; a footnote mentioned that he had been involved in writing for the *Glasgow Herald*, working with venues and managing bands. In 1989 he had joined with a group of people including promoter and studio owner Craig Tannock and academic and journalist

Simon Frith to plan a music conference to be held in Glasgow to coincide with the city's 1990 status as the European Capital of Culture. The city council would fund their New Music World conference, and a trip to New York to launch the conference at 1989's New Music Seminar.[9]

It was raining outside and everyone in the coffee shop waiting to be served was dressed in damp rain gear. I was sitting at a small table when Williamson arrived. A reflective man who weighed his words carefully, Williamson had recently completed a PhD in music studies and was now a postdoctoral fellow at the University of Glasgow. He precisely analysed his own career and its relationship to the wider music industry, telling me that in essence he learned as he went along, and was assiduous in seeking help when he found himself in an unfamiliar situation. He had begun writing about music as a teenager. 'I did fanzines, which I think was the traditional pre-internet way of getting involved without actually being able to play anything or do anything.' That led to freelance work for newspapers, writing for the *Evening Times* and the *Herald*. At the time he was writing, in the late eighties, he could see a trend: major-label pop bands like Wet Wet Wet, Hue and Cry and Deacon Blue weren't moving away once they became successful, but were staying in Glasgow, rehearsing in the city and sometimes even recording there. This generated more outside interest in the city from record labels and internally from Glasgow City Council, who, Williamson said, from the late eighties well into the nineties thought that building a big recording studio in the city was the way forward and carried out feasibility studies with that end in mind. Eventually, after several years, the plan was dropped. 'The obsession with recording was completely out of kilter with what was going on in the Scottish music business,' Williamson told me. 'The key thing has always been live music.' Venues are 'absolutely integral to explaining what ultimately has happened in Glasgow'. Even the city's record labels are often closely tied up with venues.

There's no obvious cause and effect, no straight line you can draw linking the 1990 Capital of Culture award and what happened next in Glasgow. Nevertheless, it's true that most of the venues that became key sites for live music were founded in the early nineties. Breweries were increasingly open to funding live music venues, both independent and mainstream local print media were keen to cover the music scene, and local radio was supportive, contributing to the success of the new venues. In 1991, Craig Tannock, with whom Williamson had worked on the New Music World conference, and who had previously owned and run other rehearsal rooms and studios in Glasgow, opened the Apollo, a combined venue, rehearsal room and recording studio. Williamson helped out with that venue and Tannock's next venture, the 13th Note, which opened first in Glassford Street in 1993 and then moved to its current site at King Street. (It's no longer owned or run by Tannock, who went on to run a string of bars and venues including Mono and Stereo.) Other venues that opened around this time included Nice n' Sleazy's and King Tut's, which are still key venues in Glasgow indie music. Instead of live music being an afterthought, Williamson said, 'suddenly there were places that actually were putting live music on because they really wanted to and not just because it might bring in a few extra punters on a quiet night in their pub or their club'. Williamson worked with the 13th Note for a year or so as the bar manager. During this time, bands were able to book the venue and put on nights. Alex Kapranos, later of Franz Ferdinand, put on the Kazoo Club at 13th Note, and a series of bands such as Urusei Yatsura and The Delgados played at the Glassford Street venue. The Delgados decided to found their own Chemikal Underground label to issue records by some of the bands who regularly played the 13th Note. The first release on the label was their own song 'Monica Webster', a tumble of buzzing guitars overlaid with early signs of the vocal interplay between Alun Woodward and Emma Pollock that would characterise their later work.

Chemikal Underground's second and third releases were from Bis, a trio of teenagers who went under the monikers Manda Rin, Sci-Fi Steven and John Disco. Their high-tempo pop made a virtue of their limitations, which included a tinny drum machine and no bass player. Their records paid tribute sonically and visually to DIY aesthetics and the band produced a string of memorable pop records that avoided the clichés of much guitar-based pop of the time. Their second release for Chemikal Underground, which was the label's third record, was *The Secret Vampire Soundtrack* EP – four tracks issued on multiple formats including seven-inch and twelve-inch vinyl and CD. This was 1996, when multiple formats were seen by major labels as a way of charting as highly as possible – the theory being that fans would go out and buy two different CDs sold at a budget price to get the B-sides, and that would be enough to push the single up the charts, or at least gain a marginal advantage over a competitor. That an indie label from Glasgow was able to achieve something similar with their third release pointed to an ambition for greater success, a practical knowledge of the music industry, and links with distributors to ensure that it would reach its audience. Chemikal Underground weren't messing around. Before the EP was released, the producer of *Top of the Pops* approached Bis to make an appearance on the programme, and at the time it was reported that they were the first unsigned band to do so. (They had a verbal agreement with Chemikal Underground.)

During this time, Bis were being managed by John Williamson. He had known them since the young Steven and John Clark rehearsed at Tannock's Tower Studios, where he had an office. He knew their parents, 'so I was probably the only person who had any connections with the music business that their mum and dad knew at the time. And I mean I thought they were brilliant as well, but that was kind of secondary to all the circumstances.' On their success, he said, 'that was something that happened really, really quickly. They went from playing the 13th Note and Nice n' Sleazy and places like that to being on international tours within the space of six months. Six months to a year. And they'd gone from these sorts of venues to playing on *Top of the Pops* within a year and they'd signed a big record deal.' I told Williamson about seeing Bis in Dublin around this time. I had talked to John and Steven, who were hanging around after they had performed. 'I remember some of the chaos that was going on around the gig.' He recalled the difficulty of working out how to get the band and its gear to the Irish capital: 'How do you go to Dublin?' At the time it seemed 'the biggest logistical challenge in the world'.

I was wondering how you go from being a journalist, writing about the industry from the outside, then being involved in venues in Glasgow, to managing a band who are selling tens of thousands of records and touring. The gig in Dublin had been part of Tony Wilson's In The City music industry convention, held in September 1996. Ahead of the conference, Williamson rang Wilson for advice. 'I was in the throes of being offered all these recording contracts, and it seemed like every company in the world wanted to sign the band and I had no idea what was going on.' Wilson explained some of the foreign licensing deals he had done with New Order and Happy Mondays. As a manager 'you were always being faced with challenges that you had no idea how to deal with', he said. 'But my first resort was always to find someone who had done it before and try to ask them.'

Among the people he shared advice with and sought it from were Neil Robertson, the manager of Belle and Sebastian, and Colin Hardie, Mogwai's manager. They 'were both in pretty much the same situation I was. They were mates of the band who'd started managing them, and then suddenly things started happening, and then you have to work out how to try to deal with it without any training or expertise. You'd bump into Neil, you'd bump into Colin, and they'd be doing things six months after you that you'd already done, and vice-versa, there'd be things that they'd done before we had. And again, you would ask people. It's very easy to be connected even for people who are essentially quite antisocial, which lots of managers are.'

Around 1999, Williamson decided that he would move on from the music business. He started his PhD and returned to freelance journalism. But when Neil Robertson moved to Australia, Belle and Sebastian needed a manager. The band had been formed by Stuart Murdoch and Stuart David while on a programme for unemployed musicians in Stow College. Each year the music business class at the college would choose as an end-of-year project a record to produce and release through their Electric Honey label, and Belle and Sebastian's rich, folky, funny and deeply ambitious debut album, *Tigermilk*, resulted from this process. Williamson had already written about the band, had put on gigs by them, and had 'known them for pretty much the whole time they existed as a band. Because I liked them so much as a band, and I liked them as people as well, when I was asked if I would do it, it was extremely tempting.'

Williamson took the job. The challenge was different from Bis – Belle and Sebastian were already well established with several albums behind them, and they were playing big, prestigious venues. 'One of the first gigs I went to when I was managing them was when they played at the Hollywood Bowl with the LA Philharmonic, and it was sold out and there were eighteen thousand people there or something. And I remember standing there and thinking: there's only one way I can take this, and it's not upwards. Even if I was the best manager. Because you're looking at it and you're thinking this is utterly amazing. I think it's pretty close to a fully realised version of what they probably wanted to do at the start.'

The concert at the Hollywood Bowl was held on 6 July 2006, almost ten years after the release of the band's debut. They had been touring with a large line-up, and not making much money as a result, although they had sold a significant number of records. But the record industry was shifting beneath their feet, mainly because of the internet. From now on bands would rely on touring for a large portion of their income, while record sales, as a result of the wide availability of music for free on digital platforms and the shrinking of the traditional industry, would be less reliable. Belle and Sebastian's triumph at the Hollywood Bowl 'was right at the cusp of where that was changing, where the record sales were diminishing, but the demand and the amount of money that could be made from touring was increasing'. When compared to Bis's meteoric rise, managing Belle and Sebastian at their peak at a time of wider changes in the industry 'was a very different journey,' Williamson said.

It seemed to me that the Glasgow scene that Williamson described was both a society of mutual support – people would advise each other, play in one another's bands and generally help one another out – but that at the same time there were some remarkable individuals who were forced by circumstance to improvise, to become entrepreneurial in some way. Williamson said: 'I think one of the problems is that the whole notion of entrepreneurship was so tied up in right-wing, Thatcherite ideology that people were always resistant to it. So it was like they were behaving entrepreneurially but they'd totally deny they were an entrepreneur. Conventional rhetoric wants to make music and art a much more collective operation.'

Perhaps it was both. There was no denying that key individual figures were hugely important in Glasgow. But the level of co-operation between musicians was obvious. I felt that Francis Macdonald embodied many of the things we had been talking about: he bridged the gap between musician, manager and record label boss. When I talked to him he was getting ready to release an album of classical music he had composed for a string quartet, and had recently written the scores for Scottish television programmes. He continued to play drums with Teenage Fanclub, and when we talked he mentioned that Tracyanne Campbell from Camera Obscura was recording new material with another songwriter. (The band had been on hiatus since the death of their member Carey Lander from cancer in October 2015; the project became the *Tracyanne and Danny* album, recorded with Danny Coughlan of Crybaby, released in 2018.)

Talking to Macdonald, I asked him if part of the challenge of creating and maintaining a career in music, especially in an era where so much of the traditional major-label infrastructure had fallen away – advances were smaller, the returns were lower – was that you had to, in effect, become your own industry? 'I suppose people form bands because they don't want a proper job. That's part of it as well, which you can't discount,' he said. He recalled hearing a quote from John Sullivan, the creator and writer of *Only Fools and Horses*: 'he was saying it's a joke: this guy Del Trotter, he doesn't want a proper job, so he ends up working harder than anyone else that's got a proper job. And I thought: Oh God! Am I doing that? Am I working harder for less pay because I'm trying to avoid a proper job?' A few minutes later he said his goodbyes, left the café, climbed on his black mountain bike and cycled off. Back to business.

Glasgow shows the importance of independence to creating and sustaining a city's music scene. While an individual sense of entrepreneurship plays a part in this independence, it's accompanied by motives that go beyond profit – to enable fellow musicians to release records, to provide a social space informed by one's own ethical values, to provide employment. The breakthrough for Glasgow was the rise of the DIY ethos that was communicated through punk and exemplified by Postcard Records, which exercised an influence not only on future Glasgow labels such as 53rd and 3rd, but also on the important indie Creation, who played a key part in promoting Glaswegian bands nationwide. Creation tapped into a pre-existing scene in the city that included the bands Teenage Fanclub and BMX Bandits, whose members were drawn from the nearby post-industrial towns of Bellshill and Motherwell, and Primal Scream, whose singer Bobby Gillespie had helped organise the influential Splash One club in the eighties. As time went on the crucial role of small venues became clear – they provided a place where local bands could play and improve, and where musicians could meet. These venues helped to foster a scene without which a record label like Chemikal Underground may not have happened. What's perhaps most interesting is that the Glasgow music scene persists, not just as a memory but as a living, breathing thing. Many of the bars and venues are still around in some form, and there have been new additions to the musical infrastructure of the city. The continued success of the post-rock band Mogwai enabled them to invest in their own record label, Rock Action, and their own recording studios, Castle of Doom, which is used by not just the band but many local acts too. I had no doubt that Glasgow's distance from London and its distinct Scottish identity helped to influence a sense of independence in its music scene. Whether that national identity would eventually lead to full political and administrative independence from Britain continued to be an open question.

I was heading next to Northern Ireland, a corner of the island of Ireland and a region of the United Kingdom. Here the competing allegiances of British and Irish identities led to a maelstrom of sectarian conflict and bloodshed from which the local music scene provided an escape, and a sense of possibility.

8.
BELFAST

Northern Ireland is not a familiar place to me, although I can just about navigate through the centre of Belfast on foot, especially the trek between Central station and Donegall Square, which I have come to know from the handful of times I've travelled the hundred or so miles between the two capitals of my divided nation. Growing up in Dublin in the eighties, my knowledge of Northern Ireland was initially mediated through Irish and British television news. Seen through the screen of our Philips TV, the North was a world of controlled explosions carried out by caterpillar-tracked robots and RUC Land Rovers bearing metal grilles and rubber skirts to protect them from petrol bombs. I can recall watching the television news on cold winter mornings before school and seeing video footage of incidents in Belfast from the night before. The effect was to characterise the six counties of Northern Ireland as abnormal, as a place apart; to make them feel completely unconnected to my everyday life as a child who was about to leave the house to go to school in a not particularly salubrious but generally riot-free Dublin suburb.

The first trip to Northern Ireland that I can remember was for the Belfast Marathon, held on the May bank holiday in 1986. My mother was a runner and, having run the Dublin marathon a couple of times, decided to sign up to the Northern Irish event. Northern Ireland in 1986 wasn't a particularly attractive day-trip prospect. After the signing of the Anglo-Irish Agreement in the November of the previous year, there had been a significant amount of trouble: protests from the Unionist population over cancelled parades, bombing of the houses of Catholics and police, and on the first day of the year the assassination of two Protestant RUC officers by a remote-controlled bomb detonated by the Provisional IRA. A few weeks after our visit the Northern Irish Assembly would be dissolved and wouldn't return until after the Good Friday Agreement of 1998.

Watching the TV news undoubtedly coloured my experience of the visit. Yet, somewhat inevitably, the trip was fine, banal and uneventful in the same way that a lot of childhood outings were. It rained, for example. And my enduring memory is of the strangeness of the red tarmac that surfaced the streets and the red post boxes that contrasted to the Republic's green ones. Such superficial details were enough to emphasise its foreignness. I was, after all, a child who had never left his own country, and I returned home unsure whether this counted as a trip abroad.

Another detail, from a few years later: driving north on the way to the port of Larne, our family's car is stopped on a rural road at a checkpoint manned by machine-gun-toting British soldiers. I look to the hedgerow and see a camouflaged soldier with the barrel of his rifle trained directly at me. We're waved onwards. The anxiety I had felt at the checkpoint didn't depart until we got on the ferry to Scotland. This minor incident is obviously mild compared to what residents of the six counties underwent, but the fact that I can recall this with great clarity – as could my brother when I asked him – is a sign of how unusual and disturbing it was to us, and, most likely, to many others from the Republic beyond the border counties.

One of the events that haunted the imagination when travelling from the Republic to the North was the murder of three members of The Miami Showband, a group of Catholic and Protestant musicians from both sides of the border. Showbands were essentially covers bands who plied their trade around the dancehalls of Ireland, playing to large rooms of sometimes a couple of thousand people. And the Miami were arguably the biggest and the best of that era. In the early hours of 31 July 1975, after the band had played a gig in the Castle Ballroom in Banbridge, County Down, Northern Ireland, they had been stopped at what at first appeared to be an army checkpoint consisting of members of the part-time Ulster Defence Regiment, a majority Protestant infantry regiment of the British Army established in 1970 that was easily infiltrated by loyalist paramilitaries. The soldiers who stopped The Miami Showband were also members of the Ulster Volunteer Force, an anti-Republican paramilitary organisation who wanted to maintain Northern Ireland's status as part of the United Kingdom. Their plan was to plant a bomb on the Miami's bus which would go off later, perhaps south of the border or in Dublin. Was the aim to frame the band as terrorists, or just to create fear and mayhem? Surviving members of the band recall the arrival of a commanding officer with a posh English accent, and his presence hints at the dark collusion between the British state and paramilitaries that haunts the Troubles. During its installation, the bomb was triggered, killing the two men carrying out the task. The five members of the band who had been travelling in the van were standing with their hands on their heads, facing a ditch, when the force of the explosion threw them into a field. Three of the band members were brutally slaughtered – singer Fran O'Toole, the heartthrob of the group, was shot with a machine gun twenty-two times, mostly in the head – while the other two, assumed by the gunmen to be dead, survived. Terrorism creates huge waves of fear that, over the ensuing years, become ripples of doubt that never quite leave you, and are passed often unintentionally from one generation to the next. The Miami Showband massacre was one of those forbidding lessons of the Troubles that people found difficult to forget.

From my childhood I remember the edginess that would descend on me as I reached the border: the guns pointed at you as you passed across by car, the helicopters making deliveries to army posts on misty hillsides that you could see from the train. But now, as I passed across the border on the coach, it was completely invisible. The only tangible sign that you had crossed from the Republic into Northern Ireland was that the motorway got considerably worse. Arriving in Belfast along the Westlink motorway, I got a clear view of the Milltown cemetery, recognisable from numerous news reports of Republican funerals. I thought especially of the surreal, violent rampage of the loyalist Michael Stone, filmed on news reports throwing grenades and firing shots into the crowd at the funerals of three IRA members who had been killed by the British Army in Gibraltar while they had been planning an attack on troops. Stone had attempted to escape on foot along the motorway before being arrested, and his attack killed three people. Such images flashed before me as my bus neared the city centre. While things were undoubtedly different now, I was still aware, for example, that the Europa Hotel had once been called 'the most bombed hotel in Europe'. The last time it had been bombed was 1993.

It appeared that the hellishness of the past had been successfully put behind Northern Ireland thanks to the long-term efforts of many within the six counties, and on the island of Ireland as a whole, as well as a concerted international drive towards a peaceful solution. But twenty years on from the Good Friday

Agreement a continued peace was by no means assured. The vote to leave the European Union and the Conservatives' coalition with the Democratic Unionist Party, who had opposed the Good Friday Agreement, put the agreement's achievements in doubt. The possibility that the Irish border would become a rigidly enforced frontier between the EU and the UK had raised the spectres of the past once more. What would a new border look like? More army posts and random checkpoints, perhaps. The British government talked of advanced technological solutions but were unable to offer any tangible examples, and tensions over the future of the North as part of Brexit-era Britain grew after my visit. Among the tangle of fiendish problems thrown up by Brexit the future of Northern Ireland appeared to be the most difficult to resolve.

When I climbed from the coach at its terminus next to the Europa Hotel, it was a bright spring morning. Although I had been to the city centre before, I had never seen it in sunshine. All of a sudden, I felt relaxed, like a day-tripper on a city break – a feeling that was reinforced when I reached Donegall Square, where tourists were buying tickets for bus tours around the city. Belfast City Hall sits proudly in the square, its baroque flourishes, such as the lanterned towers at each of its four corners, offset somewhat by its construction in austere Portland stone. The Union Jack had been flown from City Hall every day of the year since 1906; in December 2012 the council decided – in line with UK-wide guidelines – to limit the number of days it would be flown to eighteen. Loyalist protest resulted, and riots ensued. Which more or less brings us up to the contemporary impasse: a suspended Northern Ireland Assembly, and a national government hell-bent on pushing through Brexit at all costs, one of which could conceivably see the return of a militarised border.

For the last twenty years Northern Ireland has enjoyed relative peace, but now concern grows about what the future might look like. Before that peace, it endured thirty years of the Troubles. And before that? I wondered what the pre-Troubles era was like. An idyll cruelly ended, perhaps. The Northern Irish critic and filmmaker Mark Cousins wrote that the Troubles 'forced people's lives, and their imaginations, underground [but] we're an outgoing people'.[1] It's tempting to see the pre-Troubles era as a golden age, corresponding to the 'never had it so good' post-war era in Britain. And there's much truth in that comparison. The years after the war were relatively prosperous for Belfast, an Indian summer of sorts, before its main industries went into decline in the sixties and the Troubles began.

I was in Donegall Square to catch a bus to East Belfast – or 'loyalist East Belfast' as I felt compelled to think of it, deeply conditioned as I was by years of hearing exactly that phrase in news reports. Frankly, I didn't know what to expect. My purpose in making the trip to East Belfast was to see Van Morrison's family home. Belfast's bus fleet is painted a shade I like to think of as Peace Process Pink: neutral, in the sense that it can't be mistaken for either the tricolour of the Irish flag or the Union Jack. But in other ways not neutral at all: bright neon pink, like a big highlighter pen. At this point I looked down at what I had chosen to wear: an oatmeal-coloured sweater that vaguely resembled one of the Aran jumpers favoured by the late Martin McGuinness, and a dark-green parka with a bright-orange lining. As the sun rose, the day got warmer, so I had taken to leaving the coat unzipped. When it swung open in the light breeze I was suddenly aware my top half was adorned in the green, orange and white of the Irish tricolour. I was still worrying about this when the bus swung across the Lagan into the Short Strand, a small nationalist area surrounded by loyalist neighbourhoods that is one of many flashpoints in the city. I spotted an Irish tricolour, felt a little better about my clothing faux pas, but then the bus quickly moved into the loyalist area. When murals heroically portraying the British Army's Parachute Regiment began to crop up on the end walls of terraces, I resumed my worrying. The nationalist Short Strand is surrounded by so-called peace walls, tall barriers that divide one community from another for the sake of safety.

After the bus crossed a bridge over a small stream, I got off at the next stop and crossed the road, walking up Hyndford Street past the Bloomfield Gospel Hall. On the frosted glass above the hall's entrance was the phrase 'Ye Must Be Born Again', words which Van Morrison would invoke in the title track of his album *Astral Weeks*. Further along the street is a simple two-up, two-down redbrick terraced house in which Morrison grew up. A small brass plaque to the right of the door reads:

SINGER SONGWRITER
VAN MORRISON
LIVED HERE
Belfast Blues Appreciation Society

Morrison's parents, George and Violet, had been married at the nearby St Donard's Church on Bloomfield Road on Christmas Day 1941. Violet's mother had recently moved to the house on Hyndford Street, and by 1944 the young couple had become the main occupants. The following year their son George Ivan Morrison was born, on 31 August, three days before the Second World War officially ended. The war had ravaged East Belfast – its shipyards made it a target for Luftwaffe raids on the city in 1941, and many streets and buildings had been destroyed. Both George and Violet were the children of shipyard labourers, and George became an electrician at Harland & Wolff, the shipyard whose yellow gantry cranes still loom above this part of the city as icons of its industry. Founded in 1861, the company had famously built the *Titanic*, and was dominated by the Orange order, which ensured that recruitment policies favoured their own kind. In July 1920 a mass meeting of Protestant workers decided that Catholics were no longer welcome and descended on Harland & Wolff, hunting down Catholic workers, beating some and throwing others in the river, and after that the company remained a Protestant stronghold, drawing its workforce from the terraced streets of loyalist East Belfast. While George worked in the shipyard, Van's mother Violet worked in one of Belfast's linen mills. The couple were in many ways typical of their time and of their religious, social and economic background. But that background had rich imaginative possibilities that George and Violet would explore before their son would realise his vision: his father's American odyssey that was symbolised by the jazz and blues records he brought back to Belfast; his mother's talent for music and dance. To be born again implies a second chance, an opportunity to rise above the mundanity of the everyday, while being animated by some transcendent spark. The strangeness and multiplicity of Northern Irish Protestantism created conditions in which not just the firebrand bible-thumping of Ian Paisley could thrive, but also the mellow hippy fantasia that would evolve from Van Morrison's early blues years. The tough, uncompromising Protestantism of working-class East Belfast undoubtedly helped to shape Morrison's obstinacy, but also his spirituality. Yet his work is also an escape from that place, an enigmatic dreamscape that is lyrical, poetic, rapt: a richly imagined world that Morrison imposed on the most familiar streets of his home city.

The young Morrison was by all accounts already something of a dreamer. But his quietness and seeming aloofness barely hinted at the rich imaginative life that would later emerge in his music. He would venture out to play cowboys and Indians in the adjoining fields with his friend Gil Irvine, but often stayed in the house to pursue his hobby of stamp collecting. His father emigrated for a short period to America to become an electrician on the railroad in Detroit, leaving the family behind in Belfast, and later returning home to take up a job in the Shorts & Harland munitions factory. He brought back with him a huge collection of jazz and blues records that would provide a musical education for his son. While his father was quiet, his vivacious mother Violet was a trained dancer who would perform high-kicks at parties. Later, Van Morrison would attempt a similar move during his performance of 'Caravan' with The Band, filmed in Martin Scorsese's documentary *The Last Waltz*. It's a surprising moment of joyful physical freedom from a performer who's better known for his static stage presence. Rock critic Greil Marcus writes that Morrison kicked 'his right leg into the air like a Rockette. He shot an arm up, a dynamo, the movements repeated, repeated, repeated, and shocking every time.'[2]

Violet was undoubtedly as influential on her son's musical interests as his father – she played harmonica, as he later would, and she joined local Orange bands to play bagpipes. In line with the general shift in post-war Belfast away from traditional industry towards the commercial sector, she took a job as a store detective in C&A when her son was a teenager. Morrison's father didn't show much interest in religion, but his mother joined the Jehovah's Witnesses for a few years during his childhood. Such an affiliation was far from unusual in East Belfast, where Protestant sects and nonconformist churches flourished. 'Protestantism takes in everything', the journalist Sam Smyth, an East Belfast contemporary of Morrison's, told biographer Johnny Rogan. 'Just *not* to be a Catholic was almost enough for the real adherents', so being a Jehovah's Witness 'wouldn't have been noticed really'.[3] The young Van was brought along to services, but later he was keen to explain away his mother's membership of the organisation as an example of her free thinking. In interviews Morrison has been keen to stress that he is not religious, and rather refers to a spirituality that's free of institutions, although in May 2017 he turned up in the congregation of a Los Angeles megachurch, the Agape International Spiritual Center, before climbing onstage to perform his hit 'Have I Told You Lately' with the church's house band. Nevertheless, he continued to insist on the primacy of his own personal spirituality over organised religion.

I continued walking, from Morrison's old house on Hyndford Street through streets of redbrick terraced houses, past a memorial that at first appeared to pay tribute to local men who had died during the First World War. Poppies and little wooden crosses decorated a small park. A mural on the wall commemorated the 36th (Ulster) Division of the British Army, which had been formed from the Ulster Volunteers, a militia that had been assembled to block Home Rule for Ireland. An oval plaque below the mural read 'UVF: For God and Ulster', and under that plaque were four posters, decorated with images of poppies, commemorating dead UVF members. One poster paid tribute to Robert Seymour, convicted for the 1983 murder of leading IRA member James Burns, shooting him in his sleep. A few years later, Seymour was killed by the IRA, shot in the alley behind his video shop in East Belfast. The implied continuity of the memorial garden was clear: from the Ulster Volunteers and their sacrifice in the First World War to the loyalist gunmen shooting IRA members in their beds, all was the same struggle. The centenary of the First World War had been marked on both sides of the border: many soldiers who fought and died in the

British Army had been from what later became the Republic of Ireland, and such commemorations were viewed as a necessary part of a post-Good Friday Agreement normalisation. Yet when I looked at this memorial I couldn't help but feel a shiver of dread about the sectarian hatred that pulsed beneath the surface of peacetime Belfast.

Although they're indicative of a hatred that's probably not going away very soon, to concentrate exclusively on these symbols when walking around East Belfast would be a mistake. Van Morrison's genius, I think, was to be able to see beyond them. In a way, he was lucky to have a mother whose religious interests tended towards the esoteric end of Protestantism – becoming a spiritual and visionary tendency in his own work – and to have come of age in Belfast before the Troubles descended on the city. These influences make his version of East Belfast enraptured, pastoral, vibrating with the freedom and possibility of childhood. There's a child's eye cast on the landscape, picking out the natural spaces of the industrial suburb: the fields and rivers that had captured his youthful imagination. Yet there's a persistent uneasiness, a dark side to the world he conjures. It feels like Morrison is walking on enchanted but unstable ground, and that memory might collapse into a catastrophic present at any second. You can hear hints of this in the song 'Cyprus Avenue' from Morrison's 1968 album *Astral Weeks*, recorded after Morrison had moved to America and while the world that he had known in Northern Ireland was turning towards violence.

I walked uphill along Bloomfield Avenue, reaching a roundabout surrounded by a cluster of small shops: hairdressers, takeaways and newsagents. A lamppost across the road from Bloomfield Methodist church bore a sign that displayed a Union Jack above which was the text 'Welcome to Orangefield'. My nerves couldn't face any more UVF murals, and anyway I was heading in the opposite direction, along the North Road across the hill towards Cyprus Avenue, which gave its name to the song. If you go in this direction, you pass larger houses and the area becomes noticeably leafier. This is middle-class East Belfast, sitting in high ground above the cluster of working-class streets that tumble towards the docks.

I turned down Cyprus Avenue, a broad, tree-lined street that slopes downhill towards Beersbridge Road. The *Astral Weeks* album is a widescreen hippy odyssey, its musical backing creating an atmosphere of enraptured bliss. On 'Cyprus Avenue' a strummed acoustic guitar is joined after a couple of bars by a harpsichord and an acoustic bass. Later a flute and string section ease into the mix, and a renegade fiddle that's pitched in the space between jazz and bluegrass picks out melodies in the right-hand channel. The music journalist Lester Bangs described the lyrical content in this way: 'a man sits in a car on a tree-lined street, watching a fourteen-year-old girl walking home from school, hopelessly in love with her'.[4] Johnny Rogan in his biography of Morrison adopts a little more nuance than Bangs, pointing out, in a perceptive reading, that the 'arresting final meditation on a seemingly forbidden love for a 14-year-old' is made complex by the unusual timescale the singer is using and the way his lyrics skip from place to place, making the geographical location unclear. What happened where and when? It's difficult to know. Rogan fixes on Morrison's use of the line 'My tongue gets tied/ Every time I try to speak/And my inside shakes just like a leaf on a tree', taken directly from Elvis Presley's 1957 hit 'All Shook Up'. The song begins with the narrator 'conquered in a car seat' as schoolgirls walk by on Cyprus Avenue. If you follow Bangs's reading, he's waiting for one of them. If you follow Rogan's, it triggers in him a reminiscence about the past. For me, surely it is a case of the older Morrison looking back to the year of

Presley's song, when his twelve-year-old self fell in love with a girl two years his senior.[5]

The compression of space and time seems the result of memory's role in rearranging the past. The song transforms the street into a deeply personal mythological space, with mere fragments of the specificity that would characterise his later East Belfast songs. The scattering of details that make the real Cyprus Avenue recognisable drift into something uneasily dreamlike. The lush musical setting circles around Van's vocal acrobatics, tightening claustrophobically around the thwarted lust of the lyrics. Another reference to Cyprus Avenue comes in the song 'Madame George', beginning on that street before widening its scope to become an overwhelmingly cryptic piece of Dylanesque stream-of-consciousness that includes memories of throwing coins from the Dublin to Belfast train at the Boyne viaduct in Drogheda. There's an abiding sense that his vision of the world of East Belfast, by turns poetic and flamboyant, is by intention hermetically sealed, but it's a miniature world that can't help but incorporate the instabilities of the real one.

The atmosphere around Cyprus Avenue was leisurely in the way only a truly well-heeled area can be. A man walked his dog along the footpath, and while the morning sun shone brightly, the street was shaded by its tall trees. I dawdled along, forgetting where I was for a while, daydreaming a little bit about what might have drawn Van Morrison to the street. It was an escape, an idyll, just a short walk away from his home. The sun shone through the trees, as it did in the song, and all along the street stood big houses that the narrator refers to as mansions.

The street was, for a long time, the home of Ian Paisley, the founder of the Free Presbyterian Church and the Democratic Unionist Party, the first a fundamentalist riposte to the supposed liberality of mainstream Presbyterianism, the latter a fearsome loyalist political reaction against growing nationalist demands for civil rights in the late sixties and early seventies. It was surprising, to say the least, to observe his 2007 ascension to First Minister of Northern Ireland, which involved a close working relationship with his deputy, the former Provisional IRA leader Martin McGuinness. If such long-standing enemies could put their deep and abiding hatred aside, anything seemed possible, and the uncharacteristically grinning Paisley seemed to capture the uneasy optimism of that time better than anyone. Now both Paisley and McGuinness were dead, and the legacy of their late-career bridge-building seemed increasingly uncertain.

After he had finished up in Orangefield High School, Morrison was looking around for work. He had been playing in bands, including his first, The Sputniks, and made the acquaintance of the older Geordie Sproule, formerly a worker at Harland & Wolff, who was himself playing in bands and drifting between jobs. Having tried out and rejected an array of jobs, Morrison inherited Sproule's window cleaning route (he would commemorate those carefree days in the deeply nostalgic song 'Cleaning Windows'), learned some stagecraft from his older friend and played saxophone (and only occasionally sang) in a showband called The Monarchs, playing locally at first, but later touring Scotland and Germany. Many musicians made lucrative livings pursuing a career on the showband circuit, but for others it was a stepping stone to performing their own work. When The Monarchs broke up in late 1963, Morrison joined with Sproule in another showband, The Golden Eagles, before answering a newspaper advert and joining Them, the group with which he would enjoy early success.

Even though his solo work frequently returns to the past to evoke the geography of youth, it sometimes feels like Them were the thing itself: the distilled, joyful present, a direct portal into a time and a place that was the Belfast of the sixties. Already Morrison was interested in recording, even mythologising the geography of Belfast – not yet his childhood landscapes, but a shared geography of common venues and reference points that were familiar to both sides of what would, during the Troubles, become a frustratingly unbridgeable divide. In 'The Story of Them', Morrison sang of the Maritime Hotel, the Spanish Rooms and the City Hall. Working west to east, the Spanish Rooms was a bar on Divis Street, near the end of the Falls Road (the song places it directly on the Falls), that sold scrumpy cider from the barrel – Morrison refers to the drink in his song. On the edge of a nationalist area, the bar was frequented by people from both communities, in part because of the scrumpy's cheapness and strength – according to Morrison's lyrics, four pints were enough for intoxication. Later in the sixties, fewer Protestants would venture into the pub, reflecting the increasingly sectarian geography of the city.

A short walk, or stumble, away was the Maritime Hotel. Run by three entrepreneurs, Jimmy Conlon, Jerry McKenna and Gerry McCurvey – known collectively as the 'Three Js' – the club was unusual in that its promoters assembled a band to play there rather than choosing an existing band as the resident act. Van Morrison, who had been looking to move beyond showbands, answered an advert in the *Belfast Evening Telegraph* seeking interested musicians. The result was the band Them, named after a 1954 B-movie in which giant ants attack Los Angeles. Their first gig, without Van Morrison, who had commitments to fulfil with his previous band, took place on 10 April 1964 at the Maritime. The following week, Van took to the stage, playing sax and singing. 'Van would be pushed on stage and come gliding across out of his brains, but once he stood up and sang it was absolute magic,' one audience member recalled.[6] The Maritime was an old police station that had been, as the name suggested, converted into a seamen's mission. It held variety shows and a regular trad jazz club. Belfast-born poet Gerald Dawe, in his book about Van Morrison, described its layout. 'On the ground floor, a café faced a flight of stairs, and along the narrow, institutional-like painted passageway, there was a small dance hall' with a low stage. Bands would walk through the audience to get to the stage, and after their set, which was usually thirty to forty minutes in length, would step down into the audience 'and mill about with the crowd'.[7] As it wasn't licensed to sell alcohol, audience members would drink in nearby establishments such as the Spanish Rooms before queueing up along College Square North, drawn there to hear the band and to witness Morrison's stage antics. The singer's act often involved pretending to be drunk, or actually being drunk, to throw an extra element of drama and unpredictability into the routine. He would take off his shoes and throw them into the crowd, or fling sets of maracas into the crowd, or hurl himself into the drum kit. Onstage, Morrison came alive.

Morrison would look back on the time at the Maritime with nostalgia, as would many who witnessed the band's performances. Things moved quickly for Them. The band had been signed to Decca mere weeks after their Maritime debut, recording their first songs for the company in London in July 1964. They scored UK hits with 'Baby, Please Don't Go', which reached number 10 in February 1965, and 'Here Comes The Night', which reached number 2 in late April of the same year. Their records had enjoyed some success in the US charts, and they embarked on a tour of the country in 1966, where a dispute over money led to the band's break-up. Morrison returned to Belfast and soon embarked on a solo career, signing a contract with Bert Berns of the New York-based independent Bang

Records. Morrison recorded a number of songs in a two-day recording session in late March 1967, one of which was 'Brown Eyed Girl', which became a US Top 10 hit. But the contract he had signed with Berns was so poor that Morrison claimed he had never received royalties from the hit song. Berns died of a heart attack at the end of 1967, and the singer became embroiled in a contract dispute with Berns's widow, Ilene. Eventually, Warner Brothers were able to free him from the contract, and he set about recording *Astral Weeks* in New York in autumn 1968.

Over the next few years things would change dramatically in Northern Ireland. The growth of the civil rights movement, inspired by black activism in the United States, gave the Catholic nationalist community a voice. But the movement was met with hostility and violence by the authorities. Tensions rose and terrorist activity increased. On Sunday, 30 January 1972, British soldiers shot twenty-eight unarmed civilians in Derry, fourteen of whom died as a result of their injuries. Soon afterwards the Provisional IRA stepped up its bombing campaign in the city, leading to the horrifying Bloody Friday of 21 July, when twenty-two bombs exploded in the city over an eighty-minute period, killing nine. By this time Morrison was living in Marin County – the picturesque headland between San Francisco Bay and the Pacific Ocean that's linked to San Francisco by the Golden Gate Bridge – and was working on his sixth album. Not long after Bloody Sunday, Morrison had been asked by an interviewer about returning to Ireland. 'I don't think I want to go back to Belfast,' he said. 'I don't miss it with all the prejudice around. We're all the same and I think it's terrible what's happening.'[8]

Northern Ireland was on his mind when he came to pen the song 'Saint Dominic's Preview', from his album of the same name released in July 1972. He claimed that the words came before he really understood their import, or their connection with what was happening in his home city, that it was some kind of mystical coincidence. First he wrote the song, he said, and only then did he notice an advert in a newspaper for a mass for peace in Northern Ireland that would be held in St Dominic's Church in San Francisco. 'So to me that *wasn't* coincidence and I worked out in my head that "Saint Dominic's Preview" was me seeing that before I looked at the paper. That's what I thought it meant.'[9] By framing it as a vision, one that he didn't fully understand, Morrison was able to sidestep the notion that he had written a political work about the contemporary situation in Northern Ireland. But by linking it with the peace mass in San Francisco, he opens up a potential reading, as if to say: well, I didn't mean it, but you can think this if you want.

As with *Astral Weeks*, the stream-of-consciousness narration links multiple geographical locations. Beginning with an image of window cleaning, the career he had pursued in East Belfast before stardom, the song is told from what seems to be his own perspective as an rock star in San Francisco thinking of how far he's travelled from his home city. His thoughts inevitably drift to Belfast, before musing broadly on empathy, selfishness, doors closing, and mentioning chains, badges, flags and emblems – lyrics that were allusive enough to relate to the events in Northern Ireland, yet vague enough for Morrison to claim that he didn't know what the words meant. There's a music industry thread that runs through the song: the rock star composing lyrics in his notebook, the complimentary wine paid for by the record company, and the after party in a 52nd Street apartment where he unsuccessfully tries to explain his perspective to fellow party guests whom he suspects of being too high to understand. The song ends with the image of people marching for freedom, a potent one if you were to link it to the civil rights movement in Northern Ireland. This was undoubtedly a link that Morrison wanted to avoid, and so he framed the song as an opaque vision. Yet the unease, the preoccupation with home, and the inability to explain the incomprehensible nature of the Northern Irish situation make this a song that captures a rock star trying to wrestle with the ambiguity of the Troubles without resorting to sloganeering or sectarianism. Perhaps the 'preview' given at the mass in San Francisco was of an idyllic future of peace and prosperity. But here I'm just reading between the lines, imposing a restrictive meaning on the song, one that's both invited and avoided by Morrison. In any case, the peace in Northern Ireland that they prayed for in St Dominic's wouldn't come for a long time.

After I left Cyprus Avenue, I took a bus from the Newtownards Road back towards the city. I was thinking about the extent of Van Morrison's Belfast, how it didn't just stop on the east of the city, but stretched into the city centre, the pubs and clubs that were filled, during Them's brief heyday, with audience members who came from east and west, from Catholic and Protestant areas. When Morrison came to mystically channel Northern Ireland's unrest, he was drawing on a pain that was shared on both sides of a newly hardened divide. The divisions of the city are still glaring in some respects – the tall peace walls that zig-zag between Catholic and Protestant areas still stand – but in other ways more subtle. In travelling from east to west, I couldn't find a bus route that would bring me directly from one side of the city to the other. Instead, I had to change in the city centre, walking from Donegall Square around the corner to a side street from which buses in the direction of the Falls Road would leave. Bus routes were divided by corridor – which main road they would take out of the city – and this structure appeared to replicate the sectarian divides of the city in ways that seemed difficult to repair. (A few months after my trip, a high-speed cross-city bus part-funded by the European Union was scheduled to follow a route that linked the loyalist east with the nationalist west.)

The journey though short took me past West Belfast landmarks such as the Divis Tower, the top two floors of which the British Army had once used as a surveillance post to observe paramilitary activity in the area. To my right were murals that rehearsed key moments in the history of Irish Republicanism – the 1916 rising in Dublin's General Post Office, the hunger strikes, the execution of Roger Casement – alongside a gesture of contemporary solidarity: 'Ireland Stands With Catalonia'. Further along, the bus passed the towering Royal Victoria Hospital, and a series of pubs that appeared to have more in common with rural Ireland than the bars of central Belfast. Once I passed the West Belfast tourist office – established to promote visits to the area and provide locals with jobs as tour guides – I got off the bus at the next stop and walked back in the direction of the city centre, passing Irish language shops and pubs, GAA clubhouses, and the construction site of what would become an Irish language radio station.

The sense you get from walking the Falls Road having just spent a couple of hours in East Belfast is of a wholly distinct culture, one hemmed in to the south by the Westlink motorway, and to the north by the huge peace wall that cuts along the streets and back gardens of the area adjoining the Falls Road, dividing it from the unionist estates off the Shankill Road. The Falls Road, or nationalist West Belfast, if you prefer, is a strip that stretches south-west from the city centre, and naturally enough feels most intense in its displays of identity near its intersections with Protestant areas. While other nationalist areas are surrounded by Protestant neighbourhoods, the Falls is the gateway to the most extensive and continuous nationalist part of Belfast, much of which is bordered to the north-west only by rolling hills. It's like a parallel city.

Having passed the Irish language graffiti along Falls Road ('*díchoilínigh d'intinn*' – decolonise your mind), I walked down a side street to take a look at one of the peace lines, which stretched along a residential street, looming above the houses. On the other side of the wall was Cupar Way, a road in the loyalist Shankill Road area. On top of the concrete wall, which was perhaps twenty or twenty-five feet in height, was a fence that seemed of equal height. It was a piece of military-grade infrastructure that cut through an otherwise normal-looking suburban street. Near the Irish language graffiti I had seen a plaque that commemorated the role of the Irish speakers from the Belfast Gaeltacht in rebuilding the houses on Bombay Street that had been destroyed during the riots of August 1969, when loyalists made incursions into nationalist areas and burned homes. This escalation of sectarian conflict led to the peace walls being erected that same year. Battles raged between the IRA and the RUC on Divis Street, where loyalists also burned houses. The relative peace that reigned just a few years before, when people from both communities frequented the Spanish Rooms before heading down the street to watch Van Morrison throw himself around the stage at the Maritime, was now just a memory.

I diverted from my walk along the Falls Road down a back lane that led to a cluster of redbrick housing surrounding St Peter's Cathedral, a nineteenth-century Catholic church that stood not far from Divis Tower. Inside the church was a memorial to two priests who had been killed in 1971 and 1972 while ministering to wounded and dying parishioners in the Ballymurphy and Springhill massacres in West Belfast. At Ballymurphy, eleven people were killed by the British Army; at Springhill, five.

Then Bloody Sunday in Derry, carried out by the same Parachute Regiment as the Ballymurphy killings; then, in the same month as the release of the *Saint Dominic's Preview* album, the Bloody Friday bombing campaign by the Provisional IRA. How do you even begin to write a pop song about such a catalogue of horrors? And should you? Van Morrison, I think, tried in his own way, writing from a position of honest confusion and good intentions. And it stands as one of his finest works.

Meanwhile, back in Belfast, the Troubles continued. Passing along the Falls Road to Divis Street, and then past the brick wall that stands on the site of the Maritime Hotel, I reached the city centre once more, walking through the shopping streets and down towards the Cathedral Quarter's pubs and venues. I wandered into Belfast's central library to sit for a few minutes, before heading down a back street past the Sunflower pub. The security cage and CCTV camera that guards its front door is a relic of the Troubles, kept, the pub's website says, 'as part of the city's social history'. At a bus stop, I took a look at the circular map of the city's bus routes, its concentric rings resembling a dart board. The city was divided into twelve segments, each named after the major road the routes followed out of the city: 10 for the Falls Road, 11 for the Shankill. As I looked at the white line dividing segment 10 from 11 I recalled the peace wall that stood between the two.

It was almost time for my bus back to Dublin, so I made my way back towards Great Victoria Street. I had an hour to kill, so I wandered down the street in the direction of where Good Vibrations, the record shop run by Terri Hooley, had been located. Hooley was an ex-hippy whose left-wing ethos – his English father George was an active trade union member who had run for election for the Labour Party – informed his anti-sectarian outlook. A key figure in the cultural life of the city during the

Troubles, Hooley famously issued 'Teenage Kicks', the debut single by Derry band The Undertones, on his Good Vibrations record label, along with a number of local punk bands such as The Outcasts and Rudi. The Harp bar on Hill Street became a focal point for punk gigs. *Good Vibrations*, the 2013 film adaptation of his memoirs, captured Hooley's active role in fostering a vibrant youth culture across the sectarian divide during a time of deep hatred. The shop was a symbol of independent culture, certainly, but also of an alternative, peaceful future. His hatred of sectarianism has won him many friends but continues to be unpopular with a vocal minority: in 2012, while walking his dog in East Belfast, he was accosted and pushed over by two men, who called him a 'Fenian lover' and 'a disgrace to the Protestant community'.

In the late seventies, after a decade of the Troubles, punk had provided a grassroots way for young people to overcome sectarian divisions. The Clash had begun their 'Out of Control' tour in Belfast in October 1977, staying in the Europa Hotel and playing the nearby Ulster Hall. In the downtime before their soundcheck the band were taken on a tour of North and West Belfast in a minibus that belonged to the Northern Ireland Polytechnic Students' Union, the promoters of the gig, calling in to the Ballymurphy estate where the 1971 massacre had taken place, to Crumlin Road gaol and to the city centre, then surrounded by fences and gates, a security measure known as the ring of steel. In photos of the band taken at these locations they appear slightly confused and edgy, on unfamiliar territory. 'I just felt like a dick,' guitarist Mick Jones would later say. 'I thought the group stuck out like sore thumbs.'[10] Back at the Ulster Hall, groups of young punks had begun to gather, including Jake Burns, soon of the punk band Stiff Little Fingers. At the eleventh hour, the insurers of the concert, fearing punk's reputation for mayhem, refused to let it go ahead, and the large crowd standing outside became restless and trouble ensued. A teenager taking photos of the police was arrested. A last-minute effort to move the gig to Queen's University fell through, refunds were organised, and the band returned to the city in December.

Even though the Clash gig at the Ulster Hall didn't happen, the crowd outside acted as a Belfast punk show of force. There were more punks in the city than anyone had previously imagined. 'The important thing about punk was the DIY thing,' Brian Young, the guitarist of East Belfast punk band Rudi, said. 'Like the girl at The Clash riot who had a kettle for a handbag.'[11] Initially a glam fan who had caught the ferry to the Isle of Man in 1975 to see Marc Bolan's T-Rex – Belfast journalist Stuart Bailie calls this 'a formative moment for Belfast punk' – Brian bought The Ramones' debut album on import and the band moved towards the speed and directness of punk music.[12] Young and Rudi's bass player, Gordy Owen, who came from Sandy Row not far from Good Vibrations' location on Great Victoria Street, used to hang out in the shop, where they would talk to Terri Hooley. After the cancelled Clash gig Young and Owen had met the band, and this prompted Rudi to write a new song, 'Cops', about the heavy-handed policing on the night of the concert. Beginning with a chant of 'SS-RUC!' – referring to the Royal Ulster Constabulary – the song was in the band's set the first time Hooley saw them live, at the first punk night in the Pound, a club down by the Lagan dockside. Hooley, up until then no big fan of punk, was impressed, and decided to release two of Rudi's songs, 'Big Time' and 'No One', as a seven-inch single. It was the debut release on Good Vibrations Records recorded in Templepatrick Studios in early February 1978, pressed in EMI's Dublin plant (one of the ladies working in the plant asked Hooley if she could keep a copy) and issued in April 1978.[13]

Later that month the Harp Bar, owned by Patsy Lennon, a Catholic, held a gig by the Belfast punk band Victim. For safety, the bar was surrounded by scaffolding, chicken wire and a security camera – the pub had been bombed in 1975, and shots were fired inside and outside it on at least two occasions. It became a centre for punk, attracting a mixed crowd from across the city and beyond. 'We knew people came from all sides of the city, and eventually they started coming from all parts of the country,' recalled Maureen Lawrence, a teenage punk at the time. 'Nobody asked too many questions. The idea was, you made it, you got here, we don't need to know any more than that.'[14] If the Troubles had driven the social life of the city underground, as Mark Cousins said, then punk nights at the Harp provided a chance for an escape from sectarianism, the rare opportunity to be outgoing once again.

As my bus sped south along the Westlink, between Catholic West Belfast and Protestant South Belfast, I wondered what the future held for Northern Ireland. The Troubles had lasted thirty years; the subsequent peace had held for twenty. More strife seemed simultaneously unthinkable and very possible. By the time the coach reached the borderlands it was night, and, in the darkness, I couldn't judge exactly where I was. I thought about checking the map on my phone but decided against it. Just at that moment it didn't really seem to matter where the dividing line lay.

9.

BIRMINGHAM

Birmingham city centre, or at least the area around the Bull Ring shopping centre and New Street station, is the half-revived corpse of a peculiarly dated kind of space-age streetscape, one that originated in the second half of the twentieth century. The contemporary façades of the buildings barely hide their brutalist origins. The area, bombed during the Second World War and later cast in concrete with sixties certainty, feels bolted on to ground level in the manner that so many post-war urban planners fantasised about but never fully realised. It looms over the surrounding older streetscape like the spaceship in the sci-fi film *District 9*. These buildings, the station and the shopping centre, described in a Pevsner guide to the city as 'the two largest 1960s schemes [which are] also the worst', have been recently repaired, adjusted, and clad in chrome and glass panels.[1] You emerge from New Street dazed. The overall impression of the station, now modernised to within an inch of its life, is that of an airport terminal whose runways are subterranean. Outside it's all hard surfaces – plazas lined with chain coffee shops and minimal strips of shrubbery. Above you, looking like a bulbous silver slug, looms the new station gateway, having replaced the sixties brutalism of the previous New Street building. Despite the signposts directly outside the station that provided basic directions, I spent my first hour in Birmingham wandering blindly. And that sense of confusion never quite left me as I meandered through the city centre over the next couple of days. Later, when coming from my hotel, I approached the Bull Ring with the sense of anticipation and anguish of one about to climb a mountain, trying various approaches to see which one was the least difficult. New Street and the Bull Ring remained unknowable and unfamiliar, and perhaps that's why they continued to fascinate me during my visit. Try as I might, I couldn't use the Bull Ring as a point of orientation, as you would a traditional landmark. I never had a sure sense of where exactly I was in relation to it. As it turned out, it wasn't a bad state of mind in which to try to get to grips with Birmingham's multiple cultural identities and multifaceted musical history.

Birmingham's status as a market town was secured by a charter obtained in 1166 by Peter de Bermingham, the lord of the manor, who laid out the market around the area that's now the Bull Ring. During the medieval period it was never fully incorporated as a borough, so it wasn't controlled by the guilds that would have imposed restrictions on trade, and thus attracted migrants who could freely establish themselves as traders. Most migrants were drawn from the surrounding countryside, but some came from further afield – from Wales or France. Birmingham's position on the south-east edge of the iron- and coal-rich Black Country made it a natural gateway for trade with London. Initially, small-scale industries – goldsmiths, ironsmiths and gunmakers – flourished. In the eighteenth century the town became the centre of a canal network, enabling further industrial growth, its population doubling to 74,037 between 1760 and 1811. It became a centre for banking – Lloyds Bank was founded there in 1765 – and its professional classes grew. By the nineteenth century, Birmingham's industries were highly diversified and entrepreneurial; its highly skilled workforce was well paid. Birmingham's industries, such as iron smelters, cotton spinners and chemical manufacturers, drew more workers to the city so that by the beginning of the twentieth century the population was over half a million people. Some of these inhabitants of Birmingham – it had been granted city status in 1889 – were Irish immigrants who had come to the city after the mid-century famines in their home country. From the mid-twentieth century onwards, the city attracted new migrants, many from the Caribbean and south Asia (by 2011 Birmingham's population was over a million, 42 per cent of whom were non-white). In the seventies, Birmingham's industries suffered a calamitous collapse, with hundreds of thousands of jobs lost and wages in steep decline.

The multiple cultures of twentieth- and twenty-first-century Birmingham inevitably prompted a consideration of the multiplicity of identities in contemporary Britain. At the time of my visit, multiculturalism was venerated – especially in terms of sporting achievement – while, simultaneously, racism and xenophobia drove government policy. This contradiction didn't seem likely to resolve itself soon.

I made my way from the hotel, having decided that the best place to start was in Smethwick, a suburb to the north-west of the city centre that I could reach by tram, which I was able to pick up in a side street that runs alongside New Street station. I found it difficult to plot the trajectory I should take through the streets around the station, so thought it better to walk straight through New Street's main entrance. But I can't be certain which exit I used to reach the tram, and I'm not sure I could draw you a map of how I got there. The West Midlands Metro runs through the streets of the city centre before climbing above street level as it reaches Snow Street station, and follows an old railway cutting all the way to Wolverhampton – a distance of thirteen miles – passing through Handsworth, West Bromwich and Walsall on its journey.

Without the General Election of 1964 Smethwick might have enjoyed a relatively unremarkable history of the sort that most suburbs do. Instead, it became the site of unrestrained, righteous white rage against immigration, an anger that was, troublingly, successfully channelled by a mainstream political candidate into electoral success. For a long time it probably seemed a shameful, isolated episode consigned to the past, but it doesn't appear so now. After the war, a significant number of immigrants from Commonwealth countries had settled in Smethwick. Against a background of declining local industry and increasing pressure on housing, Peter Griffiths, a Conservative councillor, defeated the incumbent Patrick Gordon Walker, Labour's shadow home secretary. Walker, who lived far from his Smethwick constituency, in London's Hampstead Garden Suburb, had opposed the 1962 Commonwealth Immigration Act, which proposed to restrict entry by, and limit the rights of, migrants from the Commonwealth. He was easily caricatured by his opponent as a cosmopolitan who was aloof from the concerns of his constituents: 'How easy to support uncontrolled immigration when one lives in a garden suburb,' Griffiths said of him. When posters and stickers bearing the phrase 'if you want a nigger for a neighbour, vote Labour' were distributed by neo-Nazi groups, Griffiths refused to condemn the sentiment, telling *The Times*: 'I would not condemn any man who said that. I regard it as a manifestation of popular feeling.' When challenged in the Commons by Labour, the Conservatives backed Griffiths.

Griffiths would go on to write the book *A Question of Colour?*, published in 1966, in which he suggested that apartheid could be a viable alternative to integration. He had practical local experience of trying to implement such a policy. In 1964, white residents had successfully petitioned the local Conservative council, of which Griffiths was the alderman, to carry out compulsory purchases of the houses on Smethwick's Marshall Street, so they could be let only to white families. The move, blocked by the Labour government, came to nothing.[2] In 1965, black American civil rights campaigner Malcolm X visited Marshall Street, having been invited by the Indian Workers' Association (UK) to show solidarity with the black and Asian minorities of the area.

I had travelled some distance from the tram stop at which I had disembarked, walking under a motorway overpass, crossing a canal, then passing the remnants of an old glass factory and a Hindu cultural resource centre that sat next to a roundabout. Further south, I reached the west end of Marshall Street, pausing to take a photo of the blue plaque commemorating Malcolm X's visit. As I took the photo, I noticed three Asian teenage lads walking in my direction. 'All right boss, you taking a picture of me house?' one of the lads joked. 'Is that your house?' I said, cautiously aware I was being made fun of. 'Yeah, do you wanna come in for a cuppa?' he said. I politely refused, said goodbye, and headed on my way, passing the Marshall Street terraces that had been a flashpoint half a century before. I turned from Marshall Street onto St Paul's Road, which leads to Smethwick High Street. At a junction near a car dealership, turbaned Sikh men sat on the steps outside a white and gold, three-storey Sikh temple, and, further on, crowds thronged the pavement. As I passed by, I noted the shops I saw: Asian supermarkets with fruit and vegetables arranged in stands on the pavement outside, Indian sweet shops, phone shops, takeaways, travel agents, an Asian funeral home, and a women's clothes shop selling saris. Further along the street is Smethwick's main Sikh temple, which played a key role in the development of bhangra music in the city.

The partition of India in 1947 had cut through the Punjab region, forcing five million Muslims to move from India to Pakistan and three million Hindus and Sikhs to migrate in the opposite direction. The displaced Sikhs who moved to East Punjab found that the land they were offered was significantly poorer than the land they had farmed in West Punjab, and those already resident saw their holdings divided up to accommodate the newcomers. When the 1948 British Nationality Act offered citizens of the newly formed Commonwealth the same rights as those of the United Kingdom and its colonies, a significant number of already displaced Punjabis on both sides of the border saw it as an opportunity to start anew, embarking upon a journey to England that historian Clair Wills calls 'the latest in a series of migrations' for the already displaced Punjabis.[3]

At the time of the 1964 Smethwick elections, two brothers, Dalbir and Balbir Singh Khanpur, were living in the area having emigrated from Punjab in the fifties to work in local factories. They were nicknamed at the time of their arrival 'bhujhangy', or children, on account of their relative youth: they were still in their teens when they made the journey to England, and were only later joined by their families. They began to attend Sikh history classes in the temple on Smethwick High Street and were taught to play the tabla and harmonium. Calling themselves the Bhujhangy Group, they played religious hymns, with most of their performances taking place at the Smethwick temple. In 1968 they recorded an EP, *Teri Chiti Nu Parah*, which they brought to local pubs to sell. Seeking distribution for the record, they approached Oriental Star Agencies, an Asian record shop and distributor that operated from an electronics shop on the Moseley Road in Balsall Heath in Birmingham's south inner city. Its founder, Muhammad Ayub, set up the label in response to the Birmingham Asian community's demand for Indian and Pakistani songs. While some cinemas occasionally showed Asian films, there were few radio programmes or record shops that catered adequately for the demand that Ayub had identified. The shop began to stock imports, which were hugely popular, and OSA soon become a wholesaler that distributed records to other shops around the country. Its first releases came in 1969, with records from the Bhujhangy Group and Anari Sangheet. Later, Ayud would sign the Pakistani Qawwali singer Nusrat Fateh Ali Khan to OSA, releasing over a hundred of his records. Over time, the Bhujhangy Group began to incorporate Western musical instruments alongside traditional ones, anticipating bhangra's use of hip-hop and reggae. Bhangra, though named after a traditional Punjabi folk dance, has come to refer to this hybrid musical form, underpinned by the boom of the dhol drum and the throb of tabla.

Shops run along only one side of Smethwick High Street – the other side is separated from a dual carriageway by a wide grass verge. I was planning on continuing my journey on the other side of the dual carriageway, so crossed by means of a footbridge that spanned not just the main road but a railway line too, and left me at the south end of Brasshouse Lane, which led north in the direction of The Hawthorns, West Bromwich Albion FC's home ground. Next to the railway line were two canals that ran side-by-side, part of the eighteenth-century network of waterways that had been so important to the city's, and Smethwick's, industrial development. A redbrick pumping station, now a waterways heritage centre, perched on the bank of land that divided one canal from the other.

My next tram journey, from The Hawthorns station, was brief: a single stop, to Handsworth. As a music fan I knew

Handsworth primarily from the reggae group Steel Pulse's debut album *Handsworth Revolution*. The band was formed in 1975 by three friends at Handsworth Wood Boys School: David Hinds, Basil Gabbidon and Ronald McQueen. Hinds was the son of Jamaican immigrants who had come to England in the 1950s. That decade saw a substantial migration of West Indians, especially Jamaicans, to England by boat. Unemployment had grown after the war, and seasonal employment in the Americas had ceased to be an option, so, as with the displaced Punjabis, a more permanent emigration to England became increasingly attractive. Over half a million people from the Caribbean emigrated to England in the post-war era. As was common with many families, Hinds' father had come over first, followed a year later by his mother, and subsequently other family members arrived. Reaching England was a shock: the drabness and the cold. Employment was invariably in low-skilled jobs, ones the English didn't want to do themselves. Although born in England, Hinds struggled to reconcile his Jamaican identity with his British one, telling an interviewer that 'it was like I was trying to wear different heads at different times because the upbringing that we had didn't originate out of Britain'. He recalled, as a child, receiving a toy gun set that included a passport, and instead of filling in his English address he wrote in the Jamaican home town of his parents. He explained the reasons for this yearning for Jamaica: his father, who worked in a factory, would come home in the evenings speaking of the racial tensions that he experienced in the workplace. 'I grew up being accustomed to that kind of negativity,' he said. When visitors came from Jamaica their luggage often contained food and the latest records from the island. Reggae was a constant presence at any social gathering – christenings, weddings, birthdays. 'Someone would bring their sound system with their amplifiers with speakers as big as wardrobes [...] and play music all night long.'[4]

I had reached Handsworth Booth Street tram station, and walked up Booth Street in the direction of Soho Road, Handsworth's main street. As I walked I could hear in the distance a deep bass boom, and as I neared the source of the sound I could see that there was a party taking place in a small car park next to a two-storey redbrick building that housed both a Pentecostal church and a hair salon. It was Bank Holiday Monday, and a well-dressed crowd wearing what looked like their Sunday finery – flowery dresses and hats for the women, suits for the men – stood around a smoking barbecue while the music boomed and echoed around the street. At the crossroads of Booth Street and Soho Road stood a stubborn concrete building, a chunky office block that had been designed to integrate a petrol station at street level. The upper storeys hung suspended above a canopy and forecourt that must once have accommodated fuel pumps. At first glance it appeared disused, or at least under-used, but signs signalled that the forecourt functioned as a car wash and a coach station, and that the upper storeys served as a community college and gym. Two coach firms operate routes through the bus station, linking Handsworth to Southall, Slough, Gravesend and Bradford, providing a direct transport connection to other Asian communities around England.

I walked for a mile or so along Soho Road in the afternoon sun, passing mostly black and Asian faces as I went. On the pavement next to a Caribbean restaurant a group of men tended an oil-drum barbecue. As with Smethwick High Street, there were Indian takeaways, sweet shops and travel agents, but this time they extended along both sides of the road, sweeping towards the dome of a huge Sikh temple on the horizon. Near the temple is where Soho Road becomes Soho Hill, and it was also the point from which I would get a bus in the direction of the city centre. As I stood at the stop my mind drifted a little, and when I cast my gaze back down the hill towards the bustling Soho Road I thought again about Steel Pulse's music. The title track of the band's *Handsworth Revolution* had pointed to the poverty and lack of equality experienced by black residents of the suburb, suggesting that such problems will be overcome through rebellion, which might even involve the use of force. This was a prescient diagnosis of the problem.

In July 1981 the riots that took place in black neighbourhoods across Britain included three days of disturbances in Handsworth. In 1985, around the corner from the bus stop I was standing at, further riots occurred. The Irish travel writer Dervla Murphy, who had rented a flat in Handsworth to carry out research about race relations in the area, found that her new home was at the epicentre of the riot. She had noticed that tensions were growing in the days leading up to the events. Leaving the house in the early evening of Monday, 9 September to post a letter to her daughter, she saw three traffic cops on motorbikes arguing with a man who had parked his car on a double yellow line outside the Acapulco, a café frequented by Rastafarians that had a reputation for drug dealing. This was the relatively small event that triggered the riot. In Murphy's account, a crowd of about sixty Rastas gathered around the police, shouting insults at them. The situation became violent as punches were thrown, and then police reinforcements arrived by car. Murphy returned home, then a couple of hours later ventured out to the Villa Cross pub. The bingo hall next to the Acapulco was on fire, so firemen arrived to quell the blaze, then found themselves under attack from bricks, bottles, verbal abuse – and petrol bombs hurled from the forecourt of the Villa Cross. At this point, battle lines were drawn between thirty or so police and around two hundred black locals on the street. Murphy went into the pub to get a pint of cider, and helped the landlord draw the curtains before he shut early. The pub would never reopen. 'At 8.20 [I] was the last person to leave the Villa Cross before it closed – for ever,' she wrote.[5] Later that evening shops along Lozells Road were looted, with Asians, blacks and whites joining in to help themselves to the goods, or even to help others to the loot: Murphy recalls a young black looter arranging shoeboxes on the pavement outside an emptied shoe shop and asking a white woman what she needed. 'The atmosphere was totally free of any threat of inter-personal violence, racial or otherwise; it was not even a quarrelsome – far less a "murderous" – night.'[6] Nevertheless, Murphy wrote, 'it felt as though a vast reservoir of repressed resentment of White racialism had suddenly burst its dam'.[7] Like Steel Pulse's David Hinds, Roger Charlery (Ranking Roger) of the multi-ethnic ska-punk was the son of West Indian migrants to Handsworth. Formed in 1978, the band signed to Coventry's 2 Tone label, and their music drew on reggae while combining it with a new-wave urgency and a politicised edge. And young Handsworth poet Benjamin Zephaniah drew directly on the political, class and racial implications of the events in his neighbourhood on his spoken-word 1982 *Dub Ranting* EP, and 1983's *Rasta* LP, which included the song 'Dis Policeman Keeps On Kicking Me to Death'.

The story of how Black Sabbath guitarist Tony Iommi lost two fingertips from his right hand has assumed the status of a heavy-metal superhero origin story. A man is injured and as a result gains special powers. It's frequently told – indeed Iommi himself tells it twice in the first thirty pages of his autobiography – but it's worth revisiting here. It imbues the working-class industrial context from which Black Sabbath emerged with the kind of direct causation that you can rarely trace in these stories, and that you can frequently compress into a persuasive if debatable simplification: that heavy industry directly influenced the sound of heavy metal. He was aged seventeen and working in a sheet-metal factory as a welder. It was his last day on the job before going on a European tour with his band, The Birds & the Bees. This was a big break, his first job as a professional musician. At lunchtime, he went home and told his mother that he wasn't going to go back in the afternoon. 'Iommis don't quit,' she told him, and he returned to the factory to see the day out. (His story can also be read as a warning of the dangers of over-commitment to paid work.) The woman who worked further up the production line wasn't there that day, so Iommi took her place, carrying out the unfamiliar job of using a guillotine press to bend pieces of metal. Dreaming already of his band's European tour, the press slammed down on his fingers. He pulled his hand away and left the tips of his middle fingers beneath the machine. When the fingertips were brought to hospital in a matchbox, doctors tried but failed to reattach them, instead grafting on skin from his arm. After the accident it hurt when he pressed his fingertips against the strings when he played guitar. He had to find a way to work around his limitations, using lighter strings and making thimbles for the affected fingers by melting and shaping the plastic from washing-up liquid bottles.[8] His style changed as a result: chords were less easy for him after the accident, so he made his guitar sound fuller and concentrated on playing riffs.

Black Sabbath's home territory is in Aston, a suburb a couple of miles away from Handsworth, just north of Birmingham city centre. Iommi was the child of Italian parents; his grandparents, who owned ice cream parlours in the city, were emigrants to England. When he was ten years old, his parents bought a sweet shop in Park Lane, Aston, which the family lived above. Attending the nearby Birchfield Road Secondary Modern School introduced him to the future singer of Black Sabbath, John 'Ozzy' Osbourne, whom Iommi bullied. 'I used to hide when I saw him coming,' said Osbourne.[9] The dynamic between them was underpinned by class. While Iommi's family were middle-class shopkeepers, Ozzy was the working-class son of a toolmaker father and a factory-worker mother. His father worked night shifts at the GEC factory near the Aston Villa football ground, while his mother worked during the day at the Lucas factory, suppliers of components to the car and aerospace industries. Told by his father about the Luftwaffe bombing raids during the war, Ozzy didn't have to go far to see the effects of such attacks. 'Aston had taken a pounding during the Blitz,' Ozzy writes in his autobiography *I Am Ozzy*. 'On every other street corner when I was a kid there were "bomb building sites" – houses that had been flattened by the Germans when they were trying to hit the Castle Bromwich Spitfire factory.'[10]

While Ozzy was bored by Aston, Geezer Butler found an imaginative landscape among the bombed-out sites. Born Terence Michael Joseph Butler, the son of Dubliners who had moved to Birmingham for work, Butler was the youngest in a family of seven children and would be the youngest member of Black Sabbath. 'I had a very adventurous childhood,' he recalled. 'I had air raid shelters and destroyed buildings to play in. It was great for the imagination.'[11] A fan of science-fiction, especially the works of H. G. Wells and the way futuristic fantasy could be employed to dramatise and critique contemporary issues, Butler would become the band's lyricist, specialising in apocalyptic fables that fitted their Satanic popular image.

After a spell working in a slaughterhouse, a job from which he was sacked for attacking a colleague with a pole, Ozzy turned to burglary. He was caught, imprisoned, and after a few months was freed, in the winter of 1966. He was keen to become a singer and put an advert in a music shop window: 'OZZY ZIG NEEDS GIG', with a line below pointing out that he had his own PA system, and where and when he could be reached. (Ozzy Zig was his attempt at a mysterious stage name.) Ozzy's father had bought the Vox PA system from George Clay's music shop in the centre of town for £250 – a significant amount of money at the time. 'To this day I've no idea why,' Ozzy wrote.[12] Perhaps his father saw it as a chance for his son to escape from the life of dead-end jobs and petty crime that he had been living up until that point. It seems fairly likely that the PA system was what drew musicians' attention, rather than the untested singer whose previous bands were either fictional – he wrote 'The Black Panthers' on a guitar case, but there was no band to go with the name – or The Music Machine/The Approach, who while they actually existed never played a gig. Ozzy's ad in the window of the music shop was an attempt to finally make something tangible happen. It had the desired effect. The first person to call to Ozzy's house was Geezer Butler, who was the rhythm guitar player in a band called The Rare Breed; then came Iommi and drummer Bill Ward, whose psychedelic band Mythology, based in Carlisle, had fallen apart after a high-profile drugs bust by the Cumbria Constabulary. Both had returned to Birmingham in search of a singer and a bassist.

Geezer switched to bass, and together they formed a group, The Polka Tulk Blues Band, a six-piece including a saxophonist; according to Ozzy they were named after a Pakistani-owned shop in Handsworth. After two gigs they were pared down to four members, becoming The Earth Blues Band, and then Earth. Their heavy, bluesy rock was a precursor of Sabbath's sludgy riffing, and they played numerous gigs in the thriving live music scene in the West Midlands – clubs and pubs like Henry's Blueshouse, where they saw an early incarnation of Led Zeppelin and got a support slot with Jethro Tull. (According to Ozzy, in 1968 he and Butler had been wandering around the Bull Ring shopping centre when they met Robert Plant, who told them he had been recruited by the New Yardbirds, who were soon rechristened Led Zeppelin.) As a result of playing together, Tull's lead singer Ian Anderson invited Tony Iommi to join the band, which he briefly did, appearing with them in *The Rolling Stones Rock and Roll Circus* film, albeit hidden under a giant hat that had been handed to him by Anderson. By this time Iommi had decided to rejoin Earth, and he returned to Birmingham with a renewed focus, having learned from Anderson the importance of a band leader. They booked a room to rehearse in Aston's Newtown Community Centre, with the aim of starting at 9 a.m. every morning. This new regimen had an almost immediate effect: the band began to write songs, starting with 'Wicked World' and 'Black Sabbath'. Jim Simpson, who ran Henry's Blueshouse, became their manager. Still named Earth, they played gigs around the country, including as support for Van Der Graaf Generator at the Bay Hotel in Seaburn, along the seafront north of Sunderland. I mention this not merely because the site is near my house – the building was recently knocked down and replaced with apartments – but because it's where the band first met the Radio 1 DJ John Peel, who would later become their champion, playing them on his show and bringing them in to record sessions. Simpson booked them overseas dates in Denmark and at the Star Club in Hamburg, where the Beatles had spent their early years, and where they were required to play two forty-five-minute sets a night. This punishing schedule encouraged them to improvise onstage, and from their extended instrumental jams came material that they could shape into songs back at the rehearsal room in Aston. Butler estimated that most of the songs from the first two Black Sabbath albums originated from these Hamburg performances.

Earth were renamed Black Sabbath in 1969 to avoid being mistaken for another Midlands band of the same name. Their song 'Black Sabbath' predated the band name. They were inspired, at least at their inception, by the dark stuff. Geezer Butler's interest in the occult reflected a vogue for magick among hippydom. Raised an Irish Catholic, he was deeply spooked by the arrival of a dark apparition late one night in his Aston flat. The lyrics to 'Black Sabbath', written by Butler and Osbourne, recount the vision. ('We were trying to get away from traditional boy-girl lyrics,' Butler explained to one interviewer.)[13] Afterwards Butler, taking what he had seen to be a sign that he must choose between Satanism or Christianity, took to wearing a cross, as did other members of the band. But a song intended as a warning against black magic was inevitably interpreted as an endorsement, much to the band's dismay. Pro-Satan or anti-Satan, Black Sabbath's darkness perfectly suited the times as the idealism of the sixties turned sour. Yet they didn't at that point seem like a commercial prospect. Two showcase gigs organised by Jim Simpson in London failed to generate interest from record companies. Eventually, Tony Hall took a chance on them. A former A&R man for Decca who also presented radio programmes about pop music – he can be heard interviewing The Beatles on their *Live at the BBC* compilation – Hall had become an independent promoter and producer. Although no longer directly involved with a label, he offered to lend the band's manager Simpson £500 to fund the recording of a debut album. Recorded at Regent Sound studios on Denmark Street – London's Tin Pan Alley – the album took a mere twelve hours to commit to tape, proof of how well drilled the band had become through touring and rehearsing. Signing first to Fontana, a subsidiary of Philips, for a one-single deal, they moved on to Vertigo, another Philips imprint, for their debut album. *Black Sabbath*, released on the suitably hexed Friday, 13 February 1970. It immediately reached the charts without any reviews from the music press – although John Peel had been playing tracks on his radio show. Succeeding without the press's approval ensured its enduring rancour, but the band's success grew, the album moved up the UK charts, and, when released in the US, did the same there. Sabbath were on their way.

As with Birmingham's bhangra and reggae scenes, Black Sabbath's story is also in part influenced by migration. Tony Iommi's grandparents had come from Italy to England, Geezer Butler's father was an immigrant from Dublin. After the war, the largest immigrant group to come to the UK was from Ireland. My grandfather was among their number, leaving his family in the port town of Drogheda on Ireland's east coast to spend periods working in car factories and pubs in England. This temporary emigration was a direct result of workers being laid off: they would lose their jobs in Ireland on a Friday and be in England by Monday. My mother recalled her family walking to the phone box at the end of the street to await calls from him. He would return when Irish factories began recruiting again. Emigration, temporary or permanent, continues to be a fact of Irish life, but it has been most pronounced in times of crisis. The Great Famine of the nineteenth century killed between one and one and a half million people; about the same number emigrated, with around 200,000 going to Britain. During the Second World War, people from Ireland, which was officially a neutral country, were recruited in large numbers to work in the UK. Afterwards this trend continued, and by 1961 almost a sixth of the total population of the Republic of Ireland was living in Britain.[14] The population of the west of Ireland was particularly depleted by emigration from the famine era onwards. Taking the train from a station in Galway or Mayo to get the boat from Dublin was a grim rite of passage for many families. 'Somebody always seemed to be arriving or going away,' said playwright Tom Murphy of his home town, Tuam, Co. Galway. 'A lot of emotion centred around the little railway station.' Journalist John Healy wrote of the slamming of the train doors signalling 'the finality of the old life' in Charlestown, Co. Mayo.[15]

For emigrants, the separation between the old life and the new one wasn't necessarily as final as it might have initially seemed. A portion of the money earned in England was sent home, holidays were often spent back in Ireland, and sometimes whole families, or family members, returned permanently, or at least for a few years. Shane MacGowan of The Pogues, born in Kent in 1957 to Irish parents, spent several years in Tipperary as a child before his family returned to England. Kevin Rowland of Dexys Midnight Runners was born in Wolverhampton in 1953. His parents were from Mayo – his father was a builder – and, once Kevin was born, moved back to their home town of Crossmolina for several years, before returning once more to Wolverhampton. When Rowland was ten, the family moved again, to Harrow in north London. The early experience of Ireland stayed with Rowland, who returned to its landscape in the handful of autobiographical songs in which he wrote about negotiating the complexity of his Irish identity in England.

After a series of jobs in London, Scotland and Liverpool, Rowland returned to the West Midlands, working in a shop in Birmingham and eventually buying a house on Apollo Road in Oldbury, a short walk away from Smethwick's Marshall Street. As a teenager Rowland had become a soul fan and a style obsessive – his first job was in a clothes shop – and he had been a member of a mixed-gender gang called the Young Kingsbury Team. These influences would be processed and deeply stylised by Rowland for the initial model of Dexys, the punk soul revue. His desire to be a pop star, he said, was a 'last-ditch attempt to prove that I wasn't completely useless'.[16] It was born of him transforming his self-loathing into a motivational tool. 'I felt not very good about myself,' he told an interviewer. 'And I felt a desperation to do something, to prove myself.'[17] Invited to join his brother's country band as a guitarist, Rowland learned to play. He followed this with a proto-New Romantic band called Lucy & the Lovers before forming The Killjoys, a punk band who enjoyed decent sales of their debut single, 'Johnny Won't Get to Heaven', leading to a Radio 1 session for John Peel. After The Killjoys split – 'too many people wanting to do different things', he explained – Rowland and Killjoys guitar player Kevin Archer went about assembling a new band.[18]

What's particularly striking about the advert that they put in the *Birmingham Evening Mail* during the summer of 1978 – seeking musicians for a nine-piece 'new-wave soul band' – is how perfectly they would realise their vision.[19] Rowland's obsession with fashion extended into an ability to foresee trends. While still with The Killjoys he had predicted that there would be a reaction against the uniformity of punk, and after that band's demise he had returned to the soul he had loved as a teenager – classic works from Stax and Motown, but also the Northern Soul that had been played in dancehalls across the North and Midlands since the late sixties. Assembling a band that included a punchy brass section, Dexys began to rehearse from nine-to-five every day in a lock-up garage in a south Birmingham suburb, a routine of rigorous self-discipline that recalled Black Sabbath's rehearsals in Aston. They began to play gigs in venues around the city, eventually securing a Friday night residency in Mr Sam's, up a narrow lane, the superfluous-sounding Needless Alley, in the city centre. And they played Saturday lunchtime shows at the Midland Hotel, where in 1968 the Wolverhampton Conservative MP Enoch Powell had made his 'Rivers of Blood' speech during which he infamously outlined his opposition to Labour's Race Relations Bill in the most vehement and lurid terms.

In 1974, the Provisional IRA's mainland terror campaign reached Birmingham. Bombs exploded in two pubs, the Mulberry Bush and the Tavern in the Town, killing twenty-one and injuring nearly two hundred people. The response was swift: the government introduced the Prevention of Terrorism Act, making membership of the Irish Republican Army illegal. Supposedly temporary, the Act stayed in place for the next fifteen years. It allowed for the arrest of individuals without a warrant if they were suspected of terrorism, which was defined in the legislation as an exclusively Irish Republican activity. Six Irish men were arrested soon after the bombings and false confessions were extracted by the police through torture and abuse. They were remanded in custody and beaten by prison officers. The case went to trial the following year, when they were convicted and sentenced to life imprisonment, convictions that were not overturned until 1991.

One of the effects of the bombings was the increased discrimination against the Irish in Britain. 'I was actually in one of those pubs the night before,' Rowland told Éamon Sweeney of the *Irish Times* in 2016. 'I had just moved back to Birmingham.'[20] By the time of Dexys' formation, the stereotype of the backward Irishman had been joined by an image of the Irishman as terrorist, a threat to the state. 'Dance Stance', a punchy horn-led stomp over which Rowland barked out a roll call of Irish writers – Oscar Wilde, Brendan Behan, Laurence Sterne – was a defiant blast of pride in the face of Irish-joke ignorance. 'It was the 70s when the thick paddy jokes really were at their most intense,' Rowland said. 'They go into your psyche, and a part of me did feel second class for being Irish.'[21] The cover image used on the band's debut album, *Searching for the Young Soul Rebels*, was a photo of a teenage boy with a stuffed suitcase tucked beneath his right arm while in his left he clutches a holdall by its handles. Behind him, children and young men are caught in various states of agitation. The photograph was of a Catholic child, Anthony O'Shaughnessy, in the Ardoyne area of Belfast in 1971, during the feverish days that followed the introduction of internment – imprisonment without trial – of suspected members of the IRA. In Ardoyne, which had up until then been religiously mixed, the boundaries between Catholic and Protestant communities were redrawn brutally during sectarian clearances. Protestant families leaving their houses in Cranbrook Gardens turned on the gas and set the terraces alight so that Catholic families couldn't move in. It was on that street that the photo was taken. O'Shaughnessy and his brothers were being moved by men identified by historian Gareth Mulvenna as loyalists Roy Stewart and Robert 'Basher' Bates.[22] (The latter would go on to become a member of the notorious Shankill Butchers gang which was responsible for the deaths of at least twenty-three people between 1975 and 1982, with the majority targeted because they were either Catholic or suspected of being Catholic.) 'I thought it was a dream and in the morning everything would be okay,' O'Shaughnessy said in 2010. 'I don't even remember the photographer doing the picture.'[23]

The bewilderment and confusion of the Belfast teenager in the photo captured an atmosphere that Rowland wanted to communicate. It's tempting to think that, shorn of all historical context, the photograph speaks for itself, a vision of the tumult of a departure from the familiar to the strange, a universal image of migratory distress. Perhaps Rowland identified with the child in the photo, saw in him his own peripatetic movement from country to country and city to city. But Rowland knew that his experience was far from unique, that it had wider resonance with other Irish people in England, and with other immigrants. 'I wanted a picture of unrest,' he said. 'It could have been from anywhere but I was secretly glad that it was from Ireland.'[24]

In the buildings of Birmingham's centre you can see the late-twentieth-century efforts to remake the industrial city. In its suburbs you find working-class communities that included new migrants from Commonwealth countries, and in Black Sabbath's case from Ireland and Italy, who created distinct musical cultures – reggae, heavy metal and bhangra – that helped to change the course of British popular music. Being confronted with racism from locals and heavy-handed, often violent, policing encouraged a defiant cultural pride in migrant populations that led to a deeper exploration of one's own culture and the growth of a distinct cultural infrastructure – clubs, record shops, record labels – to sustain it. Kevin Rowland of Dexys Midnight Runners, in reaction to anti-Irishness, was moved to make a series of soul-derived albums that often explicitly addressed the Irish experience. The cultural influence of reggae in particular came to shape British music from the late seventies onwards, and this could be clearly seen in the ska revival in nearby Coventry.

2 TONE RECORDS

THE SPECIALS

33 1/3 RPM

SIDE

CDL TTX 5001–

825646336050

1. **A MESSAGE TO YOU RUDY** (R. Thompson)
2. **DO THE DOG** (R. Thomas, arr. J. Dammers)
3. **IT'S UP TO YOU** (J. Dammers/Specials)
4. **NITE KLUB*** (J. Dammers/Specials)
5. **DOESN'T MAKE IT ALRIGHT**
   (B. Goldberg /J. Dammers)
6. **CONCRETE JUNGLE** (R. Radiation)
7. **TOO HOT** (C. Campbell)

*Backing vocals by CHRISSIE HYNDE

Produced by ELVIS COSTELLO

Publishers: 1. Carlin Music Corp. 2. Warner
Chappell Music Ltd. 3-6. Plangent Visions
Music Ltd. 7. Melodisc Music Ltd.

Digital remasters ℗ 2014 The copyright in this sound
recording is owned by Chrysalis Records Ltd.

10.

COVENTRY

You step from the train at Coventry station and pass across a bridge that opens into the ticket hall, a bright, airy box made of concrete and glass that speaks of an illustrious recent past that rose phoenix-like from the bombed ruins of the war. The city's late-twentieth-century reconstruction was driven by investment by the state and the wealth that accrued from Coventry's manufacturing boom. Now both were mourned, and increasingly politics was being driven by a nostalgia for the higher wages and relatively secure jobs of the industrial era and the need to preserve the role of the state in towns and cities against the threat of government-imposed austerity.

At its height, Coventry had been a thriving city. In the nineteenth century it had been home to numerous bicycle manufacturers, and many of those companies went on to build automobiles: cars, motorbikes, trucks, tanks. Its manufacture of military vehicles, aircraft and armaments during the Second World War made it a natural target for the Luftwaffe, who bombed it relentlessly between 1940 and 1942. The air raids of 14 November 1940 destroyed most of the buildings in the city centre, a good number of Coventry's factories, and the city's cathedral, which was left in ruins as a cautionary reminder of the destruction of war and the importance of peace.

Before the bombing, Coventry had been a pretty market town. You can picture it, or certainly I could, as I walked along the road leading from the station to the city centre. The elegant three-storey redbrick buildings that sweep towards a concrete plaza that leads to the pedestrianised post-war shopping precinct put me in mind of Norwich, a medieval market town of lanes and churches. Elsewhere I would catch a glimpse down a narrow lane of a row of old buildings and be once again transported to a past beyond the twentieth century. For the most part, Coventry is new – but the kind of new that now feels rather dated. There's a touch of the regional German city to its juxtaposition of sixty-year-old concrete with medieval sandstone. But it now lacks the wealth of somewhere like Stuttgart, which continues to manufacture high-end cars. Coventry, although it continues to manufacture London-style taxis and is home to start-ups focused on future transport technology, is dependent on low-paid work in warehouses and retail.

The post-war miracle had served Coventry well; reconstruction had been a success. In the fifties and sixties the average wage in Coventry was 25 per cent higher than the national average.[1] But since then manufacturing had moved on. In the late seventies and eighties the top fifteen employers in Coventry cut their workforce in half. Subsequently more manufacturers had pulled out, with Peugeot leaving in 2007. I walked past a job centre outside which a scattered crowd of people, mostly young and middle-aged men, stood looking at the list of available jobs hanging in the window. Inside, representatives of Amazon were delivering a presentation to jobseekers. It was a similar scene to those I recall from Dublin when the global economic crash hit Ireland in 2008. Although the crash had affected Britain less severely, the longer-term legacy appeared to be a slow-motion version of the scenes I had witnessed in Dublin of 2010.

I had come to Coventry because of a record label, 2 Tone, and its most famous band, The Specials, a multiracial seven-piece whose music took the laid-back swing of Jamaican ska and reinforced it with the steely urgency of punk. 2 Tone had been the centrepiece of Coventry's campaign to become UK City of Culture 2021, the title the city had been awarded on the night I left Hull. The Specials' crowning achievement was their final single, 'Ghost Town', a stark lyrical depiction of the destruction wrought by deindustrialisation, a haunted and distorted regional British reggae recorded by a band on the verge of break-up. Rather than being a cultural remnant of the past that could be looked to with nostalgia, the song continued to feel uncannily relevant.

From the job centre I walked through a gap beneath a building into a small square that was surrounded by squat two-storey buildings containing sandwich shops, greengrocers, mobile phone stores, travel agents and betting shops. A kidney-shaped canopy sat on pillars next to a seating area surrounded by shrubbery. Above the adjoining street stood two tall and forbidding concrete towers linked together by a central glass reservation. The towers, known as Coventry Point, were scheduled to be pulled down and replaced with a new department store, new retail units and a hotel and cinema in the next few years, a sign of the attempts underway to modernise the post-war streetscape. The streets of the precinct aren't as oppressive as they might have been, in part because of their scale – they're relatively narrow, and designed not for cars, but for pedestrians. They're also softened by the presence of rows of mature trees running along their centre.

A little further along the street is Coventry's Central Library which was once the Locarno, opened in 1960 in the newly constructed city centre as one of a chain of ballrooms owned by the

Mecca agency. It's a peculiar building, reached by climbing a couple of flights of stairs, which open on to a large main room. In this, it's slightly different from the original Locarno, which was accessed by climbing a staircase up a glass tower located in the centre of the street. The clean lines of its sleek modernism anticipated by a couple of years a similar glass box, Coventry's new station, which opened in 1962. Once you reached the top of the staircase you followed a bridge across to the main building, and, I assume, checked your coat and went looking for a drink. (The glass tower and bridge have been removed, replaced with the new staircase that I climbed.) Photos from the early sixties show a rainswept modernist external scene that you can imagine being soundtracked by Joy Division or some of Bowie's Berlin-era instrumentals, whereas photos from inside the building show a resolutely traditional scene: ballroom dancing competitions – the men in black tie, the women in ball gowns – taking place to the sound of a big band. Looking at the pictures now there appears to be a disconnect between the future that was implied by the architecture and the traditional use to which it was put, like finding out that an incidence of Morris dancing took place during one of the moon landings.

The Locarno played an important part in the evolution of the local music scene, and a surprising role in the mid-career success of a rock 'n' roll trailblazer. On 3 February 1972 the Lanchester Arts Festival hosted Chuck Berry, along with Slade and a comedian called Uncle Dirty. The young rock critic Charles Shaar Murray was there to cover the concert for *Cream* magazine, a short-lived alternative monthly. 'The sign by the door of the Coventry Locarno read "No Jeans. No Leather Jackets. Gentlemen must wear collar and tie",' he wrote. The dress code was temporarily waived by the dinner-jacketed doormen guarding the venue's entrance. Berry took to the stage and led the crowd, who had been harangued by Slade for not dancing, in a set of his hits. Murray was excited. Cover versions by The Beatles and The Rolling Stones back in 1963 had encouraged him to investigate Berry's originals. By the time of the concert, Murray was a certified fan. 'Three, four or so feet away was Chuck Berry with his clean cherry red Gibson and his psychedelic satin shirt and his immaculate white trousers and his two-tone sharpie shoes,' Murray wrote. When Berry reached 'Roll Over Beethoven', he let the crowd take over the singing. 'We sang loud enough to wreck the tapes being made for a live album,' Murray wrote. To conclude the gig, Berry invited the crowd to take part in what Murray called 'a singalong piece of sexual hokum' called 'My Ding-A-Ling'.[2]

As Murray pointed out, the concert was being recorded for release – three songs from the gig would make up the B-side of *The London Chuck Berry Sessions* LP, issued in October 1972. The album was preceded by the release of an edited version of the live 'My Ding-A-Ling', which became a huge hit, getting to number one in the UK and America, Berry's only single to top the charts. It's difficult to know whether to be horrified or amused by the fact that Berry, whose own songwriting was a model of wit and sophistication that perfectly suited the consumerist boom years of the fifties and sixties, finally reached number one with a risqué tune that he didn't even write himself. (It was written by Dave Bartholomew, although arranged by and credited to Berry, who had rewritten it as 'My Tambourine', but switched back to lyrics that were much closer to the original for the Locarno performance. It's not clear if Berry ever made a royalty arrangement with the songwriter.) Nevertheless, the success of the song drove up Berry's fee and created a huge demand for his appearances. In Berry's autobiography, he meticulously records the sales of the single, as per his royalty statement in December

1972, as 1,295,075 copies, and claims that he received a cheque for a quarter of a million dollars as a result. 'Everybody wanted it,' Berry wrote of the single, 'with the exception of some person in England named, I believe, Mary Whitehouse, who wanted it banned.'[3]

Berry's single wouldn't be the last number one record to be associated with the Coventry Locarno. The Specials' first number one, the *Too Much Too Young* EP, had on its B-side three songs recorded in Tiffany's Coventry, as the Locarno had by then been renamed. (The rear of the record sleeve reproduced a *Coventry Evening Telegraph* article about the gig that quoted singer Terry Hall's father, who worked at Coventry's Rolls-Royce plant: 'I've seen him on television, but it was never as exciting as this,' Mr Hall said.) Their second number one, the 'Ghost Town' single, had on its flip side a fatalistic and bleakly hilarious song by Terry Hall called 'Friday Night, Saturday Morning'. Its lyrics traced with notable ambivalence a drunken and desperate journey through Coventry's nightlife, including a trip to the Locarno, where the inebriated protagonist buys a drink and pulls a chair up to the side of the dance floor. There was, too, an element of nostalgia involved: when the song was recorded the Locarno was about to shut down. The lyrics of 'Ghost Town', which on first listen seem universal and unspecific, are changed by their context. Given the band's Coventry roots, and the demise of the Locarno, it feels like the band have written about the city as a microcosm of wider British industrial decline. But they were also drawing on what they had seen in other cities. 'We were touring, so we saw a lot of it. Liverpool and Glasgow were particularly bad. The overall sense I wanted to convey was impending doom,' said the writer of the song, keyboard player Jerry Dammers.[4]

*

Leaving the old Locarno site at the Central Library, I walked further along the pedestrianised area and emerged on Corporation Street, a curving thoroughfare lined with a block of post-war office buildings that were now used as student housing. The offices of the *Coventry Evening Telegraph* were located at one end of the block, but there were few shops, and the street was quiet when compared to the lively, packed precinct. A little up the road you could find, slotted among the car parks and office buildings, a fragment of what this area of Coventry might have been like before the bombing. A red sandstone church building, formerly part of the fourteenth-century hospital of St John the Baptist, sat across the road from a mock-Tudor-fronted pub that was built in the interwar years and had recently been renamed after the poet Philip Larkin. Along one side of an adjoining street, The Burges, is an uneven row of redbrick buildings through which an arch gives access to a back lane. These buildings are reminders of the city's previous form, a city that's a little easier to visualise when you walk among the fragments surrounding its post-war centre – the towers tucked behind pubs and restaurants, and the ruined remnants of medieval priories.

Not far from the red sandstone church is the Coventry Transport Museum, a cavernous maze of warehouses containing bicycles, cars and trucks manufactured in the city over the years. A whole wing is devoted to vehicles manufactured by Jaguar, the luxury car company whose headquarters are located on the edge of the city. (Manufacturing was moved from Coventry's Browns Lane plant to Castle Bromwich in Birmingham, but that too will close, with operations to be concentrated in Halewood, Liverpool.) Walking through the museum might make you feel nostalgic not just for the days of British-made shiny motorcars and matt green military vehicles (or, in my case, the BMX bikes from my childhood) but also for the society that produced them.

I walked through a room in the museum that attempts to reproduce something of the atmosphere of Coventry during the war: a vintage car sits askew in a hole surrounded by broken pavement while smoky vapour and an odour that's similar to burning rubber hang in the air. The next room is fitted out to resemble the offices of the post-war planners who rebuilt the bomb-ravaged city. A map of the city centre encircled by a red ring-road lies on a desk surrounded by scattered photographs and plans for pristine, modernist buildings. The map is titled 'THE FUTURE COVENTRY', and from where I stood it seemed to resemble the city I had just walked through. So complete had been the destruction that it offered what was essentially a blank canvas for the construction of a new city.

That new city was informed by the assumption that urban planning should be centred around the motor vehicle, a view that fitted car-manufacturing Coventry perfectly. The narrow lanes of the medieval city were replaced with broad streets linked to a ring-road that circled the centre. There was a pedestrian shopping quarter, certainly, but if you were on foot it wasn't long before you found yourself channelled into forbidding concrete underpasses, or crossing at a motorway off-ramp. Before the war, Coventry's City Architect's Department, under Donald Gibson, had developed proposals ('Coventry of Tomorrow') for the future of the city. After the air raids, implementing the plans became imperative: only thirty-five of 975 buildings in the city centre were unharmed by the destruction. Building began in 1948, stretching out to the suburbs, where public buildings, schools and housing estates were constructed. Many of the architects working for the council would later take up prominent and influential roles in other cities, including Wilf Burns, who drew up the plans for Newcastle's redevelopment in the sixties.[5]

It was new architecture for a growing city. The population of

Coventry had more than doubled between 1921 and 1951, from 114,197 to 260,285, as workers moved to the city to take up jobs in its automobile and aerospace factories. By the mid-sixties, 45,000 people in Coventry worked in the car industry.[6] Coventry in the mid-twentieth century, therefore, was a prosperous and growing city with well-paid jobs in thriving industries and a new city centre in which to spend your leisure time. (When the giddy, flugelhorn-enhanced middle eight of The Specials' 'Ghost Town' references the good old days of the boomtown, it's hard not to think of this period of Coventry's history, the era in which the band members were born.) While the majority of those who migrated to the city to take up industrial jobs were from elsewhere in Britain, a good number were Irish, or had come from Commonwealth countries, mainly from India and Pakistan. 'I grew up in an environment where you didn't really know where you were from,' Terry Hall said in a *Guardian* interview in 2003. 'Coventry was built on immigrants because it was an industrial city looking for cheap labour. I don't think it's an accident that a group like the Specials came out of that.'[7]

Neville Staple's father had moved from Jamaica to Rugby, a town not far from Coventry, where he worked in a cement factory before going on to take a job at the Ford plant in Leamington. 'He was cheap, keen to work, and insecure in his new life,' Staple writes. Like many, his father found that 'the mother country had not extended the warm embrace he had been expecting'.[8] The young Staple began to attend under-18 discos on Saturday mornings in the Locarno, organised by Pete Waterman, a Coventry-born DJ employed by Mecca, the company that owned and ran the ballroom. Waterman described Staple as a 'cheeky West Indian who had a twinkle in his eye [and] was full of mischief'. He encouraged him to perform, bringing Staple onstage to 'toast' – a reggae style of rhythmic talking or chanting over a record – or to dance, and often took the young man's advice on suitable records to play. In 1973, Waterman opened Soul Hole Records under a boutique on Hales Road, and Staple would go to the shop to hang out, listening to music and drinking free coffee. Increasingly, Waterman was importing rare soul and reggae and playing it at the Locarno. 'To say that Pete Waterman had his finger on the pulse of what was going on in Kingston would be putting it mildly,' Staple wrote of Waterman's interest in reggae. 'His musical antennae were finely tuned to everything that was coming out of my home country.'[9]

In the late 1970s, Staple, who had been sent to borstal for burglary as a teenager, began to attend the Holyhead Road Youth Club. The youth club, which had been funded by sponsorship from Cadbury, was located in a basement and run by Ray King, a local singer who had enjoyed success in the sixties. Staple, who was by now dressing in a sharp rude boy style of tonic suit and pork-pie hat, had become interested in the sound system scene in Britain, and had first experienced it in Rugby, where his cousin Alvin had his own sound system, called the Messenger. Sound systems had originated in West Kingston in Jamaica in the late forties, and existed in most British cities with a significant Afro-Caribbean population – London, Leicester, Huddersfield, Bristol. DJs would drag their huge speakers and valve amplifiers to parties, or they would rent halls in which two sound systems would compete in 'battles'. Sometimes a friend of the DJ would 'toast' over the record, as Staple sometimes did at his cousin's parties. Staple was keen to have his own system, and he saw the Holyhead Road Youth Club as his opportunity. Persuading King to buy the equipment using some of the money from the Cadbury sponsorship, Staple set up the resident sound system for the youth club. He named it Jah Baddis. Teenagers from across the Midlands were drawn to the club as a result, and Staple continually searched for new sounds to keep them happy, travelling to London and the St Paul's area of Bristol, where in the Bamboo Club he first met the great Jamaican ska trombonist Rico Rodriguez.[10] One day, he opened a door in the youth club and found a band rehearsing. 'There was a bit of reggae, a bit of punk, and a guy with a deadpan vocal style,' he wrote.[11] At the time, the band was known as The Automatics, but they later became The Specials.

I had walked from the transport museum through the ruined foundations of a priory, among which teenagers furtively smoked cannabis, to Coventry Cathedral. The cathedral is an incredible spectacle, a work of both commemoration and of hope. The ruins of the fourteenth-century St Michael's cathedral, bombed during the war, sit alongside its vast, modernist replacement. Strolling around the roofless ruins of the old cathedral, I couldn't help noticing in some of the windows the remnants of stained glass that had been melted by the heat of the bombing. It was obvious that this was intended as a site of peace and forgiveness, of post-war reconciliation. A canopy linked the old cathedral to the new one, and inside the modern Coventry Cathedral the effect was overwhelming: the volumes of space above you, the sheer scale of the eighty-foot-tall stained-glass windows, and the complexity of the ribbed concrete and wooden slatted ceiling. My first few minutes in the building were spent staring upwards.

In 1965, Horace Dammers was appointed as canon and director of studies at the cathedral. Dammers had previously been a chaplain and lecturer in St John's College, Palayamkottai in South India, a posting on which he was accompanied by his wife Brenda, and their son Jeremy was born in India on 22 May 1955. Known as Jerry, he attended the King Henry VIII school in Coventry, before becoming an art student at Lanchester

261

Polytechnic (now Coventry University) during which time he played in a soul band led by Ray King, later forming his own band with fellow art student Horace Panter.

Adopted at the age of six weeks, Panter was brought up in Kettering, Northamptonshire, in a middle-class family. He played bass in some short-lived bands as a teenager before moving to Coventry to take up a place studying Fine Art at Lanchester Poly, where he first encountered Dammers. 'I remember Jerry in tartan trousers, grown-out mod haircut, complete with sideburns, walking into the art studios on the fifth floor, singing "I shot the sheriff" at the top of his voice,' Panter wrote.[12] It was while Panter was in Breaker, a funk and soul band that often played working men's clubs in the North – 'Newcastle upon Tyne, Sunderland and Middlesbrough, the graveyard of light entertainment' – that Dammers approached him to join a new band, which was influenced by reggae.[13] A third member of the group, rhythm guitarist Lynval Golding, who had moved to Gloucester from Jamaica aged eight, showed Panter how to play reggae bass lines. Golding was the first black person Panter had ever met. They brought in Silverton Hutchinson, a drummer originally from Barbados, and Tim Strickland, who worked at the Virgin record shop, and played their first gig, as The Hybrids, at the Heath Hotel on Foleshill Road in October 1977. Already they had written songs that would form the backbone of The Specials' first, self-titled, album: 'Do The Dog', 'Little Bitch', '(Dawning of A) New Era'. All around Coventry people were picking up guitars and forming punk bands, two of which were Roddy Radiation and the Wild Boys, and The Squad, featuring the deadpan singer Terry Hall. Both became members of the newly christened The Automatics. It was around this time that Neville Staple stumbled on them rehearsing in the Holyhead Road Youth Club. Becoming their roadie at first, he later joined the band as a vocalist, toasting over their songs as he had over the records played on the city's sound systems. Staple saw the connection between punk and ska. 'For black kids, the punk attitude was something that infected us and we understood where that anger was coming from. After all, if white kids' lives were shit, ours were doubly shit.'[14] Ska often had a political element – a vocalist would 'sing about everyday issues in a matter-of-fact manner [. . .] like a musical newspaper', Staple wrote.[15] In drawing from these two influences, The Specials were combining the anger of punk with the political commentary of ska.

Ska originated in Jamaica in the late 1950s, an approximation of American rhythm and blues. It reputedly drew its name from the characteristic 'ska' sound of the rhythm guitar's upstroke on the afterbeat, which emphasised the choppiness of the music, and lending it an additional urgency. Beyond Jamaica, the music was particularly popular in Britain, where, in the early sixties, Jamaican-owned sound systems began to play ska instead of the American jazz, R&B and calypso they had relied on up until then. Emil Shalit, the owner of Calypso label Melodisc, launched a subsidiary label, Blue Beat, making UK rights deals with Jamaican ska artists and labels, and recording sessions with many of those artists in London. 'Suddenly ska became the official soundtrack of black London,' music journalist Lloyd Bradley wrote.[16] The volume of demand for ska was huge: the singer and producer Prince Buster, originator of the ska afterbeat – the second half of a musical beat that would often be punctuated by a stab of brass or guitar upstroke – released over six hundred singles in Britain between 1962 and 1967, and his tours were packed with Jamaicans and white mods.[17] When The Specials tried to combine punk with reggae, they were drawn to ska – the sped-up bluesy R&B of punk seemed to mesh better with the higher-octane reggae subgenre of ska. (Dammers had been a young mod in the 1960s.) Sonically and lyrically, they were drawn to Prince Buster in particular, whose character-filled songs embodied the kind of kitchen sink drama that The Specials would emulate. Indeed, their debut single 'Gangsters' drew on the riff of his song 'Al Capone'.

Behind the formation of The Specials, and the 2 Tone label, founded by Specials member Jerry Dammers in 1979, was an explicitly anti-racist ethos. This ethos was, I think, an accurate reflection of the multicultural milieu Dammers found himself working in as a musician in Coventry. But it was also, I believe, drawn from a deeper strain of idealism. Simon Reynolds, in his peerless post-punk overview *Rip It Up And Start Again*, calls Dammers the 'rebellious son of a clergyman'.[18] But perhaps his pop vision was merely a new take on the family business. As canon of the cathedral, his father had worked for peace, bringing a cross made from nails retrieved from the ruined cathedral to Northern Ireland at an early stage in the Troubles. He had also worked with immigrant communities in the city and built relations with peace groups, and was a life-long Labour Party member and a campaigner for nuclear disarmament. As I had walked around the cathedral it was impossible to avoid the fact that a symbol of hope had been built from the ruins of war. Horace Dammers' story bore comparison with that of the building in which he worked. Severely injured during the Second World War at the battle of Monte Cassino, he found himself lying on a stretcher alongside a German soldier who had lost his family in the RAF bombing of Hamburg. Seeing the bible that Dammers was reading, the German said that the book had brought him comfort after their deaths.[19] War had planted in Dammers the desire for an enduring peace, one that could be secured only through relentless activism. Jerry Dammers' vision for his band and label was motivated by an idealism that was certainly reminiscent of his father's.

In an interview, Dammers described racism as 'like some kind of mental illness, like fear of spiders'.[20] His label 2 Tone, and its bands, demonstrated the logic of multi-ethnicity. The label's artwork purposefully limited its palette, as if to make a wider point: a black and white check stripe ran across the centre of the record against which leaned a stylised rude boy in tight-fitting suit, slip-on shoes, sunglasses and a pork-pie hat. A large number 2 sat neatly atop the word 'TONE'. The figure was nicknamed Walt Jabsco, and based on an image of reggae icon Peter Tosh. 2 Tone's anti-racist implications were clear, especially when combined with the line-up of the label's bands: The Specials, The Beat, from Birmingham's multi-ethnic Handsworth, and The Selecter, who boasted a mainly black line-up that included the singer Pauline Black, who had been training as an NHS radiographer before the band's success. The bands adopted a mod style of tight suits, pork-pie hats and brogues that was itself drawn from black rude boy fashion.

By early 1979, The Specials had gone through a couple of managers, including the former Locarno DJ Pete Waterman, all the while writing songs and improving as a live act. They ended up sleeping in rehearsal rooms in London's Camden Town while being managed by The Clash's Bernie Rhodes, before being sent on a disastrous tour to France that became the subject of their debut single, 'Gangsters'. After dismissing Rhodes, they returned to Coventry and recorded the song in the city's Horizon Studios in January 1979. Lacking a suitable B-side, they decided to use an instrumental that had been recorded by their friend Neol Davies and new Specials drummer John Bradbury in producer Roger Lomas's garden shed. The instrumental was titled 'The Selecter', and credited to an artist of the same name, but it would be another six months before Davies assembled a full band.

The record's label incorporated what would become iconic

2 Tone imagery, while the sleeve was a simpler affair: a generic white sleeve stamped with the names of the artists. The band had ordered two rubber stamps with which to imprint the band names, so that the sleeve read: 'The Special AKA: Gangsters VS The Selecter'. Panter chose 'versus' as his way of paying tribute to a poster he had seen advertising competing reggae sound systems. Using cardboard sleeves supplied by John Bradbury from his workplace, the Virgin record shop, Panter and Terry Hall stamped the 1500 record sleeves over the course of a single day.[21] Rough Trade distributed the first run, then took over the pressing. The song was played relentlessly by John Peel on his Radio 1 show and praised by Elvis Costello. In the month after the May 1979 release of the single, the band enjoyed music press attention, including making the front cover of the *Melody Maker* and an interview in the *NME*. Their new manager, Rick Rogers, fielded approaches from numerous major labels, but the band signed with Chrysalis Records, a British independent label founded in 1968 that had begun to diversify into new wave and punk by signing Generation X and licensing American band Blondie. The signing took place on 8 June, barely a month after they had independently released 'Gangsters'. Their records would still be released under the 2 Tone imprint, but would be marketed by Chrysalis. A clause in the contract allowed 2 Tone to release up to ten singles by other bands through Chrysalis, with a budget of £1000 per record.[22] After an agreement between Chrysalis and Rough Trade for 'Gangsters', the single went to number 6 in the charts.

Part of what made 2 Tone so attractive to record labels was that it had all the appearances of arriving fully formed. It had a distinct identity on the sleeve, on record and onstage. 'We sat up in Coventry thinking of ourselves as the UK's Tamla-Motown,' Panter wrote. 'To make a "label-sound" like that was our dream

– to hear a tune and immediately be able to say, "That's a 2 Tone record/band".'[23] At first there was only one 2 Tone band – after all, the label had been created to put out The Specials' first single – but soon there were many more.

The runaway success of 'Gangsters' had a direct effect on the band who supplied the B-side: The Selecter quickly went from fiction to fact. They recruited a lead singer, Pauline Black, a mixed-race child who had grown up in Essex having been adopted by a white working-class family as an infant. She had moved to Coventry to attend Lanchester Poly but quit to work full-time in the hospital. During this period she began to perform as a singer in a folk club that was held in the back room of a local pub, initially doing cover versions of Bob Dylan songs, but later writing her own material. 'I led a double life,' she wrote. 'By day I was mild-mannered Pauline, the hospital radiographer, in a fetching white uniform and matching clogs, and by night I was Pauline the singer/guitarist, clad in a yellow linen shirt and brown corduroy dungarees.'[24] She met a black politics student, Lawton Brown, with whom she discussed politics and black identity, and listened to reggae. 'Lawton was my conduit into Coventry's black community,' she wrote.[25] They went to see the local reggae band Hardtop 22 and began to collaborate on songwriting. This collaboration led to them assembling a reggae band that included drummer Silverton Hutchinson, who had recently been replaced as The Specials' drummer by John Bradbury. At one rehearsal, Lynval Golding, of The Specials, 'a slick, bespectacled young black guy sporting a natty porkpie hat', turned up.[26] Golding suggested to Black that she meet friends of his who were looking for a lead singer, and the following evening she went to a house in the Hillfields area of the city to meet them. Crammed inside the narrow house on Adderley Street, rolling joints and listening to a Bob Marley record, were the group of people who would become The Selecter: Neol Davies, Desmond Brown, Charley Anderson, Compton Amanor, Arthur 'Gaps' Hendrickson and Charley 'Aitch' Bembridge. With Black's addition to the line-up they had one more member, bringing the total to seven. Neol Davies took the Bob Marley record off the red Dansette and put on the B-side of 'Gangsters', then played it again. The B-side had been played by John Peel, thinking it was also the work of The Specials. Davies had phoned Peel to correct him. At the end of the night, Davies turned to the group of people he had assembled: 'I need a band to build on the success of my single,' he said.[27] It was July 1979, and the instrumental B-side of a Specials single that would soon break the Top 10 now had a band to go with it.

2 Tone, newly bankrolled by Chrysalis, made other additions to their roster. They issued a single by the London ska band Madness – 'The Prince', a tribute to Prince Buster. It was followed up by a single by The Selecter, 'On My Radio', that made it to number 8 in the UK charts. Meanwhile, The Specials had embarked on a punishing schedule of recording and touring that would eventually lead to their premature demise. They had set up a two-month club tour that coincided with the release of 'Gangsters', during which Elvis Costello often turned up, standing near the front. Once that was over, they booked a 2 Tone package tour for the autumn – playing forty dates with Madness and The Selecter. It was now August. Not long after appearing on *Top of the Pops* to mime to their hit single they went to the cramped basement TW Studios in Fulham to record their first album, with Elvis Costello as producer.

The Specials' songs were observational, sardonic, and in a realist mode. They reflected the harsh realities of economically straitened and politically cruel times. They sang about teenage mothers and tacky nightclubs, and delivered tough dispatches from mean streets haunted by far-right thugs. The connection between the Jamaican ska form and their own post-punk version was reinforced by a scattering of cover versions across their debut LP, and the use of Rico Rodriguez, the trombone player Staple had seen on one of his trips to Bristol's St Paul's district. It was the product of a band who had perfected their songs and their performance on the road and was essentially recorded live in the studio by a fan who didn't see the point in tinkering too much with the sound. It still jumps out of the speakers. At times their social observation puts the listener in mind of the gentler-sounding Kinks – an influence that would become a little more pronounced on the second album. But the tough, prescriptive lyrical style adopted by the band perfectly fits the urgency of their punk-ska hybrid. *The Specials* was a political album you could dance to, made by a multiracial band who played to multiracial audiences. Terry Hall was right: Coventry's use of cheap immigrant labour drawn from around the world created the multicultural context from which The Specials emerged. Their musical influences were drawn from the mix of cultures that industry drew to the city, and, as those industries began to decline, their fate would become the theme of the band's final and biggest hit.

By the time the band's debut album was released in October 1979, the 2 Tone package tour was underway, and on 8 November The Specials, Madness and The Selecter appeared on a single edition of *Top of the Pops*. Later that month The Beat's debut single reached the charts. The vision of 2 Tone as a Coventry Motown was being realised.

Although 2 Tone was a symbolically anti-racist label, the 2 Tone look intersected with that of mods and skinheads – the suits, the Fred Perry shirts, the loafers and the pork-pie hats. These subcultures overlapped in style, but not necessarily in terms of politics. An ever-expanding group of far-right ska fans would turn up at gigs, especially those featuring the all-white Madness. Writing about 2 Tone in his 1987 book *Cut 'n' Mix*, the sociologist Dick Hebdige believed that the symbolic anti-racism of the early years of the label – multiracial bands, the black and white imagery – wasn't explicit enough. The bands 'refused to pronounce the "correct", "responsible" line on race', Hebdige wrote; they believed instead that the anti-racism of their stance was self-evident, that 'the multiracial message could be *inferred* by a broadly sympathetic audience'.[28] But there was no guarantee that they were performing to wholly sympathetic audiences and this was confirmed by the bands' growing awareness of a troubling far-right presence at concerts. (The message to black and white working-class youth of 'Doesn't Make It Alright' on their debut album is fairly direct and explicit, but it's possible that far-right ska fans weren't poring over the lyric sheets.) What changed 2 Tone's position was what you might call the mood of the times – a violent shift in the wider social and political context. The racial profiling at work in the police's use of stop-and-search – known as the 'sus law' – had created a climate of discontent and distrust that contributed to riots across England, including in Bristol's St Paul's district in 1980 and, as we have already seen, in Birmingham's Handsworth the following year. The 2 Tone groups became more explicit in their public condemnations of racism, and in June 1981 The Specials organised the Peaceful Protest Against Racism in Coventry's Butts Stadium in response to the stabbing of twenty-year-old Satnam Singh Gill in the city centre two months earlier.

My walk around Coventry led me to the edge of the city centre and under the concrete ring of the motorway, which was suspended on columns above a car park. A fog of exhaust fumes hung in the air. To the right, overlooking the car park and suspended motorway, was the neoclassical former technical college, now scheduled to become apartments. The building already incorporates a Premier Inn hotel. Beside the technical college building was Butts Stadium, the location of The Specials' anti-racism concert in June 1981.

I turned up Albany Road, in search of the flat at number 51 in which Jerry Dammers had lived during the 2 Tone era. Two people, a man and a woman, who seemed to be estate agents – they jangled keys in their hands and wore business suits – were showing a man the property next door, a defunct barber shop in whose window hung a handwritten sign directing would-be customers to an alternative address. The estate agents noticed that I was taking a photo of the building, a two-storey redbrick house with bay windows, and they looked up at the plaque fixed to the strip of redbrick above the sitting-room.

51 ALBANY ROAD
The birthplace
of 2-Tone
The ska phenomenon
was created
here by Jerry Dammers,
The Specials and
The Selecter
It also served as the HQ for the
iconic 2-Tone Record label

Jerry Dammers' vision, of a Coventry hit factory pumping out records that shared a sound and embodied a deeper anti-racist ethos, was realised so brilliantly so early on that it didn't allow much time or space to develop further. And there was the fact that not all 2 Tone bands bought wholly into that vision, that the label was just a means to an end for some, who moved on to other record companies fairly quickly. Madness released only one single on 2 Tone before moving to Stiff Records. The Beat moved on too, and The Selecter's time on the label was limited to one LP, recorded in late 1979 and released in January 1980.

The Specials' success was so all-engulfing that it destroyed them. Their American tour in early 1980 pushed them to breaking point, halting their momentum and that of their record label. Dammers seemed overwhelmed. The 2 Tone movement had become demanding and uncontrollable, a spin-off industry only tangentially connected to the label, of knock-off badges and cheap chequer. Ska was a style that could be easily copied, a fashion that could be co-opted. The cartoony Bad Manners, led by the gurning Buster Bloodvessel, whose trademark move was sticking out his tongue, were beginning to turn up on children's TV programmes, and Madness were in the process of becoming a Great British Pop Band, a cheery combination of music hall nostalgia and significantly diluted rude boy skank that left the politics aside and settled on lyrical evocations of the sentimental joys of everyday life. 'It's a monster,' Dammers confessed in 1980. 'Frankenstein's monster. I haven't had a week off for the past two years. I've been living out of a suitcase like some sort of tramp.'[29]

The exasperation with how quickly ska had become uniform presented a challenge to Dammers. How should the next Specials album sound? The exhausted band returned to Coventry to record *More Specials* at Horizon Studios, where they had recorded the 'Gangsters' single a year or so before, upstairs in an old coach house near the station. According to Horace Panter, different members were pulling in different directions: guitarist Roddy Radiation wanted the band to go rockabilly, while

Dammers was interested in an easy listening, muzak style. The sessions for the album were interrupted by other commitments – a whirlwind trip to New York to appear on *Saturday Night Live*, a journalist arriving at the studios to interview them – and the band was affected by a growing fractiousness among its members. Although songwriting duties were shared out, Dammers produced and arranged, adding verses and chords to songs. He 'masterminded the sessions', Panter wrote.[30]

I walked from Dammers' flat through a park that ran alongside the railway, crossing a footbridge that led to a shopping centre, which had been constructed where Horizon Studios had stood. *More Specials* was regarded sceptically by many of the band members who made it, and yet it yielded songs that pointed a way out of the hybrid of punk and ska that they had pioneered. Dammers' interest in synthesisers had added a layer of theremin-like spookiness to the record, particularly 'Man at C&A' and Terry Hall's sarcastically observational 'Stereotype', accompanied by mariachi horns and Spanish guitar. And the band had slowed down, moved on from ska towards a down-beat reggae that hinted at what was to come next from the band.

I imagine the 'Ghost Town' single as a three-song concept album. On *More Specials* the band had struggled to process the mix of influences and maintain their enthusiasm, nevertheless producing a compelling document of the band's evolution. There were many directions that the band could have taken from there, a variety of blueprints for its potential future. But there was a sense of things ending, of there being no future for the band, and this is made explicit in the resigned, melancholic mood of 'Ghost Town', simultaneously a state-of-the-nation address and an epitaph for a band on the brink of destruction. It was a dizzying artistic high made by a band at its lowest point. The disorder of a year before had turned to fatalism. The

Specials were on the verge of break-up, as Hall, Golding and Staple were about to leave to form Fun Boy Three. This was the end. The Specials would return without that trio as The Special AKA, a moniker they had used on their rubber-stamped debut single but not since. The name change was an admission that the original band was no more. There wasn't enough time to make an album, so a three-track EP would have to do, each track capturing a different aspect of the contemporary moment.

'Ghost Town' was suffused with melancholy, but if you flipped the disc and played the first song on the B-side, disgust was evident. 'Why?' was a direct response to an attack by National Front thugs on Lynval Golding at a club in London during the summer of 1980. Addressed to his attackers, the song questions them on their motives for injuring him, dismissing them as un-thinking followers of the National Front. The dance floor had been an important site in the history of The Specials, from the youth discos at the Locarno ballroom to the sound systems at the Holyhead Road Youth Club, up to the band's joyful per-formances in clubs around the country and across the world, playing political music that a multiracial audience could dance to. Now, the dance floor was returned to as a site of political contestation and disenchantment, violence and despair. You could no longer assume that you were playing to a like-minded audience who didn't want to pick-on someone because of the colour of their skin. The attack on Golding, and the increasingly obvious far-right presence at Specials gigs, made this difficult to ignore. Too much fighting on the dance floor.

I had earlier passed the old Locarno building that now houses the Central Library. I decided to return there, climbing the stairs to the second floor, where a doorway opens into the main room, which is cheerily functional in the manner of libraries that date from the 1980s. Looking out across the rooftops from the window at the top of the stairs, I thought again about 'Friday Night, Saturday Morning', the Terry Hall-penned song that concludes the EP. Its walking bass line, which appears to reference the Otis Redding sea-traffic observation classic '(Sittin' on) the Dock of the Bay', is soon joined by the familiar click of ska guitar and Dammers' Hammond organ chords. Later a spacy synth line joins in to emphasise the peculiarly unworldly detachment of the narrator. Having evoked a boozy night out in the Locarno – renamed Tiffany's by then and about to shut down – Hall announces that it's time to leave, calling it a 'paradise'. On the surface this is just classic Hall sarcasm, but I prefer to think of it as an unintentionally heartfelt and nostalgic tribute to a venue that had been so important to the band, its demise a microcosm of the wider decline of Coventry, whose plight mirrored that of other regional British industrial towns and cities. 'Ghost Town' was every town, but most of all it was their home town, where everything started and ended on the dance floor.

11.
BRISTOL

Those who know me well are aware of my fear of heights so won't be surprised that when I walked the narrow footpath along the edge of Bristol's Clifton suspension bridge I wasn't able to take in much of what I saw. To the east were sheer cliffs dropping to the muddy River Avon. To the west was . . . well, I wasn't sure what was there until I reached its other end, which turned out to be the location of a visitors' centre in which a semi-transparent cut-out Isambard Kingdom Brunel stood, hands shoved in his pockets, looking less than impressed to be surrounded by so many Bristol-themed souvenirs and interpretive heritage boards.

I had come to Bristol because of trip-hop, that strangely named genre – perhaps dub-hop might be a better term – that had emerged from the city's sound-system scene, particularly the area of St Paul's near the city centre, and from an assortment of hip-hop-obsessed kids who had initially called their crew The Wild Bunch. After the departure of a couple of members The Wild Bunch became Massive Attack, and their sound evolved, becoming a glacially paced, murky dub that frequently incorporated soulful vocals and whispered rapping. Once trip-hop became a style it was easily appropriated by pop acts, but the most compelling records of that ilk from that era were produced by musicians from Bristol, and many of those musicians knew each other. They had played in bands together, or been part of a sound system, or would meet up at small clubs in which they DJed, spinning the hip-hop, post-punk, reggae and soul that would eventually fuse in the records they made themselves. Bristol was a world unto itself, visiting journalists from London would note, emphasising both its exotic normality – these people don't act like pop stars! – and its laid-back atmosphere.

The graffiti artist Goldie, who would later become a star of the British Jungle music scene, had been a visitor to Bristol in the late eighties. He had first encountered The Wild Bunch's Robert Del Naja, who was also a graffiti artist, in 1987 during their participation in Dick Fontaine's documentary *Bombin'*. Goldie would often drive from his home in Wolverhampton to attend Wild Bunch club nights. 'It was almost as if hip-hop culture had dropped like a glass in England, and the glass had shattered into different pieces,' he wrote. 'Manchester had the breaking [breakdancing], Bristol had the parties, London had the breaking and a few of the parties, Birmingham and London had the graffiti.'[1]

The geography of hip-hop culture closely echoed the geography of reggae that The Specials' Neville Staple had followed during the time he spent running a sound system, when he had travelled to Bristol's St Paul's district to visit the Bamboo Club. 'The black community in St Paul's felt so in control of its own destiny' that it left Staple and his friend 'overwhelmed. There was an utterly different feel to the place, one I had never experienced before.'[2] The Bamboo Club had been opened in 1966 by Tony and Lalel Bullimore on St Paul's Street. The Bullimores were a mixed-race couple – Tony was a white Englishman and Lalel was a black Jamaican woman – who had encountered discrimination in pubs and clubs in the city, so decided to open a venue that would cater for the St Paul's West Indian community. The club played host to numerous reggae and soul artists, including Desmond Dekker, Jimmy Cliff, Bob Marley, The Ronettes, Percy Sledge and Ben E. King, while sound systems were a regular feature. The club burned down on 18 December 1977, a few days before it was due to host The Sex Pistols, and punk bands such as Wire and Siouxsie and the Banshees were scheduled to appear soon afterwards. A 1977 flyer advertising the forthcoming gigs calls the Bamboo Club 'The New Wave Venue'. Reggae, soul, sound systems, punk: the club's booking policy appears now to be a prelude to the eclecticism of Bristol artists such as Massive Attack and Tricky.

St Paul's is directly north-east of Bristol city centre, just off the hip Stokes Croft. One of the city's earliest suburbs, and a fashionable one in the eighteenth century, by the nineteenth century St Paul's housed an industrial population who worked in nearby workshops and factories. The bombing of the area during the Second World War and a general decline in its housing stock meant that it was primarily desirable only to those who had few other options, especially West Indian and Irish immigrants drawn to the city for work who had elsewhere encountered landlords unwilling to rent properties to them. As a result, St Paul's became a centre for black culture in the city. It was a hub of political activity during the 1963 Bristol Bus Boycott, a four-month protest against the Transport and General Workers Union's ban on the employment of non-white workers as members of a bus crew (i.e. as a driver or conductor) by the Bristol Omnibus Company. In 1968 the first St Paul's Carnival was held, an annual celebration of Afro-Caribbean culture that featured local reggae sound systems including, in the 1980s, The Wild Bunch. 'We would set up a big system at the end of Campbell Street and block the road off,' Robert Del Naja told a journalist in 1998. They set up next to a flat that belonged to Daddy G (Grant Marshall), a member of the crew, and drew electricity from there.[3]

Before reaching St Paul's, I walked north along Stokes Croft, past chic coffee shops, a Banksy graffito, a vegan café and an arts hub, before turning east at the intersection with Ashley Road. Stokes Croft is the kind of funky neighbourhood that the hipper guidebooks typically advise you to visit, with lots of tastefully decorated independent stores and a repurposed office building that houses creative businesses, a bar and a restaurant. I followed Ashley Road eastwards, reaching a small triangular park in which stood a bronze statue of Alfred Fagon. His open left hand, in which someone had tucked a bunch of yellow flowers, reached across his body. Fagon had come to England from Jamaica in 1955 while still a teenager, working on the railways then serving in the army, during which time he became the army's middleweight boxing champion, before travelling the country as a calypso singer and settling in St Paul's. His career then became one of a working writer and actor – his plays, which were staged in the Royal Court and filmed for the BBC, drew on his life in St Paul's, while he took roles in popular TV programmes such as *Z-Cars* and *Boon*. When out jogging near his Brixton flat in 1986, he suffered a fatal heart attack, and although they searched his flat the police claimed to be unable to contact friends or loved ones, so he was given a pauper's funeral. His remains were cremated, his ashes spread over a hedge. His death was discovered by those who knew him two weeks later, after he had failed to show up for a meeting at the BBC.[4] It was a grim and lonely end to what had been a full life.

I turned the corner from the park onto Grosvenor Road, which led me back in the direction of Stokes Croft. Alfred Fagon had said that 'the heart of St Paul's is at the corner of Ashley Road and Grosvenor Road', and that's why his friends chose that location to erect his statue. The triangular park pointed towards a crossroads that forms a commercial centre to the neighbourhood: barbers and kebab shops and Asian supermarkets. The commercial properties stretch back towards the beginning of Grosvenor Road, where there's a shop selling hair extensions, small supermarkets and a halal butcher's. I walked along the street for a few minutes, reaching a row of three-storey redbrick flats set back from the road across a patch of grass. Directly opposite the flats was a terrace of two-storey houses in the middle of which was a neatly kept home that had once been the centre of the St Paul's riots. In 1971 the Black and White Café had been opened by the Jamaican-born Bertram Wilks at number 27, and over the years it acquired a reputation (among police, admittedly) as a place of drug dealing and unlicensed alcohol sales. Frequent police raids made it a flashpoint for confrontations with locals, and on 2 April 1980 when twenty or so police descended on the café, crowds grew outside, a police van's windscreen was smashed with a concrete block and another police car was set alight. Wilks was taken away and charged with cannabis possession with intent to supply, while the alcohol on the premises was confiscated. The crowd grew and rioting spread to the surrounding streets, continuing until around midnight, by which point the police had called in reinforcements and set up roadblocks around the perimeter of St Paul's. As with the riots that would occur in black areas across Britain the following year, sustained police discrimination, especially the use of stop and search laws against the black community, helped to create an atmosphere of tension and distrust that drove the unrest. After the riots, the police continued to raid the Black and White Café periodically – a television news report from 1986 shows a line of stern police wearing custodian, bobby-on-the-beat helmets facing down a crowd who had gathered on the green space next to the flats during a raid on the café. When things become violent reinforcements are called in, and riot shields and visored helmets are handed out among police. Watching the footage reminded me of the policing during the same period in Northern Ireland: strong-arm tactics exercised as momentary compensation for the longer-term inability to effectively police a neighbourhood that was characterised by deep economic and racial inequality. The police's approach created a sense within St Paul's of a community under siege, while the café was locally viewed as one of the few social spaces available in the area.[5] Now the rapidly gentrifying area that adjoins St Paul's is sometimes referred to as 'The People's Republic of Stokes Croft' on account of its independent businesses and alternative lifestyles, but it was St Paul's that had to live with the legacy of being a place set unwillingly apart.

By now it was the early evening, and I continued along Grosvenor Road, turning up a side street, where teenagers were queuing for an under-18 drum and bass night at the Lakota nightclub, housed in an old brewery building whose external walls were decorated with graffiti of a Native American woman in tribal dress against a background of comets and shooting stars. The Lakota had been a famous techno club in the nineties, bringing in DJs like Carl Cox, Paul Oakenfold and Todd Terry. Its persistence was impressive: it had been slated for demolition in 2011, but after a public outcry the city council dropped the plans. The Lakota had been taken over by Bentleigh and Martino Burgess, whose parents, Sonia and Denzil, were immigrants from Jamaica. The elder Burgesses had arrived in Bristol in the early sixties and had later become pub landlords, putting on gigs in the back hall of their first property, the Lord Nelson in Barton Hill. In 1983 they opened the Tropic Club in Stokes Croft – now a listed building – staging a mix of live reggae, soul acts and sound systems, a booking policy that was in many ways similar to that of the Bamboo Club. The Wild Bunch had been one of the acts to play the Tropic Club, and the crew had also decorated the club with graffiti during refurbishment after a fire, but the club most associated with them was about a mile's walk away, up the hill towards Clifton.[6]

The next morning, I set out from my hotel along St Augustine's Parade, in the centre of which stands a statue of Edward Colston, the Bristol-born philanthropist and slave trader who had served as the city's MP in the early eighteenth century. Colston looks pensive, as if considering a philosophical conundrum or pondering his offences. The statue, and the many buildings in Bristol that continue to bear his name, are symbols of how the city had profited from slavery. Colston had been a member of the Royal African Company, of which King James II was governor (he had been granted the position by his brother King Charles II while Duke of York and he continued to hold it when he took the throne). The company had been given a monopoly over trade with West Africa, establishing forts along the continent's Atlantic coast, transporting increasing numbers of slaves in the late seventeenth century. Ten years after the overthrow of James II by William of Orange in 1688, the company lost its monopoly, opening the trade with West Africa, and therefore the slave trade, to merchants, who would pay a 10 per cent tariff on goods exported from Africa. The slave trade accelerated, enabling merchants to accrue great wealth. Bristol's elite Society of Merchant Venturers, which had lobbied for an end to the Royal African Company's monopoly, stood to make huge profits. Bristol was poised to profit from a triangular trade in which slavery was a key element – the same ships would transport manufactured goods from Britain to Africa, then take African slaves to America, and bring sugar, tobacco and cotton back to Britain from the new world, before repeating the trip. Half a million or more African slaves were transported by over two thousand Bristol ships, around twenty trips each year, over the course of the eighteenth century, until the trade ended in 1807–8. (The reality of the trade remained largely invisible in the city, as few slaves passed through Bristol, going straight from Africa to America.) The wealth earned from this trade shaped eighteenth- and nineteenth-century Bristol through the activities of the Society of Merchant Venturers, who helped to fund the Clifton suspension bridge, the Great Western Railway and the city's university, among many other projects.

Walking through Bristol, once you have any idea of its history, gives one a contradictory and queasy feeling. On the one hand, it's a beautiful city, one that's not merely a result of its geographical setting on cliffs that sweep steeply down to the river. A wonderful array of Georgian architecture, from terraced townhouses to grand halls and official buildings, conspire with the landscape to lend the city its character. But it's an architectural beauty that was underwritten by the global trade in human beings. Not far from Colston's statue is a venue that's named after him, Colston Hall, which Massive Attack have so far refused to play until it's renamed. (The venue will be renamed in 2020.) I sat for a little while outside Colston Hall, sipping coffee and eating an omelette roll I had bought from the nearby Greggs. Outside the venue sat a luxury tour bus that, from a quick look at the gig listings, I judged to contain Marti Pellow of Wet Wet Wet.

I was on my way from the town centre up towards Clifton, rising in altitude all the time. Not knowing the exact route, I had taken the long way around – if you were heading from Stokes Croft or St Paul's you could follow an alternative route up Jamaica Street that would eventually lead you to the heights of Park Row. I reached a terrace of shops along which was the Chinese restaurant I had been looking for. A door to the right of the restaurant's entrance used to lead down to the tiny basement club, The Dug Out, which had been around as a jazz venue since the sixties. From 1982 onwards, Daddy G was the resident DJ in the club, and he was later joined by the rest of The Wild Bunch, who had a regular night every Wednesday. (When Goldie drove from Wolverhampton to Bristol he was invariably on his way to this club.) A photo taken of The Wild Bunch in The Dug Out shows five people packed behind decks beneath a staircase: Mushroom, Daddy G, Nellee Hooper, Will Wee and 3D (Robert Del Naja). The latter two clutch microphones in their hands, with Will Wee caught in mid-flow. Hooper mans the turntables while Mushroom and Daddy G observe their rapping bandmates. (There was another member not present in the photo, DJ Milo.) The Dug Out's location, on the hill between the multiracial St Paul's and the middle-class Clifton, sitting across the road from the university, ensured a diverse crowd, a melting pot of cultures. This hybridity was reflected in the diversity of music played at the club: reggae, soul, hip-hop and punk. Later the club would add an upstairs video room, in which reggae, hip-hop and punk videos were screened. 'People would go down to Dug Out at nine o'clock at night to watch videos,' Del Naja told *Crack Magazine* in 2012. 'And then by midnight they'd be on the dance floor. [. . .] At that time, you had to go there to meet people that shared your tastes, so the social network was a more physical one.'[7] The area was also home to the independent Revolver record shop, which specialised in reggae. Daddy G worked there – it's where Mushroom first met him – and the idiosyncratic store is memorably described in Richard King's *Original Rockers*.[8]

The importance of physical locations to these music scenes cannot be stressed enough. They provided a place in which people could meet, ideas shared and bands formed. Del Naja's choice of the phrase 'social network' to describe the Bristol scene is telling: the social functions of these spaces have since been largely absorbed by the internet, mirroring the effect the web had on how music is consumed. A scene was created in part by necessity, made up of a chain of social spaces – the record shop, the venue, the bar, the rehearsal room and recording studio – in which the creation and consumption of music was deeply embedded and from which it was seemingly inextricable. But digital technology detached music and social networks from geographically physical space. It made collaboration between musicians who had never met possible, while also globalising music, making it less geographically specific. Suddenly the music scene was everywhere, and nowhere.

One of those who occasionally attended The Dug Out was Mark Stewart, the lead singer of the post-punk band The Pop Group. The Bristol band had drawn on punk and reggae to produce the jerkily funky, politically confrontational albums *Y* and *For How Much Longer Do We Tolerate Mass Murder?* in 1979 and 1980 respectively. After the band split, various members formed the groups Pigbag and Rip, Rig and Panic, who added the Swedish-born vocalist Neneh Cherry to their line-up. Stewart, meanwhile, moved to London and began to work with dub producer Adrian Sherwood's On U label, issuing downtempo dub reggae-derived records that utilised hip-hop-style sampling, under the name Mark Stewart and the Maffia. The textures of Stewart's music from this period – the space allowed for the spare instrumentation, the muted buzz of a distant, reverb-soaked guitar, the overdriven, sinister bass – foreshadow the work of Massive Attack and Tricky. Dub was central in bringing together such a variety of sounds. Dub was a subgenre of Jamaican reggae that typically consisted of an instrumental version of a track, stripping the original of vocals or using the vocal track sparingly, and typically emphasised the bass and drums, employing echo and tape loops in the studio to create a spooky, spacy sound. During the punk era, dub became influential among musicians, and many post-punk, and even some punk, records show the influence of the form. Dub put the producer at the centre of the process: it was created at the mixing desk using multitracked tapes as raw material. Often producers would integrate found sounds like birdsong or studio conversation, distorting them with effects and delays, fading each element in and out of the mix, panning it from right to left as they saw fit, exploring the possibilities of stereo sound. Dub production was an art: not merely recording the band as faithfully as possible, but taking those performances, stripping them back, warping the sound and converting it into something distinct, and often remarkably different, from the original record.

The Wild Bunch, active between 1983 and 1988, were suffused in hip-hop culture: the graffiti, the turntables, the rapping. Hip-hop had begun in the south Bronx of New York in the 1970s, and the music was characterised by a DJ mixing between two records, isolating the beats on each but also scratching – manipulating the turntable back and forth to produce a vocal or instrumental repetition or to create a percussive noise – while a vocalist raps over the DJ's improvised backing. Hip-hop had been influenced by dub in its concentration on using elements of pre-existing recordings to create something new. One of hip-hop's originators, DJ Kool Herc, had been born in Kingston, Jamaica and moved to the Bronx when he was twelve.

Bronx street-corner hip-hop performances recalled Jamaican sound-system culture, while rapping was a high-speed, incredibly dextrous version of laid-back toasting over reggae records. Mixtapes of the latest hip-hop from New York would find their way to the cassette decks in The Dug Out, and DJ Mushroom (Andrew Vowles), whose father was from New York, travelled to the city in 1985 to get a taste of the scene.[9]

The first couple of records by The Wild Bunch, 'Tearin' Down the Avenue' (1987) and 'Friends and Countrymen' (1988), showed that the group had processed the influence of American hip-hop and ably turned it to a British context, with laid-back rapping that hinted at the near conversational, if rhythmic style of Massive Attack. The B-side of their debut single was a stripped-down version of Bacharach and David's 'The Look of Love'. Here the beats were of primary importance, a tightly wrought mosaic of drum noises – it sounds like a combination of samples and drum machines – with only the occasional stab of synthesiser or sample, and no bass line. It's like a demo for a Massive Attack tune – a complex landscape of beats underpinning a soulful torch song – and as if to emphasise the parallels it was sung by the London-based vocalist Shara Nelson, who would contribute memorable performances to Massive Attack's debut album *Blue Lines*. The second Wild Bunch single was released in 1988, as was the first Massive Attack twelve-inch, the soulful 'Any Love', which was co-produced by the band and local producers Smith and Mighty. While it featured the squelchy synths and breakbeats of hip-hop, it was suffused with the slow-burning, melancholy yearning that you can hear on *Blue Lines*. As with 'The Look of Love', the record creates space for its vocal lines and fragments of samples through sections without bass – and what bass is there is incredibly low-end. Elsewhere on the record, a brief sample of bass is introduced before snatching it away, in the same way a dub producer would drop elements in and out of the mix. Massive Attack's debut single isn't typical of what they would go on to produce – it's much higher-tempo for a start – but it shows them pushing against the limitations of the hip-hop record, dragging it towards a hybrid of hip-hop and soul and pointing towards the band's future. (Producers Smith and Mighty had a couple of club hits, Bacharach and David covers arranged in a manner similar to The Wild Bunch's 'The Look of Love', that were issued on their own Three Stripe label. The duo made an album, *Bass Is Maternal*, for the ffrr label in 1989, but the record wasn't to the label's liking and remained unreleased for several years.)

While it might sound somewhat implausible, Pete Waterman, the ex-railwayman DJ from Coventry who had unsuccessfully attempted to manage The Specials, played a tangential part in Massive Attack's early career. After his abortive attempts to pre-empt the ska craze, he had worked as an A&R man in the music industry and formed Stock Aitken Waterman, a production-line of throwaway Hi-NRG dance floor pop that sent records by Bananarama, Kylie Minogue and Dead or Alive into the charts – over a hundred Top 40 singles during a ten-year period. Waterman had reputedly modelled his hit factory on 2 Tone, and the many hit singles produced by his company became a byword for cheap and cheerful eighties pop. Because of the volume of singles pumped out by SAW, many of their artists fell through the cracks if they didn't have an instant impact on the charts. One of these groups was the singer-songwriter duo Morgan McVey, whose 'Looking Good Diving' was an anodyne song that held promise in its distinctive ascending synth riff hook. The single, whose A-side was produced by Stock Aitken Waterman, failed to chart on its release in 1987.[10] But on the B-side of the single was a remix of the song that discarded almost everything but the riff. The replacement vocals, which alternated between melody and rapping, were performed by Neneh Cherry, the vocalist who had been a member of Rip, Rig and Panic. The remix was titled 'Looking Good Diving with The Wild Bunch', after the Bristol crew who had reformulated the chart miss into what would become the basis of a huge hit, Cherry's 'Buffalo Stance'. Cameron McVey, one half of the Morgan McVey duo, was Cherry's partner and manager, and he would co-produce her debut album *Raw Like Sushi*. Cherry and McVey recruited an array of musicians to produce and perform on the album, including Tim Simenon of Bomb the Bass and producer Mark Saunders, who would later co-produce Tricky's debut *Maxinquaye*. Nellee Hooper, who had left The Wild Bunch to become a producer, contributed vibraphone to Cherry's album, while two members of the newly formed Massive Attack, Robert Del Naja and Mushroom, made significant contributions: Del Naja co-wrote 'Manchild', the second single to be taken from the album, and Mushroom added programming and scratching to many tracks – and also appeared in the video for 'Buffalo Stance'. Cherry's album appears formative for Massive Attack, who were obviously in demand because of their Wild Bunch work, particularly their minimalist version of 'The Look of Love'. The string arranger on *Raw Like Sushi*, Wil Malone, would arrange and conduct the sweeping orchestral score of Massive Attack's 'Unfinished Sympathy'. Neneh Cherry would contribute arrangements and vocals to *Blue Lines*, while Cameron McVey would act as executive producer. Some of Massive Attack's debut was recorded in Cherry and McVey's home studio in London. When the band signed a record deal, having first signed a management deal with McVey, it was with Circa, the Virgin subsidiary that had issued *Raw Like Sushi*.

Although recorded in a couple of locations, many of the tracks on *Blue Lines* were committed to tape in the Coach House studio, an anonymous-looking converted stable beside a Georgian house opposite the university's students' union building further up the hill in Clifton. Leaving the site of The Dug Out, I made my way up a side street through an evidently wealthy residential area of pastel-shaded terraces. We clearly weren't in St Paul's any more. The Dug Out had closed in 1986, under pressure from the local traders' association. As I walked around I surmised that the club had probably drawn their attention and generated unease by attracting black St Paul's residents up the hill to comfortable Clifton. Del Naja said that 'the traders . . . couldn't hack it at all. And nor could the Old Bill because it meant things weren't contained in one area [i.e. St Paul's].'[11]

I reached a tall concrete building that loomed above the surrounding houses – the students' union – and circled it before finding the Coach House studio. I could see it, past the jumble of recycling boxes and parked cars, beyond the tarmacked driveway, almost obscured by overgrown trees and a house extension. It was cottage-like and appeared to have been expanded over the years, its French windows serving as a doorway, with a large gable window above. It had the look of a mews house that might get the hard sell in a glossy property section in London or Dublin, but here it seemed a little neglected. That it had played a key part in the musical history of the city was far from obvious – there was no blue plaque, nor any sign at all of what it had been.

By the time the band recorded *Blue Lines*, former Wild Bunch member Nellee Hooper had produced Soul II Soul's *Club Classics Vol. One*, which brought the polished, laid-back, hip-hop-derived dub sound that The Wild Bunch and Massive Attack had been experimenting with to a huge audience, selling over four million copies after its release in April 1989. Cherry's

'Manchild', co-written by Del Naja, was released a month later, and made the Top 10. Her earlier single, 'Buffalo Stance', had gone to number 3 in the UK and America a few months before. The Wild Bunch had spawned a sound that had vast commercial appeal. I emphasise this because Massive Attack weren't just made by the sound systems and clubs of Bristol, but also by the possibilities of fusing the hybrid sounds of Wednesday nights at The Dug Out with a growing industry demand for commercial-yet-sophisticated pop music. Their role in the shit-to-gold transmutation of a failed Stock Aitken Waterman-produced single into a pop masterpiece was an early sign of this.

I won't linger on the recording of the album, except to note that the tape operator in the Coach House was Geoff Barrow, later of Portishead, who was still in his late teens at the time, and that the rapper Tricky was then a member of Massive Attack. The Coach House was where 'Unfinished Sympathy' was composed, after the band heard Shara Nelson singing the tune while warming up. After the release of *Blue Lines*, Tricky (Adrian Thaws), an asthmatic black kid from the largely white, working-class suburb of Knowle West in south Bristol, was on a wage from the band, sharing a flat with Del Naja while also working on lyrics that would form the basis of his 1995 solo album *Maxinquaye*. Later, while sharing a house with Mark Stewart of The Pop Group, he met the singer Martina Topley-Bird. Tricky had been in trouble with the police as a teenager, spending four days in prison for passing forged notes. Before he began to rap, joining The Wild Bunch at their gigs, he was a 2 Tone fan who had practised reggae-style toasting. Next he was a member of The Fresh Four, a posse who had a hit with a cover of 'Wishing on a Star' that was produced by Smith and Mighty.

Tricky's contributions to Massive Attack feel like sketches for his first album – some of his verses on the band's second album,

Protection, released in 1994, are repeated word-for-word on *Maxinquaye*. (*Protection* was also notable for the band's collaboration with Tracey Thorn and Ben Watt of Everything But The Girl, a band who enjoyed renewed chart success at the time as a result of both the 'Protection' single and the Todd Terry remix of their own song 'Missing'.) Tricky's ability to integrate heavy rock guitar marked him out from Massive Attack, who waited until their 1998 album *Mezzanine* to explore their post-punk, guitar-driven side. Tricky's music was direct, going straight for the jugular. There's a visceral, headbanging quality to the rock side of *Maxinquaye*, especially the cover version of Public Enemy's 'Black Steel'. The whispered anxiety of Massive Attack had been transformed by Tricky into a paranoid obsessiveness that tipped into outright aggression. It's a compelling album from a singular character, and its success, both artistically and commercially, appears to have been regarded with surprise by Massive Attack. Tricky, for his part, gave interviews slagging off his former band.

With *Maxinquaye*, seemingly random elements of the Bristol music scene came together: Mark Stewart had a vocal credit on the album – he had encouraged Tricky to record 'Aftermath' – and Mark Saunders, who had worked on Neneh Cherry's *Raw Like Sushi*, produced. The result had some of the wildness of Stewart, and much of the production nous of Saunders, but overall the fine-tuned psychosis that gave the album its atmosphere was Tricky's alone. And in Martina Topley-Bird he had found a singer whose bell-clear vocals were a relieving contrast to his wheezy, claustrophobic rapping. There was an intense atmosphere to their relationship, it seemed – one that was emphasised by the record company during the marketing of the album. Promotional photos from the *Maxinquaye* era show them both dishevelled, wearing chunky trainers but otherwise clad in formal wear: Tricky in a wedding dress, lipstick slashed across his mouth, while Martina wears a groom's top hat and tails.

Neneh Cherry also had an influence on the signing of Portishead, a studio-based band named after a nearby Somerset coastal town, consisting of Geoff Barrow, vocalist Beth Gibbons and jazz guitar player Adrian Utley. Cherry had brought Barrow in to co-write and produce a track, 'Somedays', for her second album, *Homebrew*, in much the same way that she and McVey had tapped members of Massive Attack for *Raw Like Sushi*. The track, built around a piano sample of Beethoven's Moonlight Sonata, is underpinned by a breakbeat drum track and occasional rhythmic scratches by Barrow to add texture. Press reports around the time of *Homebrew*'s release mentioned Barrow's involvement and his band, Portishead – a deal with Go! Beat records followed. The jazz influence was pronounced with Portishead, especially in the smoky, after-hours atmosphere that their records sustained. Hip-hop techniques of sampling and scratching were still present, but as the background to more traditional songwriting.

As with Massive Attack and Tricky, Portishead employed the logic, drawn from hip-hop (which in turn had taken it from dub), of using a sample of an existing record to construct a new work. In doing this they were tapping into a Bristol heritage that stretched back through Massive Attack and The Wild Bunch to the reggae sound systems of St Paul's, even if the end result was remarkably different from its origin. Their debut, *Dummy*, was released in August 1994, and one of its singles, 'Glory Box', was built around a sample of Isaac Hayes's 'Ike's Rap II', from his 1971 album *Black Moses*. The same sample was central to Tricky's 'Hell Is Round the Corner' on *Maxinquaye*, released a few months later; the song also featured lyrics that Tricky had rapped on Massive Attack's 'Karmacoma'. This overlapping said something about the interlocking of ideas and the shared influences in the Bristol of the time. But it was also unusual to hear such obvious parallels. Records with unusual beats or memorable melodies would be guarded jealously by members of The Wild Bunch during their hip-hop days. It was a competitive business: the originality of the sample lay primarily in its rarity. DJs would rip the labels off twelve-inch records or glue a seven-inch on top of them to ensure that no one knew exactly what they were playing. Mushroom would arrive in the studio with a beat and refuse to tell his fellow members of Massive Attack where he got it.[12] Their paranoia about sharing their records seemed to be confirmed when, while they were still looking for a label prior to signing with Circa, they recorded a demo for Soul II Soul's label that featured a bass line from an old reggae record, 'Five Man Army'. No record deal ensued, and Massive Attack eventually released a track using the sample on their 1991 album *Blue Lines*, but by then the rare bass line had already been sampled . . . by Soul II Soul, who used it on a track on their second album. The Bristol band, who guarded the sources of their samples jealously, felt like they had been ripped off. The sample shared by Tricky and Portishead emphasised their differences rather than their similarities. Once you got past the sample, the songs were completely different, as were their subsequent careers. Portishead won the 1995 Mercury Music Prize for *Dummy*, and perhaps by dint of their jazz influences, became the choice of discerning listeners seeking a tasteful slice of trip-hop. Tricky, previously embedded in the Bristol hip-hop scene as an MC, would react against the trip-hop label almost immediately, pushing his later work towards rap and punk, challenging and often repelling the audience drawn to him by *Maxinquaye*.

Robert Del Naja, at certain points in Massive Attack's recent history the only remaining member of the band, described their records as 'like travelling through a crowded bar and stopping for a few minutes at each conversation and listening to bits and pieces and at the end of it you create a summary of what the place was like, but made up of so many different parts'.[13] This is as good a description as you can get of the application of a hip-hop, cut-up aesthetic to the production of a record. Evidently, the approach extended to how Massive Attack worked with musicians playing live in the studio: their work was sampled and looped, processed with effects and played back to them while they sat in the live room, to try to shape their performance. It sounds like a time-consuming endeavour that requires a large degree of experimentation and failure along the way. Del Naja's description of the process of making records reminded me of the kind of work involved in non-fiction writing, the kind of thing I do: assembling references and quotations, talking to people and taking photos, then making something coherent from the fragments you've gathered. You overlay that primary experience with other elements: books, interviews, historical photos. A process of layering takes place. Only then do you try to make some sense of it, stripping the layers away, leaving the traces of a journey that you've taken through a certain place at a specific time. The comparison Del Naja draws between the physical space of a crowded bar and the atmosphere of a Massive Attack record made me think of how much their records bear the imprint of a scene, and how many of their musical influences had been deeply embedded in the physical spaces of the city, from the sound systems of St Paul's to the clubs and record shops of Clifton.

I began my descent from the west side of the Clifton bridge, down a hill and along an earthen path beaten onto a bank above a pedestrian-unfriendly main road. It wasn't long before I reached the silted-up Avon, and wandered along the river past the gentrified, residential docklands, and on reaching the city dawdled in the central markets full of bric-a-brac and food stalls. A sense of leaving overcame me, expressed in a powerful desire to take one last look around before climbing on the bus to the airport. As I strolled around the shopping streets of the city centre a thunderous downpour abruptly commenced, soaking my shoes and forcing me to shelter in the nearest shop. It reminded me for a moment of my visit to Tony Wilson's grave in Manchester's Southern Cemetery a year before. I had spent the best part of half an hour trying to track down the sleek, polished, minimalist gravestone before I finally discovered it, strategically positioned among the nineteenth-century tombs. At that point the dark sky had, suddenly, broken into a roiling storm that sent me back towards the tram station I had come from, retracing my steps past the graves and along the avenues of that city of the dead. Now, in Bristol, the weather had again interrupted my plans, and forced me to acknowledge the end of my journey. I knew it was time to go.

Conclusion
THE PLACES YOU REMEMBER

I had come to the end of my journey, one that had begun at a derelict record pressing plant in Washington, Tyne and Wear. Thinking back to that moment, when I walked across the tiled, weed-pocked floor of the old factory, I again considered the relationship pop music had to industry. Music fulfilled the definition of light industry, one that distinguished it from heavy industries such as the coalmines and shipyards and bracketed it with diode manufacturers and car component factories. It's true that making a physical product was central to the music industry. It entailed manufacturing, which meant employment, and then the product that resulted from this process was sold to consumers in shops, where the money that changed hands was channelled back into the other stages. And certainly there was a tangible, physical element to music, something that you could hold in your hand. Yet there was another level to pop, a parallel industry of the imagination whose factories were recording studios, rehearsal rooms, pubs, clubs and the front rooms of terraced houses. Here, in these otherwise ordinary spaces, is where hits were made, and perhaps that's why they inspire such fascination. Pop music delivered a dream, a sense of undying possibility. It had an intangible imaginative element that you could never completely grasp.

Pop music was *there* and *not there* simultaneously.

During the writing of *Hit Factories* my thoughts would often return to The Beatles' song 'In My Life', and the way that Lennon and McCartney had removed references to the specific Liverpool locations they recalled fondly from their childhoods. What does it mean to tell the listener that you remember places but to never name them? It left me asking questions about those locations, where the band were coming from. With The Beatles, there are the earlier draft lyric sheets where Lennon gives concrete details of those places – the buses, trams and cinemas of post-war Liverpool. It makes you look at the song in a different way, brings it from the universal level of the hit record to an everyday, local context. Nothing comes from nowhere. At times during my trip around the regional cities of British pop I felt that I was engaged in an endeavour not unlike trying to unearth the origins of that Beatles song.

It seemed to be no coincidence that these musical cities were where industry had taken hold in the eighteenth and nineteenth centuries, drawing large populations from towns, villages and rural areas into the urban environment. These cities were defined by industry, and it haunts pop music as a theme. But pop music also provided an escape from that life, either imaginatively through the act of listening, of participating in pop culture as a fan, or by joining a band and trying to make your fortune. It held out the possibility of changing your life through the social mobility that success enabled. Pop music could be a reflection or a rejection of social and geographical location: you didn't have to know your place and you could consciously decide to forget where you came from.

The sound of the cities was shaped by local scenes, and those scenes varied in size, from a band operating in relative isolation, such as The Housemartins in their Hull terrace or 10cc in their Stockport studio, to a vast network of groups and venues, such as Liverpool in the sixties or Glasgow in the eighties and nineties. The influences on those scenes varied from the rock 'n' roll imports of the early days of British pop to the art schools that helped to introduce Pop Art and radical politics to bands who would draw on those ideas in their music. And the arrival of large immigrant populations in the post-war period influenced the nation's popular music immeasurably. Indian and Pakistani immigrants to Birmingham brought bhangra music to the forges and suburban houses of Smethwick. The families of newcomers from the West Indies brought reggae to Handsworth. The Specials, the children of immigrants who had come to Coventry to work in its industries, composed 'Ghost Town', an epitaph for the very industries that had brought their families to the city.

The idea of the good old days – before regional decline, before your city began to resemble the kind of place The Specials sang about in 'Ghost Town' – had become common currency in contemporary Britain. Loss of industry was a wound that wouldn't heal. At times this nostalgia threatened to strangle the present. But even in the country's darkest moments, there were signs of hope. My journey had taken me through the regional cities of a country that was on the brink of the unknown. I had been looking for the physical places in which musicians had lived, worked and imagined the future. Although some of those places remained, many were gone. But for those who passed through these places, or who had lived and worked in them – and, indeed, for those of us who listened intently and obsessively to the records that emerged from such locations – they would never completely disappear. The places – the nightclubs and bars and venues and studios and even the terraced houses – persisted in memory. Perhaps those memories were captured, maybe even revived, through the records that they made. Could a musician's career be an endless quest to recapture a moment that happened early in their lives, at a certain moment and in a certain place? The Beatles' Liverpool, Van Morrison's Belfast, Massive Attack's Bristol: these were places to remember, to explore and reassemble, for the rest of our lives.

Acknowledgements

My agent Kevin Pocklington saw the potential of *Hit Factories* at a very early stage and found the perfect home for it with Paul Murphy at Weidenfeld & Nicolson. I thank Paul for his kindness, insight and patience. Thanks are also due to Lucinda McNeile for her editorial excellence, and to Alex Wade for legal advice, John English for copy editing and Nic Nicholas for the index.

I'm deeply grateful to everyone who helped me during the writing of this book: Julie Campbell, Gary McCausland, Nathan McGough, Simon Spence, Ian Rainford, Colin White, Aidan O'Rourke, Mark Radcliffe, Pat Nevin, John Williamson, Stuart Braithwaite, Duglas Stewart, Francis Macdonald, Grant McPhee (who generously sent me a link to his excellent documentary about the Glasgow scene, *Teenage Superstars*), Geoff Davies, Sarah Stoner, Ritch Lattimore, Brian Tomlinson, Audrey Young, Brian Craggs, Tom Caulker, Eugene Brennan, Eamonn Hoban-Shelley, Conor Emerson, Garret Monahan, Jonathan O'Malley, Neil Carlin, Ernesto Priego, Gráinne Ní Mhuirí, Siobhán Kane, Harry Pearson, David Fallon, Philip Terry, André Keil, Richard Phillips, Charles Forsdick, William Mulligan, Alessandro Vincentelli, Mark Pinder, Douglas Smith and Clodagh Finn, Liam Heneghan, Paul Laity at the *Guardian* Review; Tom Crewe and all at the *London Review of Books*; Mike Herd, Chris Michael, Nick Van Mead and all at *Guardian* Cities, and to Hugh Linehan and Martin Doyle at the *Irish Times*. To Dr Graham Raftery and specialist nurse Lesley Duffell, and all at NHS City Hospitals Sunderland's rheumatology department: thank you.

Finally, I'm very thankful for the love and support of my wife Laura, my parents May and Tom, my brother Warren, and the O'Brien family: Briege, Tony and Cathy.

I gratefully acknowledge the support of The Society of Authors Authors' Foundation, whose grant helped to fund work on this book.

Notes

Chapter 1: Manchester

1. Deborah Curtis, *Touching from a Distance: Ian Curtis & Joy Division* (Faber and Faber, 1995), p. 37.
2. In *FAC! 229 The Music Week Factorial* (a *Music Week* magazine supplement), 15 July 1989, text reproduced at http://factoryrecords. org/cerysmatic/fac229.html
3. Simon Spence, *Happy Mondays: Excess All Areas* (Aurum Press, 2015), p. 130.
4. James Nice, *Shadowplayers: The Rise and Fall of Factory Records* (Aurum, 2010), p. 446.

Chapter 2: Liverpool

1. Philip Norman, *Paul McCartney: The Biography* (W&N, 2016), p. 64.
2. George Martin with William Pearson, *Summer of Love: The Making of Sgt Pepper* (Pan, 1994), p. 160.
3. Ian Macdonald, *Revolution in the Head: The Beatles' Records and the Sixties* (Vintage, 2008), p. 203.
4. Quoted in Hunter Davies, *The Beatles: The Authorised Biography* (Ebury Press, 2009), p. 83.
5. Norman, *Paul McCartney*, p. 258.
6. The Beatles, *Live at the BBC*, 1994, disc 1, track 3.

Chapter 3: Newcastle

1. Nik Cohn, *Yes We Have No: Adventures in the Other England* (Secker and Warburg, 1999), p. 269.
2. Cohn, p. 267.
3. Cohn, p. 267.
4. Nik Cohn, *Awopbopaloobop Alopbamboom: Pop from the Beginning* (Vintage, 2004), p. 163.
5. Cohn, p. 163.
6. Ted Anthony, *Chasing the Rising Sun: The Journey of an American Song* (Simon & Schuster, 2007), p. 143.
7. Charles Shaar Murray, *Crosstown Traffic: Jimi Hendrix and Post-War Pop* (Faber and Faber, 2001), p. 70.
8. Ferry talking to Michael Bracewell, *Re-make/Re-model: Becoming Roxy Music* (DaCapo Press, 2008), p. 49.
9. Cohn, *Awopbop*, p. 164.
10. Bracewell, *Re-make/Re-model*, pp. 22–3.
11. Bracewell, p. 48.
12. Bracewell, p. 69.
13. Sting, *Broken Music* (Simon & Schuster, 2003), p. 274.
14. Jonathan Paul Watson, 'Beats apart: a comparative history of youth culture and popular music in Liverpool and Newcastle upon Tyne, 1956–1965', Doctoral thesis, Northumbria University, p. 236.
15. Ian Ravendale, 'Makin' Satan', *Kerrang* 3 (September 1981), 26.

Chapter 4: Leeds

1. George Melly, *Revolt Into Style: The Pop Arts in Britain* (Penguin, 1970), p. 3.
2. Melly, p. 4.
3. Jim Dooley, *Red Set: A History of Gang of Four* (Repeater Books, 2018), p. 32.
4. Dooley, p. 36.
5. Simon Reynolds, *Totally Wired: Post-Punk Interviews and Overviews* (Faber and Faber, 2009), p. 177.
6. Reynolds, p. 178.
7. Reynolds, p. 178.

8. Reynolds, p. 180.

9. Reynolds, pp. 179–80.

10. Dooley, *Red Set*, pp. 18–21.

11. Betty Page, 'Soft Cell: The Big Softies', *Sounds*, 1 August 1981.

12. Dave Simpson, 'How we made Soft Cell's Tainted Love', *Guardian*, 20 March 2017.

13. Betty Page, 'Soft Cell: Sweet Cell Music', *Sounds*, 12 March 1981.

14. Simpson, 'Tainted Love'.

Chapter 5: Sheffield

1. Jon Wilde, 'Pulp: Sweet or Sour', *Sounds*, 8 March 1986.

2. Simon Reynolds, *Rip It Up and Start Again: Postpunk 1978–1984* (Faber and Faber, 2005), p. 152.

3. Reynolds, p. 153.

4. Reynolds, p. 156.

5. Reynolds, pp. 157–8.

6. Reynolds, p. 160.

7. Reynolds, p. 151.

8. Reynolds, p. 161.

9. Reynolds, p. 165; Dave Haslam, *Life After Dark: A History of British Nightclubs and Music Venues* (Simon & Schuster, 2015), p. 291.

10. Haslam, p. 292.

11. Reynolds, *Totally Wired*, p. 289.

12. Andy Gill, 'The Human League/Vice Versa: The Now Society, Sheffield University', *NME*, 29 July 1978.

13. Reynolds, *Rip It Up and Start Again*, p. 168.

14. Matt Anniss, 'Bleep: The Story of Britain's first bass revolution', *Resident Advisor*, 2 December 2014, https://www.residentadvisor.net/features/2349

Chapter 6: Hull

1. Simon Ford, *Wreckers of Civilisation: The Story of COUM Transmissions and Throbbing Gristle* (Black Dog Publishing, 1999), p. 1.9.
2. Ford, p. 1.10.
3. Ford, pp. 1.14–1.15.
4. Illustration in Ford, p. 1.18.
5. Cosey Fanni Tutti, *Art Sex Music* (Faber and Faber, 2017), pp. 73–5.
6. Ford, *Wreckers of Civilisation*, p. 2.17.
7. Tutti, *Art Sex Music*, pp. 130–1.
8. Pete Frame, *Rockin' Around Britain: Rock 'n' Roll Landmarks of the UK and Ireland* (Omnibus Press, 1999), pp. 203–4.
9. Paul Trynka, *Starman: David Bowie – The Definitive Biography* (Sphere, 2011), pp. 111–12.
10. Weird & Gilly, *Mick Ronson: The Spider with the Platinum Hair* (Music Press Books, 2017), pp. 16–17.
11. Weird & Gilly, p. 34.
12. Weird & Gilly, p. 34.
13. David Bowie introducing his song 'The Width of a Circle' on *The Sunday Show* (BBC, 5 February 1970). See *Bowie at the Beeb* (CD, 2000).
14. Mike Pattenden, *Last Orders at the Liars' Bar: The Official Story of the Beautiful South* (Victor Gollancz, 1999), pp. 51–2.
15. Paul Ashton, 'Nicholas Charles Frederick Hotham: 1947–2012, fondly remembered', Pub Mirror (Hull and East Yorkshire), 12 (Winter 2012), 30.
16. Katy Noone quote, 'Heritage', the Adelphi Club website, https://www.theadelphi.com/history/
17. Stuart Cosgrove, *Young Soul Rebels: A Personal History of Northern Soul* (Birlinn, 2016), p.10
18. Quoted in Ford, *Wreckers of Civilisation*, 1.10.
19. Tracey Thorn, *Bedsit Disco Queen: How I Grew Up and Tried to be a Pop Star* (Virago, 2013), p. 118.
20. Thorn, p. 87.

Chapter 7: Glasgow

1. Allan Brown, *Nileism: The Strange Course of The Blue Nile* (Polygon, 2010), pp. 37–9.
2. Brown, pp. 47–50.
3. Brown, pp. 61–3.
4. Simon Goddard, *Simply Thrilled: The Preposterous Story of Postcard Records* (Ebury Press, 2014), p. 79.
5. Paul Morley, 'Orange Juice: The Sneer That Says Wish You Were Here', *NME*, 4 October 1980.
6. David Cavanagh, *The Creation Records Story: My Magpie Eyes are Hungry for the Prize* (Virgin, 2000), p. 20.
7. Richard King, *How Soon Is Now?: The Madmen and Mavericks Who Made Independent Music, 1975–2005* (Faber and Faber, 2012), p. 66.
8. King, p. 67.
9. Sarah Lowndes, *Social Sculpture: Art, Performance and Music in Glasgow* (Stopstop, 2003), pp. 117–18.

Chapter 8: Belfast

1. Mark Cousins, 'Days Like These', *Sight and Sound*, July 2018.
2. Greil Marcus, *Listening to Van Morrison* (Faber and Faber, 2010), p. 33.
3. Johnny Rogan, *Van Morrison: No Surrender* (Vintage, 2006), p. 39.
4. Lester Bangs, *Psychotic Reactions and Carburetor Dung* (Serpent's Tail, 1996), p. 24.
5. Rogan, *Van Morrison*, p. 243.
6. Rogan, p. 85.
7. Gerald Dawe, *In Another World: Van Morrison & Belfast* (Merrion Press, 2017), p. 61.
8. Interview in *Spotlight* magazine, quoted in Rogan, *Van Morrison*, p. 273.
9. Rogan, p. 274.
10. Stuart Bailie, *Trouble Songs: Music and Conflict in Northern Ireland* (Bloomfield Press, 2018), p. 102.

11. Bailie, p. 110.
12. Bailie, p. 111.
13. Bailie, p. 115.
14. Quoted in Bailie, p. 120.

Chapter 9: Birmingham

1. Andy Foster, *Birmingham (Pevsner Architectural Guides: City Guide)* (Yale University Press, 2005), p. 33.
2. Stuart Jeffries, 'Britain's most racist election: the story of Smethwick, 50 years on', *Guardian*, 15 October 2014.
3. Clair Wills, *Lovers and Strangers: An Immigrant History of Post-War Britain* (Penguin, 2018), p. 56.
4. Interview with Saxon Baird, 'Babylon is Falling: David Hinds on the Early Years of Steel Pulse and His Youth in England', PRI.org (Public Radio International), https://www.pri.org/stories/2014-01-22/babylon-falling-david-hinds-early-years-steel-pulse-and-his-youth-england
5. Dervla Murphy, *Tales from Two Cities: Travels of Another Sort* (Penguin, 1989), p. 280.
6. Murphy, p. 282.
7. Murphy, p. 283.
8. Tony Iommi, *Iron Man: My Journey Through Heaven and Hell with Black Sabbath* (Simon & Schuster, 2012), pp. xi–xiii.
9. Mick Wall, *Black Sabbath: Symptom of the Universe* (Orion, 2014), p. 10.
10. Ozzy Osbourne, *I Am Ozzy* (Sphere, 2010), p. 5.
11. Alexander Milas, 'Black Sabbath's Geezer Butler: My Life Story', *Loudersound/Metal Hammer*, 18 October 2016, https://www.loudersound.com/features/black-sabbaths-geezer-butler-my-life-story
12. Osbourne, *I Am Ozzy*, p. 48.
13. Unpublished interview by Steve Turner. Accessed on *Rock's Backpages*, http://www.rocksbackpages.com/Library/Article/black-sabbath
14. Wills, *Lovers and Strangers*, p. 50.

15. Quoted in Wills, pp. 44–5.

16. Quoted in Richard White, *Dexys Midnight Runners: Young Soul Rebels* (Omnibus Press, 2005), p. 8.

17. Quoted in White, p. 14.

18. Quoted in White, p. 13.

19. White, p. 15.

20. Éamon Sweeney, 'Dexys usher in their new Irish vision', *Irish Times*, 27 June 2016, https://www.irishtimes.com/culture/music/dexys-usher-in-their-new-irish-vision-1.2696343

21. Bailie, *Trouble Songs*, pp. 199–200.

22. Gareth Mulvenna, *Tartan Gangs and Paramilitaries: The Loyalist Backlash* (Liverpool University Press, 2016), pp.110–11.

23. 'Story Behind Dexys Midnight Runners' Young Soul Rebel cover', *Express and Star*, 20 July 2010, https://www.expressandstar.com/news/2010/07/20/story-behind-dexys-midnight-runners-young-soul-rebel-album-cover/

24. Quoted in Reynolds, *Rip It Up and Start Again*, p. 296.

Chapter 10: Coventry

1. Graham Ruddick, 'It was once Britain's motor city. Now Coventry's wheels are turning again', *Observer*, 24 April 2016.

2. Charles Shaar Murray, 'Big Red Cars, Little White Chicks, and the Chuck Berry Lick', *Cream*, March 1972.

3. Chuck Berry, *Chuck Berry: The Autobiography* (Faber and Faber, 1988), pp. 261–2.

4. Hugh Montgomery et al, 'Ghost Town: The song that defined an era turns 30', *Independent*, 3 July 2011, https://www.independent.co.uk/arts-entertainment/music/features/ghost-town-the-song-that-defined-an-era-turns-30-2306003.html

5. Chris Pickford and Nikolaus Pevsner, *Warwickshire (Pevsner Architectural Guides: The Buildings of England)* (Yale University Press, 2016), pp. 222–3.

6. Pickford and Pevsner, p. 221.

7. Dorian Lynskey, 'Fun boy free', *Guardian*, 2 July 2003, https://www.theguardian.com/music/2003/jul/22/artsfeatures.popandrock

8. Neville Staple with Tony McMahon, *Original Rude Boy: From Borstal to The Specials: A Life of Crime and Music* (Aurum, 2009), pp. 11–12.

9. Staple, pp. 36–7. Pete Waterman quote is from his foreword, pp. xi–xii.

10. Staple, pp. 77–94.

11. Staple, p. 94.

12. Horace Panter, *Ska'd for Life: A Personal Journey with The Specials* (Pan Books, 2008), pp. 10–11.

13. Panter, p. 15.

14. Staple, *Original Rude Boy*, p. 107.

15. Staple, p. 109.

16. Lloyd Bradley, *Sounds Like London: 100 Years of Black Music in the Capital* (Serpent's Tail, 2013), p. 58.

17. Reynolds, *Rip It Up and Start Again*, pp. 285–7.

18. Reynolds, p. 285.

19. Alan Webster, 'Obituary: The Very Rev Horace Dammers', 31 August 2004, https://www.theguardian.com/news/2004/aug/31/guardianobituaries.obituaries

20. Quoted in Reynolds, *Rip It Up and Start Again*, p. 289.

21. Panter, *Ska'd for Life*, p. 71.

22. Panter, pp. 83–4.

23. Panter, pp. 72–3.

24. Pauline Black, *Black by Design: A 2-Tone Memoir* (Serpent's Tail, 2011), p. 112.

25. Black, p. 116.

26. Black, p. 118.

27. Dialogue recalled in Black, p. 124.

28. Dick Hebdige, *Cut 'n' Mix: Culture, Identity and Caribbean Music* (Routledge, 2003), pp. 110–11.

29. Quoted in Hebdige, p. 113.

30. Panter, *Ska'd for Life*, p. 198.

Chapter 11: Bristol

1. Goldie with Ben Thompson, *All Things Remembered* (Faber and Faber, 2017), p. 259.

2. Staple, *Original Rude Boy*, p. 90.

3. Chris Campion, 'The Wild Bunch', *Ray Gun* magazine, 1998, https://www.rocksbackpages.com/Library/Article/the-wild-bunch

4. 'Alfred Fagon, playwright, actor and poet', JISC Archives Hub, https://archiveshub.jisc.ac.uk/search/archives/79f7dfb0-422e-3d12-ad3c-72dc13054ca6. The details of his cremation, and the time it took for his friends to discover his death, are from the Black Bristolians project, https://www.sgsts.org.uk/SupportForVulnerablePupils/EMTAS/Shared%20Documents/Alfred%20Fagon.pdf

5. Simon Peplow, '"A Tactical Manoeuvre to Apply Pressure": Race and the Role of Public Enquiries in the 1980 Bristol "Riot"', *Twentieth Century British History*, Vol. 29, No. 1 (2018), 139.

6. 'The Burgess Family', the Black Bristolians project, https://www.sgsts.org.uk/SupportForVulnerablePupils/EMTAS/Shared%20Documents/The%20Burgess%20Family.pdf

7. '3D' interview, *Crack Magazine*, 26 November 2012, https://crackmagazine.net/article/news/3d/

8. Richard King, *Original Rockers* (Faber and Faber, 2015).

9. Phil Johnson, *Straight Outta Bristol: Massive Attack, Portishead, Tricky and the Roots of Trip-Hop* (Hodder & Stoughton, 1996), p. 128.

10. Mike Stock, *The Hit Factory: The Stock Aitken Waterman Story* (New Holland, 2004).

11. Johnson, *Straight Outta Bristol*, pp. 51–2.

12. Johnson, p. 117.

13. Johnson, p. 118.

Index